Unwin Critical Library
GENERAL EDITOR: CLAUDE RAWSON

POPE'S 'ESSAY ON MAN'

Unwin Critical Library

GENERAL EDITOR: CLAUDE RAWSON

Pope's 'Essay on Man'

A. D. NUTTALL
Professor, School of English and American Studies,
University of Sussex

London
GEORGE ALLEN & UNWIN
Boston   Sydney

George Allen & Unwin (Publishers) Ltd,
40 Museum Street, London WC1A 1LU, UK

George Allen & Unwin (Publishers) Ltd,
Park Lane, Hemel Hempstead, Herts HP2 4TE, UK

Allen & Unwin, Inc.,
9 Winchester Terrace, Winchester, Mass. 01890, USA

George Allen & Unwin Australia Pty Ltd,
8 Napier Street, North Sydney, NSW 2060, Australia

First published in 1984

British Library Cataloguing in Publication Data

Nuttall, A. D.
    Pope's 'Essay on man'. – (Unwin critical
library)
    1. Pope, Alexander. Essay on man
    I. Title
    821'.5   PR3627
    ISBN 0–04–800017–5

Library of Congress Cataloging in Publication Data

Nuttall, A. D. (Anthony David)
    Pope's Essay on man.
    (Unwin critical library)
    Bibliography: p.
    Includes index.
    1. Pope, Alexander, 1688–1744. An essay on man.
    I. Title. II. Series.
    PR3627.N87 1984   821'.5   83-22298
    ISBN 0–04–800017–5

Set in 10 on 12 point Plantin by Preface Ltd, Salisbury, Wilts.
and printed in Great Britain by Butler & Tanner Ltd, Frome and London

GENERAL EDITOR'S PREFACE

Each volume in this series is devoted to a single major text. It is addressed to serious students and teachers of literature, and to knowledgeable non-academic readers. It aims to provide a scholarly introduction and a stimulus to critical thought and discussion.

Individual volumes will naturally differ from one another in arrangement, and emphasis, but each will normally begin with information on a work's literary and intellectual background, and other guidance designed to help the reader to an informed understanding. This is followed by an extended critical discussion of the work itself, and each contributor in the series has been encouraged to present in these sections his own reading of the work, whether or not this is controversial, rather than to attempt a mere consensus. Some volumes, including those on *Paradise Lost* and *Ulysses*, vary somewhat from the more usual pattern by entering into substantive critical discussion at the outset, and allowing the necessary background material to emerge at the points where it is felt to arise from the argument in the most useful and relevant way. Each volume also contains a historical survey of the work's critical reputation, including an account of the principal lines of approach and areas of controversy, and a selective (but detailed) bibliography.

The hope is that the volumes in this series will be among those which a university teacher would normally recommend for any serious study of a particular text, and that they will also be among the essential secondary texts to be consulted in some scholarly investigations. But the experienced and informed non-academic reader has also been in our minds, and one of our aims has been to provide him with reliable and stimulating works of reference and guidance, embodying the present state of knowledge and opinion in a conveniently accessible form.

C.J.R.
University of Warwick
December 1979

PREFACE

An Essay on Man is, as Pope hoped it would be, the principal English philosophical poem of the eighteenth century. It is indeed written with a sprightly celerity which some have interpreted, too easily, as a signal that, whatever we have in *An Essay on Man*, it cannot be philosophy. In fact the poem – despite its tempo, for all its urbane irony – engages with a surprising number of major philosophical and theological cruces. This book takes the philosophy seriously. To do so is to find that *An Essay on Man* is also an essay on God, and to be involved at once in the problem of interpreting a half-alien culture. For many readers, and especially for those who are atheists, a deliberate effort of sympathy, across the intervening centuries, is required. It is not that one must be a fully committed Christian to appreciate the polite religion of Pope; rather, some sense of what it would be like to believe in a supremely good creator is enough, but this much is needed if one is to detect the occasional note of urgency in Pope's smart couplets.

When a particular author is in one's thoughts over a long period of time, some overlap of published material seems to be inevitable. In this book the discussion of Pope's love of incongruity in Chapter 2 repeats material which I have previously published in my article, 'Fishes in the trees' (*Essays in Criticism*, vol. 24, 1974).

I am very grateful to Anthony Thorlby for helping me with Kant's German, and to Colin Brooks, Charles Martindale and Angus Ross for corrections and improvements. Above all, I am indebted to Claude Rawson for the scrupulous care with which he read and commented on my manuscript. The errors which survive are, of course, all mine.

A. D. Nuttall
Lewes, December 1982

To
JO

CONTENTS

God . . . either wishes to take away evils, and is unable; or He is able, and is unwilling; or He is neither willing nor able, or He is both willing and able. If He is willing and is unable, He is feeble, which is not in accordance with the character of God; if He is able and unwilling, He is envious, which is equally at variance with God; if He is neither willing nor able, He is both envious and feeble, and therefore not God; if He is both willing and able, which alone is suitable to God, from what source then are evils? or why does He not remove them?

Argument attributed to Epicurus (342–270 BC) by Lactantius (*c*.260–*c*.340 AD) in his *Treatise on the Anger of God*, ch. XIII (*The Works of Lactantius*, trans. William Fletcher (Edinburgh, 1871), Vol. II, p. 28)

George Frideric Handel, *Jephtha* (1752), end of Act II

ABBREVIATIONS AND PRINCIPAL TEXTS

Corr.   *The Correspondence of Alexander Pope*, ed. George Sherburn, 5 vols (Oxford: Clarendon Press, 1956)

EC   *The Works of Alexander Pope*, ed. W. Elwin and W. J. Courthope, 10 vols (London: John Murray, 1871–9)

MM   Alexander Pope, *An Essay on Man*, ed. Maynard Mack, the Twickenham Edition (London: Methuen, 1950)

Spence   Joseph Spence, *Observations, Anecdotes, and Characters of Books and Men*, ed. James M. Osborn, 2 vols (Oxford: Clarendon Press, 1966). Reference according to Osborn's entry-numbers

References to Horace, Lucretius, Milton, Pope, Shakespeare and Virgil are to the following editions:

Horace, *Odes and Epodes*, with an English translation by C. E. Bennett, the Loeb edition (London: Heinemann, 1960); *Satires, Epistles and Ars Poetica*, with an English translation by H. Rushton Fairclough, the Loeb edition (London: Heinemann, 1961).

Lucretius, *De Rerum Natura Libri Sex*, ed. with a translation by Cyril Bailey (Oxford: Clarendon Press, 1947).

Milton, *The Poetical Works of John Milton*, ed. Helen Darbishire (London: Oxford University Press, 1958)

Pope. All references to *An Essay on Man* are to Maynard Mack's Twickenham Edition (MM). Other references to Pope's verse are to *The Poems of Alexander Pope*, a one-volume edition of the Twickenham text, ed. John Butt (London: Methuen, 1968).

Shakespeare, *The Complete Works*, ed. Peter Alexander (London: Collins, 1951).

Virgil, *Eclogues, Georgics, Aeneid*, with an English translation by H. Rushton Fairclough, the Loeb edition (London: Heinemann, 1926).

CHAPTER 1

The Poet

Twenty years ago it was fashionable to deny that knowledge of an author's life could be in any way relevant to an assessment of his work. Today still greater austerities are laid upon us. The very idea of an 'author' is itself a social fiction; literature, for all important purposes, writes itself and the name on the title-page is a mere badge, a piece of obsolete heraldry. The old claim was that the extra-literary genesis of a work was critically irrelevant; the new claim is that there is no such thing as an extra-literary genesis. The best way to deal with these unnatural taboos is (initially, at least) to submit utterly to them. For a time all seems well. One discerns an impersonal organic logic in the way literature evolves: the manner of a Cowley must give place to the manner of a Dryden, whose forensic energy must in turn be both softened and sharpened until at last we have an Alexander Pope. Yet to say this is to say no more than that English poetry was ready for Pope when he came, that he used the existing tastes of readers. It would be strangely coarse to suppose that literature produces by an inner law of its development a series of slots, each of which will inevitably be filled by a conscript author; so that if Pope had died in childhood (as he almost did) we should have had the same poems, under a different badge or name. That some-one would have written a poem called *An Essay on Man*, though far from certain, is at least plausible. That it would have contained the line 'The green myriads in the peopled grass' is simply incredible. Thus, if one conscientiously reduces one's mind to a state of unearthly neutrality and then seeks the sources of Pope's poetry, one will find indeed a great many other poems, Greek, Latin, French and English, but one will also find, quite ineluctably, a certain indi-vidual, a tiny black-coated figure with a hump back, who is not just a source but a potent, *organizing* source. This, of course, is Pope himself.

There are five things which everyone should know about Pope. First, he had a crooked spine and was four feet six inches tall. Secondly, he was so weak that he was unable to stand or sit without the support of a specially made canvas bodice. Thirdly, he had a fine head and especially fine (almost beautiful) eyes. Fourthly, he was, more than any other literary figure in England (with the possible exception of Defoe), the object of intense hatred. Fifthly, like Milton and John Betjeman, he knew from childhood that he must be a poet.

The best-known account of Pope's physical appearance is Samuel Johnson's in his Life of the poet.[1] Johnson obtained some of his information from persons who had known Pope, but he also placed heavy reliance on the account given in *The Gentleman's Magazine* for September 1775, taken from the mouth of 'an ancient and respectable domestic, who lived many years in the family of Lord Oxford'.[2] Johnson adds to the picture of diminutive stature and physical weakness an emphasis on the slenderness of his body (so different from Johnson's gigantic frame) and on his extreme, shivering sensitivity in later life to cold.

It is clear that to an unkind eye (and many of the eyes turned on Pope were less than kind) he presented an appearance which is sufficiently grotesque: a sort of cross between a monkey and an insect. Such is the imagery which recurs in the contemporary pamphlet attacks on Pope and is traceable even in the accounts left by friends (though friends, having a nearer view, tend to notice the marvellous face). Among all the splendid portraits assembled by W. K. Wimsatt in his handsome volume only one tiny drawing shows Pope's deformity.[3] The rest either idealise or tactfully suppress. Nevertheless, the breathtaking portrait busts by Rysbrack and Roubiliac exhibit at one and the same time a subtlety of form and a likeness to each other which strongly suggest that they really did closely resemble Pope himself. Sir Joshua Reynolds, one of the most verbally articulate of painters, gave Edmond Malone what seems to be the most balanced and minute description of Pope:

He was about four feet six high, very humpbacked and deformed; he wore a black coat and, according to the fashion of that time, had on a little sword . . . He had a large and very fine eye, and a long handsome nose; his mouth had those peculiar marks which always are found in the mouths of crooked persons; and the muscles which ran across his cheeks were so strongly marked as to appear like small cords.[4]

Somehow Reynolds's account of Pope's face suggests pain, though it does not assert it. In Roubiliac's description of Pope this suggestion becomes explicit: 'His countenance was that of a person who had been much afflicted with headache.' Roubiliac claimed that he would have known this in any case from 'the contracted appearance of the skin above the eyebrows'.[5] Pope's habit of dressing in black and wearing a little sword (like a sting) must have increased the insect-like effect.

It was said that Pope had once made an open declaration of love to Lady Mary Wortley Montagu, and that she had laughed at him. The anecdote is not certainly true but is nevertheless instructive. The story is told by Lady Louisa Stuart in the 'Introductory anecdotes' attached to her grandmother Lady Mary's *Letters and Works*, 1861. Lady Louisa suggests that Pope's implacable hatred for Lady Mary dates from this experience.[6] The story neatly encapsulates what is likely to have been a running trauma, a continuous psychic wound. When Pope first began to move in London society, it is clear that an image he yearned to present was that of the rake. The age was demonstrative in its cruelty to such pretensions and was in any case willing to laugh at physical deformity. We may remember Fielding's account of the laughter of the bystanders at his own swollen, dropsical body, when it was carried aboard ship at Rotherhithe.[7] Certainly Pope was strongly attached to Lady Mary Wortley Montagu and this attachment was abruptly replaced by hatred.

The two women whom Pope may have loved are very different. One, Lady Mary, was worldly, ironic, an intrepid traveller in quite dangerous countries, a formidable wit. That such a woman, with all her strength, may not have spared Pope so commonplace and yet so dreadful a humiliation is sad enough. Yet Pope's other love, Martha Blount, a more modest, less distinct personality, may have inflicted a similar hurt, but in a manner so negative as to be almost invisible. Johnson tells a curiously touching story of Pope's old age:

> While he was yet capable of amusement and conversation, as he was one day sitting in the air with Lord Bolingbroke and Lord Marchmont, he saw his favourite Martha Blount at the bottom of the terrace, and asked Lord Bolingbroke to go and hand her up. Bolingbroke, not liking his errand, crossed his legs, and sat still; but Lord Marchmont, who was younger and less captious, waited on the Lady; who, when he came to her, asked, 'What, is he

not dead yet?' She is said to have neglected him with shameful
unkindness in the latter time of his decay; yet, of the little which
he had to leave, she had a very great part. Their acquaintance
began early: the life of each was pictured on the other's mind;
their conversation, therefore, was endearing, for when they met
there was an immediate coalition of congenial notions. Perhaps he
considered her unwillingness to approach the chamber of sickness
as female weakness, or human frailty; perhaps he was conscious to
himself of peevishness and impatience, or, though he was
offended by her inattention, might yet consider her merit as over-
balancing her fault; and, if he had suffered his heart to be alien-
ated from her, he could have found nothing that might fill her
place: he could have only shrunk within himself; it was too late to
transfer his confidence or fondness.[8]

Despite the occasional sentimentalism ('of the little which he had to
give') the picture is convincing.

Even if Pope learned to bear such things, we should not suppose
that he was never injured by them. Similarly, we cannot conclude
from Pope's alacrity in satire that he was indifferent to the attacks
made on him by contemporaries. These, indeed, were extraordinary.
John Dennis in his *Reflections Critical and Satyrical, Upon a Late
Rhapsody, call'd An Essay Upon Criticism* (1711), joyously combined
the ideas of physical deformity and erotic failure, calling Pope 'a
hunch-backed toad' (a creature supposed to be equally remarkable
for its impotence and its venom) and also (referring to the line of his
back) 'the very Bow of the God of Love'. Had Pope been born in
ancient times, Dennis adds, he would certainly have been left to die
at birth.[9]

Still more offensive was the story told by Colley Cibber in 1742, in
his public *Letter from Mr. Cibber to Mr. Pope*.[10] According to Cibber,
some twenty-seven years before, he and the Earl of Warwick had
'slily seduced' Pope into a brothel. Having made sure that Pope was
engaged with one of the prostitutes, Cibber was seized with a sudden
solicitude for Pope's health and the future of English literature; he
therefore burst in upon the poet, whom he found 'like a terrible *Tom
Tit*, pertly perching upon the Mount of Love'. Cibber instantly took
Pope by the heels and dragged him to safety. The whole is skilfully
written and, at moments, genuinely funny. At the same time, the
manner in which gross sexual derision is disguised as benevolent

anxiety is very nasty. Pictures of the climactic moment of Cibber's anecdote were circulated in London.

But perhaps the most hurtful of all the attacks made on Pope was the anonymous *A Popp upon Pope* of 1728:

Last Thursday, being a pleasant Evening, Mr. A. Pope, a great Poet (as we are inform'd) was walking in Ham Walks, meditating Verses for the Publick Good, when two Gentlemen came up to him (whose Names we cannot certainly learn) and knowing him perfectly well by his Back, and partly by his Face; walked a turn or two with him; when, entring into a Conversation (as we hear on the Dunciad, a pretty Poem of the said Poet's writing) on a sudden, one of the Gentlemen hoisted poor Master Pope the Poet on his back, whilst the other drew out, from under his Coat, a long Birchen Rod, (as we are inform'd, made out of a Stable Broom) and with the said long Rod, did, with great Violence and unmerciful Hand, strike Master Pope so hard upon his naked Posteriors, that he voided large Quantities of Blood, which being yellow, one Doctor A[rbuthno]t his Physician, has since affirm'd, had a great Proportion of Gall mix'd with it, which occasion'd the said Colour.[11]

Notice in this passage how the author switches from an air of polite benevolence to violent humiliation of the subject, without any kind of reason or even stylistic warning. Here, one senses, is real upper-class bullying, rejoicing in its own gratuitousness. There is a queer nuance of snobbery in making the instrument of correction derive from a stable-broom. In view of the obtrusively male atmosphere of the piece, it is especially interesting that Pope believed it to be the work of Lady Mary Wortley Montagu. The supposition is not, however, wholly implausible. Lady Mary's 'Verses Address'd to the Imitator Of The Second Book of Horace' contain the lines

And with the Emblem of thy crooked Mind,
Mark'd on thy Back, like Cain, by God's own Hand,
Wander like him, accursed through the Land.[12]

A Popp upon Pope remains, of all the attacks, the one that seems more than any of them to have got under Pope's skin. In the *Memoirs of the Life of Garrick* we are told that Pope read Cibber's appalling

Letter aloud to his friends 'in agony'.[13] But with the anecdote of Ham Walks no such public exorcism was possible. This Pope could only seek to repress. It does not appear in the list of attacks made upon him which he gave in the second appendix to *The Dunciad* (1729). The examples I have given are admittedly extreme. Yet it remains true that Pope was the object of an amount and a degree of literate hatred which can hardly be matched by any other figure in the history of English literature. It is not enough to say that it was characteristic of the age. No one in Augustan England was attacked as venomously as Pope.

It will be said that Pope knew how to inflict pain himself, and this is undeniable. Yet he never sank as low as his enemies; they searched in vain for some example of Pope's mockery of another's deformity and could find nothing stronger than 'Roome's funereal face' in the 1728 *Dunciad*, III, 146.[14] Yet Pope's attack on Lord Hervey in lines 305–25 of his *Epistle to Dr. Arbuthnot* is expertly framed to humiliate and crush. Pope's personal satire continues to pose a problem for those who seek some ultimate identification of art and morality: it seems so plain that they are an exceptionally elegant mode of tormenting other human beings.

One suspects that Pope's greatest offence was his breathtaking superiority, his amazing skill. For a time it must have been almost impossible for a practising writer to read Pope without envy. Even his great friend Swift wrote:

> In POPE I cannot read a Line,
> But with a sigh, I wish it mine.[15]

But Pope in his turn, for all his profound consciousness of his own prowess, was eminently capable of being hurt. Jonathan Richardson told Johnson that, when a hostile pamphlet arrived, Pope would try to pass it off as amusing, but as soon as he began to read those watching were embarrassed to see his features 'writhen with anguish'.[16] Lord Chesterfield said that Pope neither forgot nor forgave, but that attacks whetted the edge of his own satire.[17]

It is clear that the ill-treatment Pope received did more than merely set his pen in motion. The picture of Pope which others drew was thoroughly assimilated by his art, became the matter of his poetry. Even the image of the insect became richly ambiguous under his hand. In the ninety-second number of *The Guardian*, Pope endorsed the comparison of himself with a spider (in this context spiders count as insects) and was able to use the image lightly enough in his letters ('I live like an insect': *Corr.*, IV, 499). Meanwhile, in the poetry we find an almost passionate identification with the spider as feeling subject, which can shatter the Augustan smoothness of the verse:

> The spider's touch, how exquisitely fine!
> Feels at each thread, and lives along the line. . .
> (*An Essay on Man*, I, 217–8)

Moreover, the running contrast between Pope's Homeric aspirations and his own worse-than-Thersitean deformity, so persistently stressed by his enemies, developed in a somewhat different manner within the mind of Pope himself. There is a curious analogy here with Pope's great predecessor, Milton. Milton, himself a short, slight man, was proud of his flowing hair. With a strange simplicity Adam in *Paradise Lost* has Milton's hair, crowning a body of heroic symmetry. In *Samson Agonistes* a darker kind of analogy is achieved: the mighty Samson, because he is blinded, irresistibly evokes the blinded Milton, mighty controversialist. Today we are trained by our teachers to repress such intuitions. Great Victorian editors of Milton like Masson were under no such restriction. Nor was Pope.

To begin with, he was immensely sensitive to the force and significance of names (his choice of classical substitutes, for example, is very clever: 'Atossa' in the second of the *Moral Essays* is a minor miracle of allusive ingenuity). He therefore knew that his own name, Alexander, was a heroic name and, because heroic, potentially ridiculous. The first Alexander, the military conqueror, is still remembered as 'Alexander the Great'. The poem of two thousand couplets which Pope is said to have written when he was about 14 (and to have destroyed later on the advice of Bishop Atterbury) was called *Alcander, Prince of Rhodes*. This was Pope's first essay in the heroic mode (an ambition which remained formally unfulfilled at the end of his life), and it may be that there is a touch of what psychologists used to call 'projection' in the choice of the hero's name, like but not exactly like 'Alexander'. Some such constellation of images undoubtedly lies behind the phraseology of Pope's letter written in January 1711 to his friend John Caryll: 'I appear not the great Alexander Mr. Caryll is so civil to, but that little Alexander the women

laugh at' (*Corr.*, I, 114). Here it seems Pope's urbane style is successfully performing its work of exorcism, dispelling the various demons
raised by Cibber, with his talk of Pope as a 'little, hasty Hero'
threatened by a sexual challenge to which he was manifestly
unequal.

Meanwhile the echoes extend still farther. Pope was not simply a
matchless verbal duellist incongruously imprisoned in a crippled
body. His very person, as I have suggested, was ambiguous, for the
twisted body was surmounted not, as one might have expected, by a
wizened, Voltairean visage, but by an authentically noble face. In
Plutarch's *Lives* the Roman analogue to Alexander is Julius Caesar.
By a strange chance Pope seems actually to have resembled the
Roman conqueror physically. Joseph Spence (no. 1464) cites a 'Mr
T.' who thought the bust of Caesar in the Grand Duke's palace in
Florence (now in the Uffizi) looked as much like Mr Pope as 'any
bust that has been made on purpose for him', and Wimsatt in our
time finds in Roubiliac's marble and terracotta busts 'convincing
presentations of Pope as the noble Roman, the laureated, the
senatorial'.[18] Pope was conscious of himself, then, as a ridiculous
hunchback and at the same time as the English Homer. But (like one
of his own couplets) each of the terms of this antithesis turns out to
contain its own internal antithesis. The hunchback is fair of face.
The English Homer somehow cannot rise to an authentic English
epic. Moreover, other tensions, of a less abstract kind, persist. The
poet who excelled at softness and delicacy, the poet with the genius
for friendship and intimacy, is excluded from the erotic.

Here the effects are, with an awful inevitability, roughly what one
would predict. Pope's letters to women notoriously combine the
most sensitive and urbane friendliness with occasional intruded
indecencies, which seem to serve the writer's needs more than the
reader's, a muted literary equivalent of exhibitionism. It is as if the
sheer physical distance between parties implied by the epistolary
form somehow begets in Pope the feeling that a brief sexuality may
after all be risked – verbally, at least. This is very nearly explicit in
one letter to Lady Mary Wortley Montagu (whom, be it said, Pope
could hardly have expected to shock – that element of exhibitionism,
at least, is missing): 'Let us be like modest people, who when they
are close together keep all decorum, but if they step a little aside, or
get to the other end of a room, can untye garters or take off shifts
without scruple' (*Corr.*, I, 384).

Similarly, *The Rape of the Lock*, Pope's great essay in urbane conciliation, written to 'laugh away' a family quarrel, is laced with an obscure sexual tension, a tension which once, and once only, breaks out in an oddly gross (almost surrealist) simplicity: 'And Maids turn'd Bottels, call aloud for Corks' (IV, 54). Elsewhere the sexual implication is fugitive, uncertain. The critic who offers examples is in danger of appearing to be prurient. But with Pope as with Sterne a prurient reading again and again proves to be critically productive. What, in the early eighteenth century, is the precise nuance of 'Trembling' in the couplet describing the dressing of Belinda?

> Th' inferior Priestess, at her Altar's side,
> Trembling, begins the sacred Rites of Pride.
> (*The Rape of the Lock*, I, 127–8)

Gradually the excitement of the adoring servant infects the mistress:

> And keener Lightnings quicken in her Eyes. (I, 144)

Notice how at II, 39, the word 'Garters' is dropped into the line with conscious impudence, and how at line 107 of the same canto

> Or stain her Honour, or her new Brocade

the idea of ruptured honour in the first half of the line can momentarily affect the second half, the half which properly supplies the 'innocent' antithesis, so that the imagination, for a fleeting fraction of a second, dallies with less creditable, more sexual ways in which brocade might come to be stained. Indeed, the very title of the poem is a nicely judged deflection of an indecent suggestion. 'Rape' in Pope's day already bore the sense 'sexual violation', but Pope's classicism reassuringly imposes the more neutral sense, 'seizure'. Meanwhile, within the poem the same defeated ambivalence may be found at the point where the Baron meditates the rape itself, doubting whether 'By Force to *ravish*, or by Fraud betray' (II, 32; my italics).

It will be said that all this is in coarse defiance of the true atmosphere of *The Rape of the Lock*, which is (amazingly, for its period) a work of childlike wonder, turning all 'to favour and to prettiness'.

That a childlike wonder fills *The Rape of the Lock* I would not deny, but will merely add that it is everywhere subtly contested by tensions which are far from childlike, in the ordinary meaning of the term. Pope, indeed, employs the vision and to some extent the persona of a child, but he does so to (largely covert) sexual ends. One senses it even at the rudimentary level of physical vision. The very eye-level of Pope, at four feet six, is little higher than the top of Belinda's dressing-table. Pope's physical presence (once the reader has informed himself of such 'extraneous' matters) insinuates itself into the light fabric of the poem, and we become subliminally aware of one who is a child and not a child, admitted (because of his harmlessness) to the intimacy of the lady's bedroom, where he can toy with fascinating combs, bottles and hair-brushes and watch – with eyes that are much too old – all that is happening. It is as if he uses his childlike persona ('little Alexander') to attain a proximity which is in fact not wholly innocent. Yet all the while the simple wonder is entirely real.

The indecent innuendoes of Pope are quite unlike the vehement scatological outbursts of Swift (see, for example, Swift's disquisition on the difference between English and Irish excrement[19]). Curiously enough, it is Swift with all his misanthropic violence who is closer to the primal antipathies of infancy; Pope in comparison is almost humane.

There remains (of the five cardinal points I laid down at the beginning) Pope's consciousness of himself as a poet. For this we need to go back to the beginning of his life, to the last decade of the seventeenth century.

It is a common error of the historical imagination to suppose that a given period contains nothing but its own products. The time will come when historians of the twentieth century will unthinkingly assume that in 1960 the scene consisted entirely of featureless blocks of flats, council houses, shopping-centres and factories. We who have lived through the middle years of this century know how in fact twentieth-century cities are full of very large, visually assertive Victorian buildings. Similarly, the eighteenth century was full of seventeenth-century survivals (and far more Gothic than is commonly supposed). Moreover, we must remember that many luminaries of the Enlightenment passed their childhood in a very different atmosphere. David Hume, the coolest of the critics of religion, was terrified when small by Calvinist sermons on Hell.

The beginning of Pope's life was much more like the beginning of Donne's than most people would expect. A little over a hundred years before, Donne was born into an intense, beleaguered Roman

Catholic family, among persons 'hungry of an imagin'd Martyr-dome'.[20] Pope likewise was brought up in a Roman Catholic family in times which were only a little less intolerant. He was born in 1688 to middle-aged parents; his father, Alexander Pope senior, a success-ful linen-merchant, was then forty-two, his mother, Edith, was forty-six. Alexander senior had one other son by a previous wife, but this child died in 1682, some four years after his mother. One daugh-ter remained from the earlier marriage. It is clear that Pope was the longed-for, the exceptionally beloved only son.

The century which followed still distrusted Popery. Today such an attitude appears, precisely, unenlightened, but to contemporary advocates of toleration Roman Catholicism was to be put down because it was infested with priestcraft, superstition and psychic intimidation: in short, intolerance. Thus, the sectarian hostility of the Protestant reformers was as much corroborated as checked by the new rationalism. We are confronted here with an old paradox of liberalism: how far should intolerance be tolerated? Locke was firm: tolerance could not be extended to Roman Catholics.[21] It is true that the reason Locke gives in his *Letter on Toleration* is political: no church which makes allegiance to a foreign prince a condition of membership can be tolerated by the civil power. But the wider problem is unlikely to have been absent from his mind. He notes elsewhere that 'some are as conscienciously earnest for conformity as others for liberty, and a law for *Toleration* would as much offend their consciences as of *Limitation* others'.[22] In the second part of the *Essay Concerning Toleration* (1667), the forerunner of the *Letter*, he says that Roman Catholics 'are not to enjoy the benefit of toleration, because where they have power they think themselves bound to deny it to others'.[23] The same reasoning lies behind that cultural anti-Semitism which is so characteristic of the Enlightenment and so surprising to modern readers.[24]

The Roman Catholicism of Pope's father had the special intensity which comes from conversion. English Roman Catholics, from the time of Elizabeth I to the beginning of the eighteenth century, were, as Basil Williams has said, 'legally little better than pariahs'.[25] The Test Act of 1673 (25 Car. II cap. 2) incapacitated from offices and places of trust under the Crown all persons who refused to take the oaths of allegiance and supremacy and to receive the sacrament according to the Church of England. In taking the oaths persons were expressly required to deny the Roman Catholic doctrine of

Transubstantiation. By this Act, Roman Catholics were excluded from public office and from the prosecution of any suit in law or equity.[26] In the very year of the poet's birth, the Protestant William of Orange disembarked at Torbay with fourteen thousand men and the Roman Catholic James II fled his country and his throne. Feeling between Papist and Protestant ran high (Roman Catholic chapels were burned to the ground), and the government, shaken, hastened to enforce old legislation designed to suppress Popery and even enacted fresh laws for the purpose. Elizabethan and Jacobean legislation aimed at recusants had remained on the statute-book through the seventeenth century. These penal laws were indeed often laxly enforced, but they were always available for revival when need arose.[27] The government was excited to action by specifically Jacobite plots and movements (the Jacobites themselves being a severe embarrassment to many English Roman Catholics, who by keeping their heads down had found a *modus vivendi* within the system). In 1715 tension increased once more as James, the Catholic Pretender, landed in Scotland. Informers were encouraged to seek out the properties of 'certain traitors, and of Popish recusants' and to discover 'estates given to superstitious uses' (1 Geo. I, St. 2, cap. 50).[28] Some of the legislation, such as that requiring Roman Catholics at all times to keep a certain distance from the Court, may seem bizarre or picturesque today, but Catholics certainly felt its force. Later in his career, when Pope had a villa at Twickenham, he was on three occasions obliged to move out, simply because the Court had taken up residence in nearby Hampton. When Pope was dying in 1744 he was seriously advised not to go into London for medical treatment.

Pope's father was never in any sense martyred by these restrictions but he was undoubtedly harassed by them. In 1700, in order to comply with regulations, the family moved to Binfield, in Windsor Forest. Some ten miles away lived Martha Blount, whom Pope was in some sense to love all his life. Already, however, he was physically broken. Described by his half-sister as having been at first an 'excessively gay and lively little boy', Pope was at the age of 3 or 4 badly injured by a wild cow (Spence, 3 and 4). Then, at the age of 12 he fell victim to the spinal tuberculosis which was to cripple him for life, probably as a result of drinking infected milk.

Pope's father retired from business in the year of his birth. In these circumstances such education as he received was intimate, private and intensely Catholic in tone. Pope was first taught formally by a priest (one John Banister) and then, at the age of 8, was sent to a seminary school at Twyford, near Winchester. Here he seems to have given some trouble; he was whipped for writing a satire and seems subsequently to have been expelled. Pope was then sent to 'Mr. Deane's seminary' at Marylebone (Spence, 15). Thomas Deane's career exhibits in a somewhat sharper form than Mr Pope's the difficulties of publicly committed Roman Catholics at the end of the seventeenth century. He left a fellowship at Oxford after refusing to take the oath of allegiance to William and Mary in 1688 and was both pilloried and imprisoned for his religion (*Corr.*, II, 428 n.).

After the move to Binfield, Pope had some further teaching from yet another priest, but from the age of 12 he seems to have educated himself by voracious reading. In 1701 his docile facility in compositon ('I lisp'd in Numbers, for the Numbers came': *Epistle to Dr. Arbuthnot*, l. 128) resulted in a tragedy on Genevieve, the French saint who dedicated herself to God at 7, took the veil at 15 and devoted herself to mortification. The story is only a little less sensational than that of Heloïse and Abelard, which the mature Pope was to make the theme of a Gothick (almost kitsch) emotionalism. The juvenile piece we may presume to have been more simply pious.

There can be no doubt that Pope's Roman Catholicism powerfully determined the shape of his life. The Test Act prevented (if ill-health alone had not) his attendance at either university, but it is hard to believe that Pope felt his genius impaired by the prohibition. He relished small horizons, small rooms, small circles of intimate friends. Yet his steady formal adherence to the faith throughout a career filled with urbane, pluralist chat remains mildly enigmatic. The evidence we possess is ambiguous or even contradictory. In September 1742, Pope told the French poet Louis Racine that he was a good Catholic, willing to submit all his opinions 'to the Decision of the Church' (*Corr.*, IV, 416). About a year later he told Warburton that he was 'convinced that the Church of Rome had all the marks of the anti-Christian power predicted of in the writings of the New Testament.'[29] When Warburton asked why in that case he did not leave the Church of Rome, Pope answered that to do so would be to make a great many enemies for himself and would do no good to anyone else (Spence, 352). In either case we may guess that Pope's real views were modified by his perennial eagerness to please. In part, no doubt, the 'there-is-much-to-be-said-on-both-sides' manner which is worked so hard in *An Essay on Man* was expressly designed to lift its author clear of the bloody sectarian dissension which had torn the previous century. Here Pope makes an interesting contrast with Donne. Donne found his way from the hot, dark world of his Roman Catholic childhood to Anglicanism and a deanery. Dame Helen Gardner has noted the studious moderation of his poem 'A Litanie', in which he reviews his religious progress.[30] But Donne's violent style continually contests the irenic content of his verse. With Pope it is otherwise. He found the required style: a soothing, transcending urbanity, antitheses which rather reconcile than divide opinion, a running insinuation that we, who are men of sense and culture, are unlikely to burn one another.

Certain lines in *An Essay on Criticism* go surprisingly far in disparaging the monastic tradition:

> A *second* Deluge Learning thus o'er-run,
> And the *Monks* finished what the *Goths* begun.
>
> (691–2)

Similarly, the lines in the 1742 *Dunciad* which describe the overthrow of the Roman Empire, ending with

> See Christians, Jews, one heavy Sabbath keep,
> And all the western world believe and sleep
>
> (III, 99–100)

seem to breathe the purest eighteenth-century scepticism. Indeed, they are Gibbonian. Gibbon describes how, on an autumn day in the ruins of Rome, he watched the barefoot friars going to sing vespers in what had once been the Temple of Jupiter Capitoline and resolved there and then to recount the decline and fall of the Roman Empire and 'the triumph of barbarism and religion'.[31]

It is not enough to point out that Roman Catholics have always enjoyed anti-clerical and anti-monastic jests. Pope's lines did actually offend people like the Abbé Southcote and his old friend John Caryll. Yet Pope stuck formally to the faith of his parents. Swift once offered Pope twenty guineas if he would change his religion. Pope answered that twenty guineas was rather low but a well-organised public subscription might just raise a hundred and seventy pounds (*Corr.*, I, 198–9). It is possible that he was, as Lord Chesterfield said, 'a Deist, believing in a future state',[32] that is, one who, like others of his time, rejected all narrowly doctrinal forms of religion and substituted a belief in a highly abstract Supreme Being, but yet retained his faith in personal immortality. Chesterfield in the same passage elegantly compares Pope's Roman Catholic death, attended by a priest, with Socrates' deathbed compliance with the old Athenian pious custom of sacrificing a cock to Aesculapius – a sort of smiling final courtesy and no more. Johnson's account is a little stronger:

> Pope expressed undoubting confidence of a future state. Being asked by his friend Mr Hooke, a papist, whether he would not die like his father and mother, and whether a priest should not be called, he answered, 'I do not think it essential but it will be very right; and I thank you for putting me in mind of it.'[33]

We should remember that the strictest Roman Catholic would agree with Pope that the presence of a priest is not essential. In the third book of Evelyn Waugh's *Brideshead Revisited* (chapter 5) a twentieth-century family of Roman Catholics endeavours to explain to an unbelieving friend how priests are clearly inessential to a 'good' death and yet how every Roman Catholic would nevertheless prefer to have one at his or her side when the time comes. Yet, when all this is said, Pope's apparent absence of mind on the matter suggests that he had moved some considerable distance from the faith in which he was educated. One cannot suppose that his father would have answered so.

If Pope's religious beliefs remain an indistinct quantity, his sense of himself as a poet, firm at the beginning, grew somehow harder and brighter as his career progressed. If one questions professional writers, one often finds that in childhood they laboriously produced, manually, the august apparatus (title-page, 'Contents', and so on) of 'proper books'. Pope was an extreme case of this loving anticipation of literary fame. He not only followed the general forms of published material, but also taught himself to reproduce with minute accuracy the shapes of printed letters (Spence, 25). Thus, nearly from the beginning, the poet who preferred the drawing-room to the forum, the poet of intimacy, of *privacy*, had an eye to *publication*. R. H. Griffith has observed that Pope was the first person in

England to accumulate a fortune from writings deliberately composed as works of art.[34] He was also the first major literary figure to publish the letters he wrote to his friends.

It is likely that the young Pope received plenty of what behaviourist psychologists call 'positive reinforcement'. Sir William Trumbull, whom Pope came to know when his family moved to Windsor Forest, used to ride out with him and together they would declaim the classics. Sir William certainly led Pope to believe (fortunately, with abundant reason) that he could write. Pope was the sort of child prodigy who clings throughout life to the special, protected status this term affords. When mature, he showed a more than Miltonic anxiety that readers should be aware how young he had been when he wrote such and such a poem, but took equal care, one senses, that any authentically childish solecism in the verse should be invisibly mended before the world be permitted to applaud.

About the year 1705, Pope began to make contact with literary society in London. He assiduously cultivated the acquaintance of such men as Thomas Betterton, the actor, Wycherley, the now ruinous Restoration rake and author of libertine comedies, Lord Lansdowne, Samuel Garth, Lord Bolingbroke and William Walsh. Perhaps the most striking thing about the list is the fact that they are all much older than Pope; they belong to another, established generation. Pope, I have said, wished to pass for a rake, and some of those he courted had been in their time notable debauchees, but in truth he was very far from being a young man out on the tiles. Even if nature had fitted him for sexual adventures, one suspects that his principal energies would have been differently employed. He was furthering, with almost professional expertise, his literary career. Later Bolingbroke was to testify to Pope's genius for friendship. The praise is just. Yet friendship is partly an art, and one suspects that Pope acquired it in his laborious and considerate cultivation of various old men. But, indeed, the root is less than the flower.

The idea of a 'career' is neither Hebraic nor Christian, but originally classical. The male Roman of the appropriate social class hoped to proceed through a definite sequence of public offices, known as the *cursus honorum*. It is unlikely that the Romans in general had an equivalent conception of the proper progress of a literary career. But they had the example of Virgil, who wrote first pastorals and then epic, and Virgil became a model for the poets of the Renaissance. In English literature both Spenser and Milton were careful to write

pastorals before proceeding to epic, so that by the time we come to
Pope the sequence is, so to speak, authoritative.

I have already suggested that Pope was never able to write the epic
of which he had always been so urgently conscious, as the proper
crown of a poetic progress. Indeed, if we follow his actual writings in
minute chronological sequence we shall see that he did not follow the
Virgilian order but, rather, was straining after epic at the very
beginning (with *Alcander, Prince of Rhodes*) and died still essaying
the same high task (with the uncompleted *Brutus*), but that all the
while, from boyhood onwards, satires flowed easily from his pen.

Of course, Pope knew his Virgil well enough to be aware that
Virgil, too, speaks of an attempt on epic made *before* he wrote the
pastorals which now stand as his earliest work. Pope told Spence:

> My next work after my epic was my *Pastorals*, so that I did exactly
> what Virgil says of himself:

> > Cum canerem reges et proelia, Cynthius aurem
> > Vellit, et admonuit; 'pastorem, Tityre, pinguis
> > Pascere oportet oves; deductum dicere carmen'
> > (Spence, 47)

Pope's careful phrase, 'says of himself', suggests that he was aware
that the Latin lines are highly conventional (Virgil is, after all, echoing Callimachus), yet in his own case the biographical truth of the
formula is indisputable. The lines he quotes are from Virgil's Sixth
Eclogue and may be translated thus: 'When I would sing of kings
and battles (that is, epic), Cynthian Apollo tweaked my ear and gave
me a piece of advice: "Shepherds should feed fat their sheep but
their poems should be slender." ' Apollo's advice was to write in the
minor genre before attempting the major. Milton refers to the same
Virgilian passage in 'Lycidas':

> Fame is the spur that the clear spirit doth raise
> (That last infirmity of noble mind)
> To scorn delights and live laborious days;
> But the fair guerdon when we hope to find
> And to think to burst out into sudden blaze,
> Comes the blind Fury with th'abhorred shears
> And slits the thin-spun life. But not the praise,
> Phoebus repli'd, and touch'd my trembling ears;
> Fame is no plant that grows on mortal soil. . .
> (70–8)

It is easy to see that Milton will be less easily deflected than Pope from the highest ambition. We might have begun to conclude from the phrase 'last infirmity' that Milton scorned the very idea of fame, but the passage taken as a whole makes it clear that Milton is against one kind of fame only: the merely human. There is another, immortal fame which he will not easily give up. The reference to Virgil is appropriately transformed. Instead of showing disapproval of excessive ambition, Milton's Apollo rebukes the poet for setting his sights too low.

Nevertheless, Pope remains, after Milton, of all English poets the most urgently conscious of his programme and his powers. One senses Pope's conception of his own place in a splendid succession in the account he gives of the time when, 'being almost twelve', he sat and narrowly observed the great Dryden in Wills's coffee-house (*Corr.*, I, 1–2; Spence, 57). Remembering the occasion, Pope quotes Ovid, 'Vergilium tantum vidi' (*Tristia*, IV, x, 51) – 'I once caught sight of Virgil' – and one feels, as it were with an Eliotic shiver, the simultaneous presence of all the great poets of our European past. Then one remembers how, a generation before, a youthful, dapper Dryden had met Milton, the blinded Samson of an earlier age, and asked if he might turn *Paradise Lost* into a kind of light opera!

I have dwelt at some length on Pope's religious beliefs, partly because we shall in due course be considering his principal religious poem. But Pope himself seems to have been in no doubt that, in him, the poet ousted the Roman Catholic. The idea is present with a curious nakedness in the passage where Pope describes his father:

> Hopes after Hopes of pious Papists fail'd,
> While mighty WILLIAM's thundring Arm prevail'd.
> For Right Hereditary tax'd and fin'd,
> He stuck to Poverty with Peace of Mind;
> And me, the Muses help'd to undergo it;
> Convict a Papist He, and I a Poet.
>
> *(The Second Epistle of the Second Book
> of Horace, Imitated*, 62–7)

The lives of authors are commonly most interesting in their earlier parts. Pope (to this writer, at least) is no exception. We have already assembled the crucial constitutive materials of a literary personality. From here on we have a steady march of major works and a most unedifying and intricate mess of quarrel and intrigue. This I do not propose to pursue. The underside of it I have already in a manner noticed in my discussion of the pamphlet attacks on Pope. The general atmosphere of the rest is perhaps best conveyed in Johnson's dexterous account of the machinations by which Pope secured the publication of his letters. Since it was not normal practice to publish letters, Pope was obliged, as Johnson put it, to contrive 'an appearance of compulsion'.[35] Accordingly he seems to have sent copies of the correspondence anonymously to two booksellers, Lintot and Curll. Curll rose to the bait and published. Pope subsequently went through the charade of a lawsuit, but complacently concluded that his only recourse was to replace Curll's faulty and surreptitious edition with an authorised version. The story does little for Pope's credit. Yet there are deeper impulses at work here than a vulgar eagerness for fame. The translation of the private into a public form lies very near the centre of Pope's art.

CHAPTER 2

Order and Disorder

(i) METRE

The eighteenth century, as every schoolboy used to know, was the Age of Reason. Yet, if a pervasive character is sought, it may be that the idea of order will serve better than the idea of reason. Reason (as we shall discover) is a troublesome term. Even the philosophy of the eighteenth century is not rationalist in certain fundamental senses of the term. According to one ancient antithesis, Locke himself, whose genius presided over the early years of the century, was by virtue of his empiricism an opponent of rationalism. To locate knowledge in the passive imprinting of the senses is implicitly to dislodge reason, formerly seen as the organ of understanding. By the middle years of the century David Hume in his *Treatise of Human Nature* had carried out a thoroughgoing attack on reason, subverting the fundamental concepts of induction and causality. With the arts, though historians still struggle to apply the term 'rational', its appropriateness is persistently elusive. In what sense is the music of Handel rational? In what sense is St Paul's Cathedral more rational than Salisbury? Certainly not by adherence to honest utility. Those who have ascended Wren's great dome and looked down upon the nave from above know how the architect made covert use of such Gothick barbarisms as flying buttresses, discreetly concealed from those who stood below by screen-walls.

With the notion of order we fare a little better. To be sure, Gothic cathedrals were minutely organised structures; the traditional conception of them as mighty remnants of medieval chaos has been overthrown. It does not follow that the eighteenth century counter-emphasis on apprehensible order should be rejected at the same time. Meanwhile, the favoured conception of the universe, common to the free-thinking Deist and the orthodox Anglican divine, was of an ordered whole. In music, in painting, in sculpture, in architecture, in literary theory, in poetry, order was prized. But it was not the only thing which counted.

With Pope it is best to begin at the level of metre. Johnson praised the 'systematical arrangement' of his language and the 'minute and punctilious observation' with which he examined 'lines and words'. 'Pope', he says, 'is always smooth, uniform and gentle.'[1] It is a description of Pope to which almost every reader gives instinctive assent. But it is not exactly true.

Every line of English verse, if we are to analyse it metrically, must be considered both in terms of its ideal formal scheme and in terms of what is actually done. It is best, therefore, to speak of the elements of a line as *positions*, which may be variously occupied. The most commonly used line in English verse is the decasyllabic. Where these lines are unrhymed, as commonly in Shakespeare, they are known as blank verse. When they are placed in rhyming pairs, as by Pope, they are called heroic couplets.

An ordinary decasyllabic line has ten positions. These may be described as either weak or strong, according as they naturally invite an unstressed or a stressed syllable. The first position is weak, the second strong, the third weak, the fourth strong, and so on alternately until we come to the last position, which is strong. Where a line is completely regular all the actual syllables occupying the strong positions will be stressed and all those in weak positions will be unstressed; for example (note that here 'w' stands for 'weak' and 's' for 'strong', and an acute accent marks the syllables which are actually stressed):

> The ínter-tíssu'd róbe of góld and péarl
>
> w   s   w   s   w   s   w s   w   s

Each of the five 'natural' stresses of the line falls in a strong position and all five remaining weak positions are occupied by naturally unstressed syllables. The line, therefore, is fully regular.

Any reader of Shakespeare, however, will soon discover many lines which do not satisfy these requirements. We do not say, for example:

> The quálitý of mércy ís not stráined.

Rather, we say:

> The quálity of mércy is not stráined.

That is, only three of the five strong positions receive a natural stress. Some readers or actors will depart still further from the ideal metrical scheme and (because of the sense of the passage) stress 'not', despite the fact that it occupies a weak position.

Notice that no one stigmatises this line as 'unmetrical' (though we *would* condemn a Latin line as unmetrical if a short syllable were substituted for a long one). On the contrary, the actor who delivers the line in a tick-tock manner with five uncompromising stresses would normally be condemned as having no ear, no sense of the proper commerce between metrical scheme and natural variation which is characteristic of English poetry. There is, to be sure, an opposite vice, the delivery of blank verse without any sense whatever of the underlying formal scheme, but that need not detain us here.

There is in fact a subtle auditory war going on almost all the time in English verse between the scheme (the positions) and the reality (the occupying syllables). Although this war should not be seen as a conflict between the metrical and the unmetrical, it is a conflict between regularity and irregularity, order and disorder. Metrical brilliance, outside the special ingenuities of comic verse like that of Benjamin Bickley Rogers, W. S. Gilbert or A. A. Milne, does not consist in the attainment of uniform regularity, but in the management of the war.

We must grant, of course, that Dryden, Pope's greatest immediate predecessor, wrote with pronounced and conscious regularity. If we compare him with the earlier Metaphysicals, this is especially true: much of Donne's verse is so irregular that it deserves to be called unmetrical, since there is no 'norm' discernible to resist the natural bias of the syllables; it is sometimes impossible to discover the metre of a Donne poem without 'cheating', by looking at the visual arrangement on the page. In Dryden the push towards regularity tends to produce one of its regular consequences in English, which is comic effect. In *Religio Laici* one can watch a poem, which sets out as an expression of profound religious feeling, being insensibly transformed in the direction of cheerful good-humour. These are the opening lines:

> Dim, as the borrow'd beams of Moon and Stars
> To *Lonely, weary, wandring* Travellers,
> Is *Reason* to the *Soul*: and as on high,
> Those rowling Fires *discover* but the Sky

> Not light us *here*; so *Reason*'s glimmering Ray
> Was lent, not to *assure* our *doubtfull* way,
> But *guide* us upward to a *better Day*.
> And as those nightly Tapers disappear
> When Day's bright Lord ascends our Hemisphere;
> So Pale grows *Reason* at *Religions* sight;
> So *dyes*, and so *dissolves* in *Supernatural Light*.[2]

And these are the last lines:

> Thus have I made my own Opinions clear:
> Yet neither Praise expect, nor Censure fear:
> And this unpolish'd, rugged Verse, I chose;
> As fittest for Discourse, and nearest Prose:
> For, while from *Sacred Truth* I do not swerve,
> *Tom Sternhold's* or *Tom Shadwell's Rhimes* will serve.[3]

The tone of the last lines is much lighter than that of the opening. It is hard to avoid the inference that sheer metrical regularity, independently of sense, has assisted in the transformation. In the very last couplet, sense turns round, looks at what has happened, and itself alludes to *versification* ('Tom Shadwell's Rhimes').

The same bouncy regularity (combined with 'cliff-hanging' punctuation) continually raises smiles in the purportedly serious *Threnodia Augustalis*:[4]

> So swift and so surprizing was our Fear:
> Our *Atlas* fell indeed; but *Hercules* was near.
>
> ii
>
> His Pious Brother, sure the best
>   Who ever bore that Name,
> Was newly risen from his Rest,
>   And, with a fervent Flame,
> His usual morning Vows had just address'd . . . (34–40)

But even Dryden is far from uniform. The most metrically regular of all the major English poets is in fact Spenser.[5] This would doubtless surprise Johnson, who, one suspects, was not careful to distinguish metrical from stylistic effects and would therefore begin by thinking of *The Faerie Queene* as a 'Babylonish' essay in literary mock-Gothic, a very monument of disorder. The effect of Spenser's metrical regularity is not comic but – perhaps because it is so regular that one loses all sense of a surprisingly *achieved* scheme – merely tedious, tending, in alliance with a profusion of inertly tautological adjectives ('dolefull drerihed'), to obscure an immensely powerful imagination.

Pope, so far from being a metronomic poet, is one of the supreme masters of the running counterpoint between scheme and natural stress. It is true, of course, that he marks off the lines as uttered with firm 'end-stopping', that is, with frequent punctuation falling at the end of a line. He deliberately rejects Milton's 'sense variously drawn out from one verse into another'[6] in favour of a coincidence of sense-unit with metrical unit. He then enforces this effect with rhyme, which Milton chose not to use. That rhyme alone does not produce a metrically assertive effect can be seen from the opening lines of Keat's *Endymion*:

> A think of beauty is a joy for ever:
> Its loveliness increases; it will never
> Pass into nothingness; but still will keep
> A bower quiet for us, and a sleep
> Full of sweet dreams, and health and quiet breathing.[7]

It is hard to remember that Keats is here writing in heroic couplets, the metre of Dryden and Pope. One is influenced, indeed, by the content (since in reading one never 'hears' the metre in abstraction from the rest), but there is no doubt that the punctuation (which aims in general at mid-line and avoids line-endings) plays its part. It is likely that a person who knew no English, having first listened to Pope, would receive a quite different auditory impression from Keats.

But, having marked off his lines, Pope proceeds to his double labour of sustaining and subverting their metrical form. The opening lines of the 'Epistle To Miss Blount, on her leaving the Town, after the Coronation' would be regarded by most readers as 'typical to good' Pope and will therefore serve as an example:

> As some fond virgin, whom her mother's care
> Drags from the town to wholsom country air,
> Just when she learns to roll a melting eye,
> And hear a spark, yet think no danger nigh;
> From the dear man unwilling she must sever,
> Yet takes one kiss before she parts for ever:

Thus from the world fair *Zephalinda* flew,
Saw others happy, and with sighs withdrew;
Not that their pleasures caus'd her discontent,
She sigh'd not that They stay'd, but that She went.

Of these lines only one (the fourth) is unambiguously regular. The
sixth line

Yet takes one kiss before she parts for ever

launches itself with perfect regularity, perhaps to assist the deliberate suggestion of cliché planted by a Pope who, in an almost trans-
parently self-protective manner, seeks at times to patronise the
delicious Miss Blount. But the line terminates with the ghost of an
extra syllable, the '-er' of 'ever', a faint metrical shimmer which
subliminally enforces a 'vanishing' effect appropriate to the line's
meaning.

There are several examples at the beginnings of lines of the
stressed equivalent of what in classical metre would be called 'choriambic substitution', that is, the substitution of x́ x x x́ for x x́ x x́. In
the case of 'Drags from the town' this seems to be firmly linked
to stylistic effect: the emphasising of the important verb, 'Drags'. In
the case of 'Not that their pleasures' the metrical irregularity assists
the impression of eager and embarrassed apology, as the poet hastily
explains that Miss Blount is no Rochefoucauldian egoist. The other
examples of 'choriambic substitution' are much less firm:

Júst when she leárns
Fróm the dear mán
Thús from the wórld

In the first and third of these it is quite possible to read with no stress
on the first syllable and with a stress on the second, which regular-
ises both, and in 'From the dear man' it is possible to avoid a stress
on 'From' and so make the line less irregular. We are here entering
the grey area of reader's discretion. What is certain is that Pope's
habitual versification does not, with educated readers, automatically
direct such hesitations to a regular solution. Meanwhile the last line
quoted

She sigh'd not that They stay'd, but that She went

is powerfully irregular, capitalising the two calculated affronts to the scheme, stressed syllables in weak positions.

In Latin verse, where the natural *stress* of the language is permitted to conflict with metrical emphasis on *quantity* (the length in time of the syllable, an element which scarcely figures in English versification), the resulting effect is known as 'heterodyne'. Virgil is the acknowledged master of the subtly managed heterodyne. In English there is no exact equivalent, but Pope's subtle manipulation, within the firmly marked couplet, of an endlessly varied metrical tension is almost Virgilian. Pope's verse is never mechanical. In metre he is enamoured of order, but never enslaved by it.

(ii) SENSE

So far I have admitted the notion of *meaning* only in order to explain or comment on the sort of irregularity which is in any case traceable at the prior level of *sound*. We may now turn to Pope's characteristic method of dealing with the smaller units of sense. Here one discovers immediately an excited and highly ingenious patterning, with frequent use of antithesis, that is, the balancing of one element against another.

Commonly the first line of a couplet is set in antithesis with the second:

> 'Twixt Plautus, Fletcher, Shakespear, and Corneille,
> Can make a Cibber, Tibbald, or Ozell.
> (*Dunciad*, 1742, I, 285–6)

Here great names in the first line are set against contemptible names in the second. This is the simplest form of Augustan antithesis. Not infrequently, however, Pope succeeds in achieving a double antithesis in a couplet, whereby the two halves of the first line contrast and the same effect is repeated in the second; for example:

> Not Man alone,* but all that roam the wood,
> Or wing the sky,* or roll along the flood. . .
> (*Essay on Man*, III, 119–20)

I mark the points of contrast with asterisks; man in his civility is contrasted with woodland creatures, and then the birds that fly above are contrasted with the fish that swim below. This scheme is susceptible of further elaboration. For example, each of the antithetical lines can be placed in contrast with the other, creating a triple antithesis; for example:

> With too much knowledge* for the Sceptic side,
> With too much weakness* for the Stoic's pride. . .
> *(Essay on Man,* II, 5–6)

Here knowledge is contrasted with scepticism, weakness with Stoic pride, and a larger contrast is proposed between man's erudition and his incapacity.

Those who like drawing diagrams can work out the scheme for a quadruple antithesis, a quintuple, and so on, but it may well be thought that even Pope's ingenuity is unlikely in practice to reach so far. This surmise is in fact quite wrong. He occasionally attains the extraordinary, glittering effect of a septuple, or sevenfold, antithesis, that is, an antithesis having fourteen terms in a single couplet. The diagram for a sevenfold antithesis looks like this:

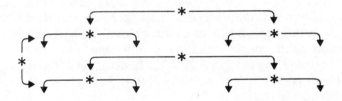

Here is an actual specimen:

> Oh! if to dance all Night, and dress all Day,
> Charm'd the Small-pox, or chas'd old Age away . . .
> *(The Rape of the Lock,* V, 19–20)

If we take the smallest contrasts first, vigorously active dancing is contrasted with night (normally a time for sleeping), dressing (usually done before the day begins) is contrasted with the day, 'Charm'd' (which, while it bears the basic sense of magical incantation, is also touched, because of the erotic context, with a hint of the modern sense) is contrasted with the disgusting smallpox, and the nimbleness of 'chas'd' contrasts with slow 'old Age'. Then dancing all night is contrasted with dressing all day, and the insinuating gentleness of charming away the smallpox is contrasted with the rough expulsion of old age. Finally, the entire idea of dancing all night and dressing all day (the first line) is set against certain grim consequences with which it is unable to deal in the second line.

When antitheses come as thick and fast as these, some of them are necessarily almost 'inaudible'. Yet Pope's mind really does slice his matter his way and that in a manner which is both dazzling and suggestive of intellectual control. In the example of a sevenfold antithesis we can actually glimpse further patternings, shimmering away into the darkness; night goes with old age and by consequence youth with day and perhaps with smallpox, 'dress' is echoed by 'Charm'd' and 'dance' by 'chas'd'. Thus, a system of similarities operates to prevent the successive contrasts from blowing the couplet apart. We can call this order if we like, but it is far indeed from mechanical order. It is brilliantly organic, a springing order endlessly branching into new life.

The terms of an antithesis may echo or contrast with one another. The poet has, so to speak, an unsymmetrical freedom within the formal symmetry of the method to vary echo with contrast or to conceal one within the other. Again and again one finds with Pope's poetry that it is only the couplet-form which is regularly double; the use made of the couplet is devious, even wanton. The first English critic to see this clearly was William Empson. In *Seven Types of Ambiguity* (1930), Empson quoted (or rather slightly misquoted) two lines from *The Rape of the Lock*:

> Here Thou, Great *Anna*! whom three Realms obey,
> Dost sometimes Counsel take – and sometimes *Tea*.
> (III, 7–8)

Empson was interested in the figure of speech known as zeugma; that is, the yoking together in a single copulative phrase of unlike objects: 'The bridesmaids all went home in floods of tears and hansom cabs.' In the lines from *The Rape of the Lock* we have a zeugma of 'taking counsel' with 'taking tea'. Empson observed that in some societies a man who says, 'Bring me my gun, the dogs and three beaters', using the same inflection of the same verb, will be laughed at as if he has made a barbarous pun (since each of the objects named

normally requires a differentiated verb). At the same time a capacity
for high abstraction (so that we not only have a word for every tree
but also the word 'tree' which applies to them all) seems to be
necessary to civilisation. Pope here contrives his subtly intermediate
effect 'by putting together two of the innumerable meanings of the
word *take*'.[8] The Popean zeugma depends for its existence and effect
on the partial defeat of a formal parallelism by things unlike, eccen-
trically unassimilable.

(iii) CLASSICISM

Some of what I have said may suggest that we have in Pope a tension
of classical and Romantic modes. Terms so latitudinarian can hardly
be ruled out as clearly irrelevant. If Classicism implies regularity and
control and Romanticism implies the opposite, then I have obviously
said as much. Certainly, many readers of Pope have been visited by
the presentiment that inside the socially vigilant, ironically cool poet
there is an unusually 'pure' Romantic, struggling to get out:

> . . . quick effluvia darting thro' the brain,
> Die of a rose in aromatic pain?
> *(Essay on Man,* I, 199–200)

Here Pope borrows the thought and some of the phraseology of a
poem by the Countess of Winchelsea (MM, 40) but makes it
thoroughly his own. In such lines the Romantic sensibility seems to
be seen from afar, ironically judged and then, most incongruously,
made the object of a profound empathy. Less than a hundred years
before, George Herbert had written in his poem 'Vertue':

> Sweet rose, whose hue angrie and brave
> Bids the rash gazer wipe his eye. . .[9]

There a skinless sensitivity to the rose's beauty finds itself in conflict
with an austere Protestantism, committed to despise all that is not
God. Pope's lines, hedged about not by theology but by social irony,
betray the different fears of a later age.

Among the underlying motives we may, remembering the way the
Richardsons watched Pope's face 'writhen' under the lash of personal
attack,[10] surmise a fear of ridicule. The man who languishes at the
sight of a rose is easy meat for the satirist. The man who describes

such languishing is less open to mockery. Yet even the first line seems to betray, with the sharpness of 'quick effluvia', a more than intimate acquaintance with the experience, and the second line (as Edith Sitwell ingenuously assumed) is ravishingly lyrical.[11]

Similarly, when Pope's lyric gift breaks through in *The Rape of the Lock* the effect is of a curiously neat, that is, an unmixed Romanticism, Swinburne rather than Browning, Shelley rather than Keats:

> Soft o'er the Shrouds Aerial Whispers breathe,
> That seem'd but *Zephyrs* to the Train beneath.
> Some to the Sun their Insect-Wings unfold,
> Waft on the Breeze, or sink in Clouds of Gold.
> Transparent Forms, too fine for mortal Sight,
> Their fluid Bodies half-dissolv'd in Light.
>
> (II, 57–62)

Much indeed must be conceded to the Classical side. Broome submitted his draft translations of Homer for stylistic 'correction' by Pope, who, unrestrained by any sense of the sanctity of personal expression, did a professional job (*Corr.*, II, 226, 269, 321).[12] Still more remarkably, Wycherley in his sixties submitted his poems for correction by a Pope not yet out of his teens.[13] For such deference (initially, at least) and such magisterial revision one can find no parallel until Eliot, in conscious rejection of Romanticism, sent *The Waste Land* to Pound, 'il miglior fabbro', for his improvements. But Eliot, despite his ostentatious deference, knew that his poem would remain Eliotic, would not become Poundian. Pope did a similar job for various dead poets, for Shakespeare in his edition, for John Donne in his 'versification' of the Satires (as if they were not already in verse), for Homer in his translation or, rather, transposition.

The anti-Romantic, Horatian *nil admirari*, 'wonder at nothing' (*Epistles*, I, vi, 1), is echoed by Pope with 'Fools *Admire*, but Men of Sense *Approve*' (*Essay on Criticism*, 391). To be sure, he is here laying down laws for critics, not for poets, but in the opening of *The Sixth Epistle of the First Book of Horace Imitated* he repeats the Horatian phrase, and this time the reference is to the writing, not the reading of poetry. But always a contrary force asserts itself. *The Rape of the Lock* is full of wonder. The world of glittering surfaces, of silver, porcelain and ivory, silken dresses and steaming, fragrant cups of coffee is in the end a profounder source of poetic energy than the penetrating exposure of folly. Mere seeing is, after all, a deeper business than satirical 'seeing through'. In the tenth chapter of *Rasselas*, Johnson's pedagogue Imlac speaks disdainfully of those who would number the streaks on a tulip.[14] It is one of the central statements of neo-classicism and one of the most ill-fated. It is not just that Tennyson and Hopkins, in their reaction against Augustanism, delighted in specificity. Pope himself, the master of the Augustans, is never so happy as when tracing minute phenomena.

In so permitting counter-classical forces to operate, Pope is not really at odds with his age. Architecture alone successfully reconciled neo-classical theory and practice. The great exception to this rule is Sir John Soane, who, in the work he did on his own house in Lincoln's Inn Fields at the end of the century, subjected the classical movement to an extraordinary, oblique redaction: cunningly placed mirrors produce illusions of height and depth, the eye is alternately satisfied and confused by unintelligible spaces, and, as one descends into the cellar (where Soane's imaginary friend, 'the Monk', was deemed to live in a Gothic grotto crowded with death-masks, fragments of temples and the actual sarcophagus of Seti the First) one seems to be entering the unconscious of the century. The elusive heterodyne of Popean versification is only a faint and exceedingly subtle last echo of something which elsewhere in the art of the period assumes far grosser forms.

Take the composition of a typical Hogarth picture – *The Lord Mayor's Show*, Plate XII, or *The Country Dance*, for example. In the upper half of the picture regularity prevails, in the rectilinear severity of the buildings. But all across the lower half flows a turbulent phantasmagoria of chaotic humanity. There is a certain correspondence between such a visual composition and the organisation of lines like

> Escape in Monsters, and amaze the town.
> (*Dunciad*, 1742, I, 38)

The eighteenth century revered Raphael, but its own greatest achievements in draughtsmanship always tended towards caricature, towards the extravagantly irregular.

It has often been observed that the Age of Reason inaugurated by Pope turns out on closer inspection to be largely populated by mad or melancholy figures. Sir Isaac Newton suffered a serious mental breakdown in 1692–3. Johnson himself was frequently the prey of disabling depression. Boswell, in a superb simile, likened the mind of Johnson to the Roman Colosseum, majestically regular in its structure but with certain, dreadful beasts lurking in the *carceres*.[15] Swift feared that he would die mad. Certainly his contemporaries assumed later that he had (Johnson wrote, 'Swift expires a Driv'ler and a Show' in *The Vanity of Human Wishes*, 318). Christopher Smart, after composing five tedious hymns on the attributes of the Supreme Being, went *happily* insane and in the asylum celebrated a Blakean universe of lyric innocence in *Jubilate Agno*. This may be the only poem in the language which renders madness enviable. It is manifestly insane and breathes the very smell of heaven. Even Collins went mad; Gilbert White of Selborne watched from the wall of Merton College in Oxford as Collins was dragged struggling along Dead Man's Walk to the local Bedlam.[16] Cowper was driven by the conviction of his damnation into paralysing depression and then, irrationally enough, to attempted suicide. We may think of the unbalanced and unhappy Chatterton, of his bizarre exercise in creative forgery followed by the terrible journey to London and suicide in 1770. The very hilarity of Sterne's *Tristram Shandy* is the natural obverse of its author's melancholia, a protracted effort of self-therapy. Meanwhile, where we do not find madness, we find extreme eccentricity. The classical scholar Porson once carried a young woman round a room in his teeth.

How far such stories really demonstrate a high incidence of mental imbalance is impossible to say. What is inescapable is that this is the richly anecdotal picture which the age itself left behind. This is the way they saw themselves. Doubtless the more austere literary critic will still reject such biographical material as so much picturesque irrelevance. Yet the same critic will be forced to acknowledge that the major literary monuments of the century are extravagantly irregular, monstrously superabundant. The method of Boswell's vast, sprawling *Life of Johnson* is utterly unlike the method of Plutarch. Sterne's *Tristram Shandy* is one of the most wantonly irregular stories ever written. No one can describe the *shape* of either work. The 'architectonics' of Fielding's *Tom Jones* are prominent, but parodic. *The Dunciad*, though full of local antithesis, lacks as a whole the proper symmetry of epic narrative structure.

Indeed, the Classicism of the eighteenth century was more a matter of aspiration than of performance. C. S. Lewis has drawn attention to the way Addison, in an essay on 'Chevy Chase', 'called the bluff' of the neo-classical movement. The age talked endlessly of truth, simplicity, reason and nature. All these characteristics were present in the old ballad, which everyone despised. Meanwhile, in the literature of the town, they were nowhere to be found.[17] Instead of the great classical genres – epic, tragedy, lyric – we find, over and over again, satire, a genre unknown to the Greeks (though they had their *iambopoioi*) and regarded by the Roman poet Juvenal as a mere 'farrago' (see his *Satires*, I, 86). The picture is too simple but is, nevertheless, not without a certain justice. A few eighteenth-century tragedies are still remembered. Addison wrote his *Cato* and Johnson his *Irene*. Many fine eighteenth-century lyrics survive, but they seem slight beside those which Marvell wrote in the century before or Keats in the century which followed. No one wrote a straightforwardly great heroic poem.

Yet the image of Rome dominated their thoughts. At the level of poetic diction it was possible to believe that a classical style had been attained. It was the boast of the original Augustus 'that he had found Rome made of bricks and left it made of marble' ('urbem . . . marmoream se relinquere, quam latericiam accepisset').[18] Dryden, it was felt, really had done a similar job on English verse. Johnson in the final sentence of his life of Dryden invokes the boast of Augustus. But how far did the English Augustan age really resemble the age of the original Augustus?

A *locus classicus* for the conception of English Augustanism is Pope's own 'Epistle to Augustus' (also called *The First Epistle of the Second Book of Horace Imitated*) addressed to George II. This poem, so far from proposing an analogy between two great patrons of literature (for the Roman Augustus was the patron of Virgil and Horace), instead depends for its wholly satirical effect on a sharp contrast between the two men. George II despised literature, and Pope in his turn hardly conceals his contempt for his philistine sovereign. The mode of the poem is not panegyric but ironic, and therefore its thesis is precisely to deny that the new age was Augustan. Yet the *stylistic* deference to Horace remains largely unironic. The Roman poet is a seriously revered model (as, after all, the Roman emperor *ought* to have been a model for the King of England) and so, at another level, the Roman analogy is, after all, a potent one. There is a likewise serious force in the way the image of Rome underlies the skirmishing of *The Dunciad*, as Aubrey Williams has shown.[19] But Pope repeatedly conveys his sense of the ways in which the English reality falls short of the Roman ideal.

When Gibbon describes how, sitting in the ruins of Rome, he had first conceived *The Decline and Fall of the Roman Empire*,[20] the scene he gives us strangely mirrors a scene in Virgil's great poem on the rise of that same empire. In the eighth book of the *Aeneid* the hero comes at last, having been driven from Troy, to the primeval site of Rome. Virgil's poem is set in what was even then a remote antiquity, and those who sat in Rome, listening to the recitation of the great epic, must have felt a growing excitement as the hero, Aeneas, travelled up the silent river towards the very spot where they then sat, so many centuries later, in the heart of the great city. Aeneas on the site of Rome meets the Arcadian King Evander, the ruler of the pastoral people. But, as he looks about him, he sees the overgrown ruins of an ancient city (*Aeneid*, VII, 355–6). The effect is uncanny, and is doubly so for those of us who live after the sack of Rome. What Aeneas sees, within the poem, is the ruins of the archaic Saturnian city which existed before Rome itself was built. Virgil surprises his Roman listeners with a ghostly effect, akin to that achieved by the superimposition of filters on pictures of places; to listeners who are even then mentally superimposing on the pastoral scene the vast urban shapes of their own time (Virgil leads them to do this by a string of reminders in the poem) the poet suddenly provides an answering image of urban forms, but one which tells not of the future but of the past. To us who come later the effect is stranger still. For what Aeneas saw and what Gibbon saw, in the same place, are virtually identical – vast shattered buildings among which trees grow and beasts graze. The scene in Gibbon's mind gradually broadened, until it became the immense, catastrophic panorama of the collapse of Latin civilisation.

This was the vision which Pope anticipated in the lines

> Lo! where Mæotis sleeps, and hardly flows
> The freezing Tanais thro' a waste of snows,
> The North by myriads pours her mighty sons,
> Great nurse of Goths, of Alans and of Huns!
> (*Dunciad*, 1742, III, 87–90)

Virgil, the poet of the first Augustus, saw Rome as the city of cities, ruined long before but now ascendant. Pope saw it as irretrievably

overwhelmed. The dark image of the frozen, sluggish river suggests
a slow numbing of the human spirit itself, a loss both of life and of
form.

Pope undoubtedly thought Roman and Greek literary models
worth imitating. Yet it is clear that he also saw the eighteenth-
century emulation of the ancients as a ruinous failure. Certainly he
was not inclined to congratulate his own epoch on its fidelity to
nature:

> The Face of Nature we no more Survey,
> All glares *alike*, without *Distinction* gay. . .
> *(Essay on Criticism,* 313–4)

Similarly, the fashionable displacement of energy into the forms of
scorn and contempt could not be right. With Horace it was otherwise, for he

> . . . *judg'd* with *Coolness* tho' he sung with *Fire*;
> His *Precepts* teach but what his *Works* inspire.
> *Our Criticks* take a contrary Extream,
> They *judge* with *Fury*, but they *write* with Fle'me. . .
> *(Essay on Criticism,* 659–67)

In Pope images of poetic impotence recur. The poets he sees round
him

> . . . Rhyme with all the *Rage* of *Impotence*!
> *(Essay on Criticism,* 609)

Still more powerful is the vision of poetry extinguished, in *The
Dunciad*:

> Keen, hollow winds howl thro' the bleak recess,
> Emblem of Music caus'd by Emptiness.
> Hence Bards, like Proteus long in vain ty'd down,
> Escape in Monsters, and amaze the town.
> *(Dunciad,* 1742, I, 35–8)

The problem of renewing in poetry the serious passion of the
ancients was hard for Pope as for the others. The great epic continued to elude him. The translation of Homer remained a brilliant
substitute, a picture of epic but not the thing itself. Yet, against all

the odds, he sometimes almost broke free. These moments of liberation are never formally docile to the old 'pure' models, however. Rather they come from the intensification of impulses originally satirical. Mock-heroic can assume various forms, but a felt discrepancy between the noble and the ignoble is common to them all. In *The Dunciad*, however, something very mysterious happens. We seem to reach a point at which the discrepancy between the grand past and the ignoble present is lost in a final intuition of hell. Ancient epic had regularly included an episode called in Greek the *nekyia*, in which the hero visits the world of the dead. Readers of *The Dunciad* find themselves, without irony, in the same place. The original attack on dull writers (hardly a major enterprise, one would suppose) is mysteriously intensified and becomes an intuition of un-being.

Something oddly similar happens in Eliot's *The Waste Land* to the image of London, at first ironically contrasted with the world of the past, but then, in the vision of the crowd flowing over London Bridge, identified with the *Inferno* of Dante. The closing lines of the 1742 *Dunciad* partly transcend the convention of mock-heroic. Pope had made his contribution to the central, running image of the Enlightenment, by wittily applying the language of Genesis to England's greatest natural philosopher:

> God said, *Let Newton be!* and All was *Light*.
> ('Epitaph. Intended for Sir Isaac Newton,
> in Westminster Abbey')

There the biblical phrase 'Let there be light', the standard example of 'the Sublime' in neo-classical theory, is lightly turned into a compliment which is both elegant and immense. The line courts and then successfully avoids blasphemy. At the close of *The Dunciad* both images – the image of the Enlightenment and the image of the world's creation – are inverted, and it is hard to feel that the inversion is wholly a matter of satiric fun:

> She comes! she comes! the sable Throne behold
> Of *Night* Primæval, and of *Chaos* old!
> Before her, *Fancy*'s gilded clouds decay,
> And all its varying Rain-bows die away.
> *Wit* shoots in vain its momentary fires,
> The meteor drops, and in a flash expires.
> As one by one, at dread Medea's strain,

The sick'ning stars fade off th'ethereal plain;
As Argus' eyes by Hermes' wand opprest,
Clos'd one by one to everlasting rest;
Thus at her felt approach, and secret might,
Art after *Art* goes out, and all is Night.
See skulking *Truth* to her old Cavern fled,
Mountains of Casuistry heap'd o'er her head!
Philosophy, that lean'd on Heav'n before,
Shrinks to her second cause, and is no more.
Physic of *Metaphysic* begs defence,
And *Metaphysic* calls for aid on *Sense*!
See *Mystery* to *Mathematics* fly!
In vain! they gaze, turn giddy, rave, and die,
Religion blushing veils her sacred fires,
And unawares *Morality* expires.
Nor *public* Flame, nor *private*, dares to shine;
Nor *human* Spark is left, nor Glimpse *divine*!
Lo! thy dread Empire, CHAOS! is restor'd;
Light dies before thy uncreating word:
Thy hand, great Anarch! lets the curtain fall;
And Universal Darkness buries All.

> (*Dunciad*, 1742, IV, 629–56)

Here the language in such phrases as 'clouds decay' and 'sick'ning stars' has a strangeness and a power which are not easily paralleled elsewhere in the Augustan period. 'Light dies before thy uncreating word' (the story of Genesis now running backwards) presumably satisfied the requirements of wit and paradox. Yet at the same time it is simply majestic. In such terms can a principal work of the Enlightenment at once undo itself and triumph. Pope wrote his epic, a black epic, made out of the very impotence of poetry.

But the end of *The Dunciad* is only one extreme moment in Pope's poetic progress. Elsewhere his relations with both order and disorder are more genial (though seldom entirely restful). Pope knew in his bones that Horace's insistence on a regular simplicity was not a maxim to be followed slavishly. Horace puts the point thus:

> Qui variare cupit rem prodigialiter unam,
> Delphinum silvis appingit, fluctibus aprum.

[He who would prodigiously diversify a single theme paints dolphins in forests, and boars in the midst of the sea.] (*Ars Poetica*, 29–30)[21]

But then Horace himself, on another occasion, could also write:

> Terruit gentis, grave ne rediret
> Saeculum Pyrrhae nova monstra questae
> Omne cum Proteus pecus egit altos
>   Visere montes
> Piscium et summa genus haesit ulmo
> Nota quae sedes fuerat columbis. . .

[He has struck terror into the nations, lest the heavy age of Pyrrha should return with new prodigies, the time when Proteus drove his whole flock of seals out upon the high hills, and the fishes clung to the tops of the elms, formerly the familiar haunt of pigeons.] (*Odes*, I, ii, 5–10)[22]

Incongruity cannot be outlawed from poetry. Horace himself found that there were times when he wished to admit it. In the *Ars Poetica* it energises the line even while it is made the matter of a prohibition. In the second ode of the first book it marvellously expresses the infancy of the world.

In France writers made a serious effort to obey the rule of Horace, to keep their fish in the sea and their sheep on the pastures. The effect of poetry which keeps to this rule was brutally summed up in a single line by Dryden:

> So just, so like tautology, they fell
> ('Mac Flecknoe', 56)[23]

The English could never sustain their belief in such taboos for long. Pope's art, even when it repeats the Horatian stricture, shamelessly exploits the incongruity it purports to condemn:

> She sees a Mob of Metaphors advance,
> Pleas'd with the madness of the mazy dance:
> How Tragedy and Comedy embrace;
> How Farce and Epic get a jumbled race;
> How Time himself stands still at her command,
> Realms shift their place, and Ocean turns to land.
> Here gay Description Ægypt glads with show'rs,
> Or gives to Zembla fruits, to Barca flow'rs;
> Glitt'ring with ice here hoary hills are seen,

> There painted vallies of eternal green,
> In cold December fragrant chaplets blow,
> And heavy harvests nod beneath the snow.
>
> *(Dunciad,* 1742, I, 67–78)

The examples of absurdity are obstinately pleasant. Where Pope
might have visited Tuscany with blizzards or Kent with sterility, he
chose instead to make the thirsty desert bloom and bear fruit. On the
other hand, the icy mountains and green valleys are merely appropriate and not absurd at all. In the last line of the quotation the sheer
power, always latent in such passages, bursts out in the surrealist
image of the snow-laden corn. Meanwhile there lurks within the
whole passage a certain ironic presence. Who was it who, more
marvellously than anyone else, mingled tragedy and comedy?
Remember the sea-coast of Bohemia. But to mention Shakespeare is
to leave the argument of Horace and Boileau in ruins.

Perhaps the most famous passage in which Pope's poetry condemns and is in its turn energised by incongruity is the description
of the house and garden belonging to the ostentatious Timon in the
Epistle to Burlington:

> The suff'ring eye inverted Nature sees,
> Trees cut to Statues, Statues thick as trees,
> With here a Fountain, never to be play'd,
> And there a Summer-house, that knows no shade;
> Here Amphitrite sails thro' myrtle bow'rs;
> There Gladiators fight, or die, in flow'rs;
> Un-water'd see the drooping sea-horse mourn,
> And swallows roost in Nilus' dusty Urn.
>
> (119–26)

Here again (as with Dr Johnson's friend) cheerfulness keeps breaking in. Pope may have disapproved of statues, but he also liked
them. The surviving inventory of his possessions includes four lead
urns, sixteen stone urns, the obelisk to his mother's memory, a
Venus, a Mercury, 'a stone statue with a wooden pedestall' and 'four
bustos antike'.[24] At Twickenham we catch the poet off his guard.
The celebrated grotto where (as in the cellar of Sir John Soane's
house) Pope's tastes could escape the control of his aesthetic super-
ego, was crowded not merely with statues but with grotesques. The
same delighted taste is evident, however, in published form, in the

sepia drawing, probably by Pope himself, prefixed to *An Essay on Man*. It bristles with truncated statues, shattered columns and fractured antique torsos.

In *Epistle to Burlington* the spirit of disorder will not lie down. She reappears with all the demonic authority of Nature itself. Absurdity or incongruity is normally opposed to nature. But in the *Eclogues* of Virgil such violent juxtapositions always had a double force. Either they connote absurd impossibility, or else they connote miracle, the Golden Age. The reader need only compare I, 59, and VII, 53, with III, 89, IV, 30 and V, 50. And in the Golden Age Nature triumphed. So in Pope's Epistle we find a second muted version of the ancient trope, called by the Romans the *impossibilia*, when nature avenges herself on the puny excesses of Timon, with her own surrealism:

> Another age shall see the golden Ear
> Imbrown the Slope, and nod on the Parterre,
> Deep Harvests bury all his pride has plann'd,
> And laughing Ceres re-assume the land.
>
> (173–6)

Yet 'natural surrealism' is a paradox which cannot be sustained for long. In the last line incongruity is swallowed up in joy.

(iv) REASON

Such was the poet, such the poetry, such the age when *An Essay on Man* came to be written. Pope, born into a family with memories and perhaps even some faint experience of the anti-Papist terror, seriously feared disorder but suspected that in many of its forms it was susceptible of genial control by the right poet.

The progress of philosophy in the eighteenth century was generally in the direction of an ever darker scepticism. At the beginning of the century the excitement of the new certainty conferred by the natural philosophy of Newton was still strong. Great thinkers were like conquering heroes in a war of intellect. The atmosphere is vividly illustrated by the story of Bernoulli's challenge in 1696 and its sequel. Jean Bernoulli was a Swiss mathematician who in an open letter to the principal intellects of Europe invited solutions to a pair of problems (the problems were, first, to determine the curve described by a body moving other than vertically under the action of gravity and, secondly, to determine a curve such that, if a straight line drawn through a fixed point A meets it at two points P_1 and P_2, then AP_1m and AP_2m will be constant). Bernoulli allowed six months for the solution of these problems, but the period passed and no solution was forthcoming. Leibniz, however, wrote to Bernoulli explaining that he was halfway there, and in return Bernoulli granted an extension of time. Newton did not receive the problem until January 1697. He at once came up with the solution to the first problem (a cycloid) and solved the second problem in a related manner. Newton's solution was unsigned when it reached Bernoulli (along with solutions from Leibniz and the Marquis de L'Hôpital), but Bernoulli at once recognised the author, *tamquam ex ungue leonem*, 'as we know the lion by his claw'.[25] With one contemptuous stroke Newton had rent the problem asunder.

The century began with the grand rationalist systems of Leibniz, Descartes and Newton – systems in which God was firmly enthroned at the centre, prior to human knowledge. In Newton's system, however, for all its evidently sincere piety, one senses that God is somehow less than he was. Newton welcomed the quasi-mystical conception of God whereby the whole of space was his *sensorium*. Leibniz wickedly insisted on taking *sensorium* to mean 'sense-organ' and in effect accused Newton of spreading the doctrine that the universe is God's nose.[26] But in the thirty-first Query appended to the *Opticks* Newton also welcomed, with an eagerness which smacks of relief, the discovery that the planets, if left to themselves, would increasingly disturb one another's orbit through varying gravitational attraction, were it not that the hand of God, extended from time to time, corrected the irregularities.[27] To be sure, such arguments are always double-edged. Leibniz pointed out that, if we suggest that God, so to speak, is obliged to run round with an oil-can keeping his creation running, we derogate from his power.[28]

As the years passed, of the two great principles of Descartes' philosophy, systematic doubt and systematic construction, the first began more and more noticeably to outrun the second. In England, Locke, in his *Essay Concerning Human Understanding* (1690), asserted the primacy of experience: the human mind begins as a *tabula rasa*, or blank sheet, on which facts are successively imprinted, and in this way our knowlege of the world is formed. Locke embarked upon his great task with high hopes of a quick resolution of all previous difficulties through an adequate philosophy of Man, which would underpin the cosmic system of Newton.

As his work progressed the forces of chaos seemed more and more formidable. Locke's *Essay* is a huge, rambling, repetitious work. There can be no doubt that it represents a major achievement in philosophy, but equally it affords at last a diminished rather than an enhanced sense of certainty. Experience is now master, and experience is a vast, confused and enigmatic thing.

Later in the century the empiricism of Locke became in the hands of David Hume an agent of deconstruction, so that the three great stabilising substances, God, mind and body, were no longer securely founded upon experience but were, rather, reduced to their psychological representatives. By the end of the first book of Hume's *Treatise of Human Nature* (1739–40) nothing is real but a flux of ideas of varying strength; the strong ones we may call percepts, the weak ones mental images. This is black scepticism, and Hume was not insensible of its terrors. He felt, he said, 'inviron'd with the deepest darkness'.[29] Was this the ironic terminus of enlightenment? 'Let there be light' becomes 'There is only darkness'. Yet the whole of this movement of thought is in a manner imaginatively anticipated in the passage (the first version of which appeared in 1729) which ends *The Dunciad.*

In metaphysical philosophy the movement of reason to dethrone itself is curiously swift. In the more popular disputes over theology the drift towards uncertainty is less spectacular but is nevertheless real. The principal movement of the century is that known as Deism. Here, as in the progress of Cartesianism, we find, if we follow the admirable analysis of Leslie Stephen, a constructive phase overlapped and succeeded by a critical.[30] Once more, it is a movement which begins with high hopes of a corroborated orthodoxy. Locke, in *The Reasonableness of Christianity* (1695), proposed that, to anyone who took the trouble to read the Gospels with an open mind, a clear and simple Christianity would immediately present itself. John Toland, in his *Christianity Not Mysterious* (1696), pushed the argument a little farther. Where Locke had said that everything in Christianity was reasonable, Toland claimed that nothing in Christianity was mysterious; for surely God could hardly expect his creation to respond with love and worship to mere gobbledegook. Matthew Tindal in *Christianity as Old as the Creation* (1730) argued that a true religion must be founded on universal principles. To impute to God a restriction of the truth to those fortuitously born at a certain time and in a certain place is to convict him of a capricious injustice.

Thus, the Incarnation of Christ and even the authority of Scripture is down-graded.

This kind of thinking in theology was powerfully assisted by the growth of trade with remote, un-Christian peoples. The rationally benevolent and fair-dealing Chinaman made a strong impression. Christ on the cross as the centre of the stage had seemed both natural and right. But now, as Leslie Stephen observed, the scenery had become too wide for the drama.[31] The stage was now so huge that most people on it could not even see the cross. By the time we reach the work of the freethinker Anthony Collins, whose *Discourse on Freethinking* came out in 1713, the tendency of the Deist movement is discernibly subversive of orthodox Christianity.

Some of the philosophical developments I have noted in this section post-date Pope. Yet it is worth remembering that he lived among people who were to think and write these things. He was not himself, despite his moments of prophetic insight, a clear-sighted philosopher. Although like others of his time he had some acquaintance with Pyrrhonian scepticism, it is most unlikely that he ever clearly foresaw the radically destructive arguments of Hume, which, not content with removing God, proceeded to dissolve His creation. Rather, placed as he was, Pope would be disposed to trust in those elements of Deism which proposed a reasonable faith, available to all fair-minded people, capable of transcending bloody sectarian disputes. Even stronger, one senses, was his faith in his own powers of epigrammatic, urbane persuasion. Also, as we have seen, he needed to produce a great poem. Perhaps, while the model of the *Aeneid* would always elude him, the model of Lucretius' great philosophical poem, *De Rerum Natura*, lay within his grasp. So, in 1730, he set to work.

CHAPTER 3

An Essay on Man

(i) DESIGN AND SOURCES

Joseph Warton, contemplating the immense success of Pope's *Essay on Man*, drew the mildly surprising conclusion that it did well because it was a didactic poem, that is, a work designed to give general instruction. He wrote:

> The moderns have produced many excellent pieces of this kind. We may mention the Syphilis of Fracastorius, the Silk-worms and Chefs of Vida, the Ambra of Politian, the Agriculture of Alamanni, the Art of Poetry of Boileau, the Gardens of Rapin, the Cyder of Phillips, the Chase of Somerville, the Pleasures of Imagination, the Art of preserving Health, the Fleece, the Religion of Racine the younger, the elegant Latin poem of Brown on the Immortality of the Soul, the Latin poems of STAY and BOSCOVICK, and the philosophical poem before us; to which, if we may judge from some beautiful fragments, we might have added Gray's didactic poem on Education and Government, had he lived to finish it.[1]

Today Warton's list seems both deeply obscure and somewhat weird. No species of poem seems as certainly dead as the treatise-poem. Where Pope's *Essay* once rode high on a wave of fashion, it now succeeds against the current.

Pope's *Essay*, like Wordsworth's *Prelude*, is in some sense a fragment, carefully polished and mounted, of a larger design which the poet was never able to complete. In the first collected edition of all four epistles of *An Essay on Man* published in 1734, Pope wrote in a prefatory note on 'the 'Design':

> What is now published, is only to be considered as a *general Map* of MAN, marking out no more than the *greater parts*, their *extent*, their *limits*, and their *connection*, but leaving the particular to be more

fully delineated in the charts which are to follow. Consequently, these Epistles in their progress (if I have health and leisure to make any progress) will be less dry, and more susceptible of poetical ornament. I am here only opening the *fountains*, and clearing the passage. To deduce the *rivers*, to follow them in their course, and to observe their effects, may be a task more agreeable. (MM, 8)

It is of course always prudent to suggest that what is offered is only a first try; the very word 'essay', started by Montaigne in 1580, proved exceedingly useful to nervous writers. It is also, however, used by writers whose inward confidence is so robust as to suggest that the formal profession of modesty is a polite fiction. In the twentieth century even sages like Eliot – or perhaps we should say *especially* sages like Eliot – have availed themselves of titles which suggest an almost ludicrously provisional character in the work: for example, *Notes towards the Definition of Culture*.

But there is no need to assume that Pope's profession of modesty is a mere smokescreen. One senses, indeed, that his project differs from that of Wordsworth in one crucial regard. Wordsworth, egged on by Coleridge, intended to proceed in due course to the grand theme of man, nature and society.[2] Pope's philosophical mentor, Bolingbroke, was, we may suspect, much less pressing than Wordsworth's; Coleridge worked in Wordsworth's mind with real power. Thus, where Wordsworth feels a certain social guilt at the way his poetry intransigently confines itself to the psyche of its author, Pope seems rather to think that he has performed the difficult part and in what lies ahead he may decently indulge himself and his reader. On 19 November 1729, Bolingbroke wrote to Swift: 'Bid him [Pope] talk to you of this work he is about. I hope in good earnest; it is a fine one: it will be in his hands an Original. His sole complaint is that he finds it too easy in the execution.'[3] There is a faint echo of Locke's 'Epistle to the Reader' prefixed to *his* great *Essay* in Pope's use of the word 'clearing'. Locke had written: '. . . in an age that produces such masters as the great Huygenius and the incomparable Mr. Newton . . . it is ambition enough to be employed as an under-labourer in clearing the ground a little'.[4] But, where Locke subordinates himself as a disciple, Pope presents himself as an original explorer of new terrain. It is as if he is more concerned to apologise for the dryness of his poem than for any intellectual deficiency. Moreover, in promising his readers entertainment, Pope was hardly engaging himself to a project at which his spirit would secretly quail.

At the same time, however, the intellectual programme of the work was immense, and Pope knew it to be so. The entire poem was planned to include, in addition to the four epistles we know today as *An Essay on Man*, four further essays which later became *The Moral Essays* (Spence, 294). In fact the eight pieces involved were published as follows:

(1) *The Epistle to Burlington* (the first to appear of the *Moral Essays*, but now generally known as 'Epistle IV'), December 1731

(2) *The Epistle to Bathurst* (which became 'Epistle III' of the *Moral Essays*), January 1733

(3) Epistle I of *An Essay on Man*, February 1733

(4) Epistle II of *An Essay on Man*, March 1733

(5) Epistle III of *An Essay on Man*, May 1733

(6) *The Epistle to Cobham* ('Epistle I' of the *Moral Essays*), January 1734

(7) Epistle IV of *An Essay on Man*, January 1734 (a week after no. 6)

(8) *Epistle to a Lady* ('Epistle II' of the *Moral Essays*), February 1735.

The four epistles of *An Essay on Man* were published together in April 1734, Pope's authorship being by this time an open secret. The *Moral Essays* were published together in 1735.[5]

The 1734 edition of the four epistles of *An Essay on Man* carried the subtitle 'Being the first book of the Ethic Epistles'. Pope told Spence in 1734 that he had in fact 'drawn in the plan for my Ethic Epistles, much narrower than it was at first' (Spence, 300). He took the trouble to add a leaf to about twelve copies of the 1734 edition, intended for special friends. Most of these were later recalled, but that sent to Bethel was not, and Spence got hold of it. It reads as follows:

Index to the Ethic Epistles

The First Book
OF THE NATURE AND STATE
OF MAN

Epistle I
– With Respect to the Universe

Epistle II
– As an Individual
Epistle III
– With respect to Society
Epistle IV
– With respect to Happiness

The Second Book
OF THE USE OF THINGS
Of the Limits of Human Reason
– Of the Use of Learning
– Of the Use of Wit

Of the Knowledge and
Characters of Men

Of the particular Characters
of Women

Of the Principles and Use
of Civil and Ecclesiastical
Polity

– Of the Use of Education

A View of the Equality of
Happiness in the several
Conditions of Men

– Of the Use of Riches,
&c.

(Spence, 300)

The 'First Book' is essentially *An Essay on Man* as we know it today. The 'Second Book' seems to contain much that is covered in the *Moral Essays*, since the 'characters of Men', 'the characters of Women' and the 'Use of Riches' appear in both. In fact *Moral Essays* III and IV did not get their subtitle, 'Of the Use of Riches', until 1735, and the *Epistle to a Lady. Of the Characters of Women* had not yet been published. A little puzzlingly, 'the Equality of Happiness in the Several Conditions of Men' seems already to have been dealt with in the fourth epistle of 'the First Book'. It is likely that the epistle on 'the Limits of Human Reason' was never completed, though Pope told Spence that some lines from it were incorporated in the fourth book of *The Dunciad* (Spence, 337). Various links exist between *An Essay on Man* as we now have it and the *Moral Essays*. Pope's note on the *Epistle to Bathurst*, lines 161 ff., refers the reader to *An Essay on Man*, II, 165 and 207. The *Epistle to Cobham*, lines 222-7, is most easily understood against the background of the second epistle of *An Essay on Man*. The *Epistle to a Lady* makes use of the theory of the Ruling Passion, so prominent in the *Essay*. The eulogy of Bathurst in the third of the *Moral Essays* connects with several passages of *An Essay on Man*. But the *Moral Essays* and *An Essay on Man* certainly do not, in their surviving form, compose a single, unified work of art.[6]

Pope addresses his poem to Lord Bolingbroke as Lucretius addressed *De Rerum Natura* to Memmius. Pope was an unsystematic thinker; Bolingbroke was a philosopher of sorts; *An Essay on Man* is a philosophic poem. The effect of these three propositions, taken in succession, has been irresistible. Bolingbroke, it is said, must be 'the key' to the philosophy of the *Essay*. In fact, the thought of *An Essay on Man*, philosophical or not, is notably unsystematic, and Bolingbroke's philosophy, as it has come down to us, is in any case not very like that of Pope's poem. Maynard Mack has exposed the weakness of the case for regarding Bolingbroke as an exclusive or overriding influence (MM, xxix–xxxi). Bolingbroke's surviving work, the *Fragments or Minutes of Essays*, cannot have been Pope's source. It appears that Bolingbroke did not begin to write the *Fragments* until after Pope had finished the first three epistles and was already at work upon the fourth. Certain tricks of expression are common to both works; but as Warburton, Pope's heavy-handed but not unintelligent apologist, pointed out in 1756[7] this is as likely as not to be the result of Bolingbroke echoing the felicitous phrasing of his highly articulate friend. They are in any case far less prominent than, say, the verbal echoes of Wollaston's *Religion of Nature Delineated*, which Maynard Mack discusses in his introduction to the Roxburghe Club reproduction of the Houghton and Morgan manuscripts of *An Essay on Man*. But Wollaston's thesis, that the evils and injustices of this world are gross and must be compensated in the next, is in unusually clear opposition to the views of both Bolingbroke and Pope!

There is, however, some evidence that Bolingbroke wrote a philosophical letter or dissertation for Pope's use. The story can be traced back to Lord Bathurst. Joseph Warton in his *Essay on the Genius and Writings of Pope* wrote: 'The late Lord Bathurst repeatedly assured me that he had read the whole scheme of the Essay on Man in the hand-writing of Bolingbroke, and drawn up in a series of propositions, which Pope was to versify and illustrate.'[8] Dr Hugh Blair dined with Bathurst in 1763 and wrote a letter to Boswell in which he described the occasion: 'The conversation turning on Mr Pope, Lord Bathurst told us that *The Essay on Man* was originally composed by Lord Bolingbroke in prose, and that Mr Pope did no more than put it into verse: that he had read Lord Bolingbroke's manuscript in his own handwriting; and remembered well, that he was at a loss whether most to admire the elegance of Lord Bolingbroke's prose, or the beauty of Mr Pope's verse.'[9] Boswell read Blair's letter aloud to Johnson. The Doctor's response is a model of temperate judgement.

Depend upon it, Sir, this is too strongly stated. Pope may have had from Bolingbroke the philosophick *stamina* of the *Essay*; and admitting this to be true, Lord Bathurst did not intentionally falsify. But the thing is not true in the latitude that Blair seems to imagine; we are sure that the poetical-imagery, which makes a great part of the poem, was Pope's own. It is amazing, Sir, what deviations there are from precise truth, in the account which is given of almost everything.[10]

It seems clear enough that some such draft existed. Pope himself told Spence that 'he had received (I think) seven or eight sheets from Lord Bolingbroke in relation to it, as I apprehended, by way of letters, both to direct the plan in general and to supply the matter for the particular epistles' (Spence, 311). We may guess, with Johnson, that Bathurst exaggerated and at the same time confess that Pope may have minimised the importance of the Bolingbroke draft when he spoke to Spence. Further speculation on a document which has not survived would seem to be pointless.

Meanwhile, if we judge by what we have, we must see that Pope and Bolingbroke differ fundamentally. Maynard Mack (MM,

xxx–xxxi) points out that Pope assimilates what Bolingbroke
excludes: the classical, medieval and Renaissance picture of the
universe as a glittering hierarchical system, extending from God
through angels down to man, and thence to beasts, plants and min-
erals. Pope assimilates the mistrust felt by the Humanist party (who
championed 'Ancients' against 'Moderns') towards natural science,
the role of intuition in the moral life, the propriety of ascribing moral
attributes to God (Bolingbroke says that everything God does is good
merely because He does it; the suggestion that, on the contrary, God
does them because they are good he rejects). Bolingbroke's 'proto-
positivist' insistence that philosophy should confine itself to what
falls within the purview of the human mind is indeed trumpeted by
Pope at the beginning of the second epistle but is merely disregarded
elsewhere. The major exception to this rule is the tormented section
following line 145 of Epistle I. There the view, strongly upheld by
Bolingbroke in his *Fragments*, that the elements of the great chain of
being exist for the sake of the scheme and not for man is pressed
hard by Pope. At the same time, this theological view is found in
many other authors.

Nevertheless, although Mack was right to point out the mass of
traditional material despised by Bolingbroke but included by Pope,
it remains true that Pope did not include in his poem the absolutely
central – one might almost say, the *vertebral* – idea of Scriptural
Christianity: the Fall of Man, the Incarnation and Redemption.
Here it is very likely that Pope was powerfully influenced, as to
atmosphere, tone and content, by his worldly friend. But scholars
who find their best security in the identification of influences are in
general ill-served by the example of Bolingbroke. The one potent
element commonly underestimated in such discussions is of course
talk (scholars often proceed as if writers were deaf-mutes, incarcer-
ated in cells, communicating with the outside world only by a sort of
inter-library loan system). Pope was personally acquainted with
Bolingbroke and doubtless exchanged enough words with him to fill
many volumes. In such conversations the threads of influence, in
both directions, may have been innumerable. I insist only that we
cannot trace them now.

One kind of source-hunting proceeds with its eye firmly fixed on
Pope's known personal acquaintances. Another instantly flies to the
principal philosophical figures of the age. The second method at first
sight looks less reasonable than the first. If Pope was not demon-

strably influenced by his good friend Bolingbroke, whom he addresses at the beginning of his poem, what hope is there that he will prove to have been influenced by the geographically and intellectually remote figure of Leibniz? Pope told Warburton that he had never read a line of Leibniz (*Corr.*, IV, 164). Yet it is a mark of major thinkers that they influence even those who do not read them. Today thousands who have never read a word of Marx think and utter Marxian maxims. Leibniz's thought was never as influential historically as Marx's, and the case is complicated by the degree to which he formalised pre-existing ideas, but it is probably still true to say that the *Essay on Man* is slightly more Leibnizian than it is Bolingbrokian.

I owe much in this discussion to Maynard Mack's masterly account of Pope's sources in the introduction to his Twickenham edition. Yet his wholly proper scepticism towards certain local sources produces at last a curiously timeless view of the poem. For Mack, *An Essay on Man* is a rich tapestry of Stoic and Christian elements, an utterly traditional fabric in which Pope is on excellent terms with his peers across the intervening centuries, easily echoing the sentiments of Epictetus, Pascal and Milton. But at the last name we must pause. The difference between Milton and Pope is over-whelming and is partly a matter of history. Mack himself notes, but lightly as if it were unimportant, the fact that Milton justifies God by telling a great remembered story, the story of Adam and Eve, while Pope instead offers an abstract rationalisation of the difficulty (MM, lxiv). This profound change of method is clearly implicit in the history of eighteenth-century Deism, which found intolerable difficulties in a merely local operation of God's love, incarnating itself for some, hiding from others. The Miltonic 'justification' of God must have seemed to contemporaries of Toland to show nothing so much as the capricious injustice of the Creator. It is likely that the sort of rebellious indignation which has visited so many readers of *Paradise Lost* played an important part in the Deist movement. Seen in this context, Pope is not so much on easy terms with Milton as the author of the great counter-Miltonic justification. Where Pope harmonises older philosophies, that very harmonisation is eloquent of the early eighteenth century. To suppose that a poem is of the same kind as its predecessors merely because it incorporates earlier material is a naïve critical error. Maynard Mack is far too intelligent to make this mistake himself but it is possible that his introduction may cause others to make it. The word 'traditional' is a trap. Eliot's *The*

Waste Land is traditional in content but wholly of its age in method. So is *An Essay on Man*.

Meanwhile there is no single key to the poem. In the circumstances, our best course is simply to begin at the beginning.

(ii)   EPISTLE I: MAN AND THE UNIVERSE

The first epistle announces itself as dealing with 'the Nature and State of Man, with respect to the UNIVERSE'. The tone of the announcement is thrasonical – almost, indeed, that of a showman – although the blustering capitals are more unusual and therefore more assertive in the twentieth century than they were in the eighteenth. But Pope knows that he has opened with trumpets, and the first task of a poet taught by experience to disarm ridicule is to fence his pride about with prophylactic ironies.

This he does in the first two lines:

> Awake, my ST. JOHN! leave all meaner things
> To low ambition, and the pride of Kings.

The poet arouses the sleeping hero to a task higher than that of statesmen or rulers. Pope deals with potential critics by confusing the ordinary categories of pride and humility. He scorns ambition and the pride of kings, but then, in order to make it clear that he is not stooping to mere shrill denial as defence, he wickedly adds that the trouble with such schemes is that they aim too *low* ('low ambition' is our first 'miniature' antithesis). Pope plants such small explosions in the couplet to start a smile in the reader; a reader who is beginning to smile finds it harder to be hostile. In like manner, the first word of the poem is, to an ear attuned to such effects, a faint but unmistakable instance of mock-heroic. Pope signals to the reader by a slight exaggeration of manner in *the first two syllables of the poem* that he is conscious of the extravagant grandeur of his enterprise. But these effects (though they do their work) are slight. The subject, lightly yet triumphantly announced, really is the greatest possible. Pope's trick is essentially to refuse to rebut the charge of pride, and to reassert instead a still greater pride, but in a form which will paradoxically conciliate the reader. He does much the same thing in an altogether more urgent, more personal manner in the famous lines from the second dialogue of the *Epilogue to the Satires*:

> Yes, I am proud; I must be proud to see
> Men not afraid of God, afraid of me. . .
>
> (207–8)

It is likely that Pope got the idea for this couplet from one of the notes on Cowley's *Davideis*. The note cites Herodotus on the statue of Sennacherib in Egypt which bore the inscription, 'Let him who looks upon me learn to fear God'.[11] Pope, the civil spider, involves the ancient starkness of the sentence in a web of ironies. The ostensible implication is that there is no pride in being able to strike terror into those who are so morally insensitive that they do not even fear God himself. Yet the lines remain taunting and obstinately retain the flavour of a boast.

At the beginning of the *Essay* the personal element is less evident. The poet starts bouncing the ball from pride to humility, varying the bounce in each line. In the first the awakening of St John is contrasted with meaner employments, in the second ambition and regal pride are undermined by the cunningly planted monosyllable 'low', then in lines 3 to 5 we are at first told of the modest confinement of Man by the brevity of human life and the narrowness of the human situation but then suddenly take an expansive breath on the marvellous word 'expatiate':

> Let us (since Life can little more supply
> Than just to look about us and to die)
> Expatiate free o'er all this scene of Man. . .
>
> (3–5)

Pope's use of the same word later in the same epistle suggests that it carried for him a connotation of release:

> The soul, uneasy and confin'd from home,
> Rests and expatiates in a life to come.
>
> (I, 97–8)

The view, at first confined, swells, as we 'zoom in' on it, to a panorama. Then, as the units of antithesis grow larger and the sense of freedom stronger, we find ourselves suddenly brought up short with the closing, admonitory words of line 6:

> A mighty maze! but not without a plan.

Here the pre-Romantic exhilaration of the 'mighty maze', with its
delight in formlessness, is suddenly arrested, as the voyage of
Dante's Ulisse into unknown seas was arrested by the sight of God's
mountain. For what has happened here is that intellectual modesty,
having chosen not to exceed a purely human scope, runs up against a
plan which is not human at all. But still the ball has not stopped
bouncing. For, after all, this plan is the subject of the poem and we
must therefore explore it.

Pope's fluid antithesis of pride and humility has swiftly grown
until it encapsulates one of the primary philosophical tensions of the
poem; that is, the tension between a view of man which confines him
to merely human concerns and the grand metaphysical overview of
man in relation to God and the creation, which at one and the same
time provides a rationale for the first view and violates it. Even the
innocent phrase, 'Know then thyself' (Epistle II, 1), by the time we
reach it, is fraught with an inner duplicity. For to know oneself
thoroughly, to be fully aware of one's lowly position in the scheme,
one must have some conception of the higher elements in that
scheme. But in that case one must be careful, after all, not to exaggerate the harsh limitations of human thought or one will fall into
contradiction. If we maintain that man is unable to conceive anything beyond his own sphere, and make that limitation of *conception*
a principal element in our low estimate of man, the view in question
can consistently be put only by a being with supernatural powers of
insight. Man, so limited, would never know that he was limited.
This is perhaps the single most important philosophical tension in
the poem. It is interesting to watch, in the opening lines, how swiftly
it grows from something as small as a passing ironic paradox. Curiously, what is tolerated – or even welcomed – as an invigorating
ironic tension on a small scale is much harder to accept at the major
level of the argument. It becomes, indeed, mere contradiction.

The phrase, 'but not without a plan', seems to have been a late
afterthought. In the Houghton manuscript, which looks as if it were
originally intended as a fair copy of the Morgan manuscript, Pope
wrote in a careful hand:

A mighty Maze of Walks without a Plan.[12]

Then 'of Walks' was deleted and the crucial 'but not' substituted (and the final full stop changed to an exclamation mark). It is sometimes thought that this change shows how far Pope's mind was from serious theology, since he could switch in a moment from a planless (Godless) universe to a God-directed one. But the earlier version need only imply that we do not possess the plan of the maze. It would be better literary criticism to point out that the word 'maze' was itself ambiguous from the beginning, suggesting as it does both a pleasing bewilderment and, somewhere beyond, a designer who has deliberately and artfully achieved this end. I have already allowed the loose word 'Romantic' to slip into the discussion; this is perhaps the place to observe, as a *caveat*, that mazes are characteristic of pre-Romantic, formal gardens and not of the 'natural' gardens which came later. The maze is not a favourite image of the great Romantic poets, probably because it makes sense only where there is some expectation of a rational solution. It returns in the modern fiction of *defeated* reason. In Kafka the idea of a maze which is without centre or exit is continually implicit. The lurking ambiguity of 'maze' reappears in the cognate phrase, 'th' amazing whole' at I, 248.

Pride is not so much a theme of the first epistle as a source of varying contrasts. It appears again at line 35 where man is called presumptuous, either for seeking metaphysical reasons for his situation or else for always asking why he is not placed higher (and never asking, 'Why not lower?'). It surfaces again at line 65 where pride and lowness are reflected in the line about the fiery horse and the plodding ox. At lines 91 ff., after a strange meditation on the way heroes and sparrows are merely level with one another in the mind of God, Pope's running contrast is marvellously transformed by a strange marriage of humility with hope, and the image of soaring flight normally applied to arrogance is adapted to a different purpose:

> Hope humbly then; with trembling pinions soar. . .

At line 99 the fundamental contrast, which is with the arrogance of knowledge, reasserts itself, but this time it is not theological overconfidence which is imagined but natural science. The humble dream of the simple Indian is favourably contrasted with the intellectual ambition of the astronomer.

In the opening paragraph of the epistle the pride–humility contrast melts into a contrast between freedom and determinism, taking its cue from the idea of the maze; thus we have a 'wild' contrasted with a 'Garden' (gardens are artificially worked and controlled). Here, indeed, Pope's unconscious gives a little shiver; the Garden, which one would expect to be commended, finally, as evidence of the benevolent hand of God, in fact seems oddly sinister. This is the first hint in the poem of Milton, who is to be plainly invoked at line 16, for the allusion is plainly to the Garden of Eden. Here, indeed, events were arranged by God, but with no good outcome for the human race.

Then, as Pope settles to the business of exploring his chosen domain (the picture, revealingly enough, seems to be that of a gentleman walking his estate, flushing occasional birds from the coverts and studying the fauna of the area), the contrast of unfettered ambition and humble confinement grows fainter and fainter. It is still there in the juxtaposition

> Of all who blindly creep, or sightless soar
> (12)

which virtually returns us to the grand opening opposition of pride and humility, but no longer with any sense of strong distinction. Presumably those who soar are those who try to pass beyond human limits. If so, one might expect the humble 'creepers' to be commended for their modesty, but in fact the line stigmatises both parties alike as blind. The final effect of this comprehensive scorn is the insinuation of a gentlemanly complicity with the reader. One senses a half-jesting assumption of 'our' superiority, that is, a superiority of poet and reader over the rest of the creation. This, perhaps, is the mode of pride which remains unexpelled from the verse. It is certainly deeply different from the *active* pride Milton showed, when he launched himself on his great design. Pope's proposal that we should walk at his elbow while he takes occasion to 'shoot folly as it flies' (line 13) suggests the social poet rather than the philosopher. Yet he knows what he is about. The growing cosiness is suddenly shattered by an open challenge.

Milton had closed the great opening verse-paragraph of *Paradise Lost* with the line

> And justify the ways of God to men
> (I, 26)

Pope's line

> But vindicate the ways of God to Man
> (16)

is his first act of truly calculated presumption. The presumption is, so far, wholly literary, not philosophical at all. The slight 'correction' of Milton's line, the further classicising of the already classical 'justify' as 'vindicate', the abstracting of 'men' to 'Man' are consciously magisterial. There is an element of sheer 'cheek' in the line but, at the same time, a firm assumption of the centre of the literary stage.

The technical term for the justification of God is 'theodicy'. The existence, on the one hand, of a God who is all-powerful and, on the other hand, of a manifestly imperfect world naturally implies that God, who made this world, is not good. In traditional Christian theology two main arguments were used to rebut this inference. First, evil springs from man, not from God, for man was created free and used his freedom disastrously; Adam, not God, removed us all from a state of blessedness. For English readers the principal representation of this tradition is Milton. Secondly, God's creation would have been imperfect, that is, it would have fallen short, if he had not filled his universe with all the possible beings. This implies that both higher and lower creatures must exist; creation itself implies degrees of subordination and subordination itself implies degrees of evil, for that which is low is less good than that which is high. The technical term for a universe so filled is *plenum*. The idea survives vestigially in the common phrase, 'It takes all sorts to make a world'. The principal names in this second tradition are those of Augustine (354–430) and Leibniz (1646–1716).

The notion of the *plenum* can indeed be traced back as far as Plato, but it flourishes most vigorously in the later seventeenth and early eighteenth centuries. The ordinary culture of the period was in any case enamoured of hierarchy. Poets and preachers delighted to explain how the universe was an immense, graduated system: plants were higher than stones, animals were higher than plants, human beings were higher than animals, angels higher than human beings. The effect of the specifically theological argument on this world-view was to invest it with a feeling of necessity; the great, analogical, ordered dance of nature turns into a *chain of being*, in which each link is necessary to the subsistence of the whole. The fullness which characterises the universe seen as a whole is felt rather as a continuous interconnectedness when its elements are taken in succession. Throughout, all is guaranteed by the nature of the Creator. This manner of accounting for the existence of evil in God's creation is generally known as theological optimism. The theory is optimistic in that it asserts that the world we inhabit is indeed the best possible. Today theological optimism is frequently treated as a remote aberration, an eccentric doctrine which was finally exploded when Voltaire created the character of Pangloss in *Candide* (1759). In fact much of the satire in *Candide* misses its mark. Voltaire assumes that he can confound the optimists by a simple catalogue of disasters. But those he attacked had never supposed that there was no pain or distress in the world. Indeed, it was just this that had prompted the entire philosophical enterprise. Voltaire, thoroughly dazed by his own brilliance, proposed to shatter the optimists with something which could almost be described as their own first premiss. The goodness of the world is in fact a direct implication of the Christian conception of God (all-good, all-powerful, creator of all things). The most famous phrase in *An Essay on Man* ('Whatever IS, is RIGHT') proclaims Pope an optimist. In one form or another these arguments will be with us for the rest of this book.

Having completed his less-than-solemn exordium, Pope embarks upon his first argument, 'that we can judge only with regard to our own system':

> Say first, of God above, or Man below,
> What can we reason, but from what we know?
> Of Man what see we, but his station here,
> From which to reason, or to which refer?
> Thro' worlds unnumber'd tho' the God be known,
> 'Tis ours to trace him only in our own.   (17–22)

As we shall find elsewhere in Pope, these lines seem clearer than they really are. A general air of brisk efficiency can have an oddly sedative effect on the intellect. Obviously a philosophical position of fundamental importance for the whole epistle, perhaps for the whole poem, is being taken up. Pope seems to be saying two things at once: first, that we are restricted to knowledge of human affairs and that any attempt to reason beyond the range of our information is absurd; secondly, that we may draw certain inferences about God and man from the knowledge we possess.

Pope's reference to 'worlds unnumber'd' recalls Lucretius' description of Epicurus, his master in philosophy, in the *De Rerum Natura*: Epicurus burst the locked doors of nature, passed beyond the flaming walls of the world and brought back knowledge (I, 66–79). Pope seems deliberately to disclaim any such wild ambition and, indeed, to doubt its possibility for any merely human agent. In effect, he ironically observes that anyone with the superhuman powers of an Epicurus could tell us why we are made the way we are, but then asks whether any of us really understands his or her own frame. This suggests that knowledge of a minute segment does not really allow us to talk about anything else at all. Thus, we might conclude that Pope's main weight is behind the first thesis: man can know only man and his own world. But then the *prepositions* suggest that the second thesis is, after all, dominant. For, if we can reason *from* man's present condition, it would appear that we can proceed thus *to* some larger conception. Moreover, Pope seems to think it consistent with his modest approach to suggest that we may 'trace' God in his creation.

Mark Pattison in his commentary opted for the second thesis. These lines, he explained, illustrate the principle of analogical reasoning in theology, that is, the assumption that, the universe being regulated by uniform laws, those laws which we can trace in that part of it which falls under our observation extend also to that part of it which we cannot see.[13] This, let us acknowledge, is likely to be at least part of what Pope, perhaps confusedly, had in mind. But the doctrine itself is full of difficulties. The word 'analogy' is properly applied to a relation of the following form: A is to B as C is to D. In such a relation A is *analogous* to C and B is analogous to D. How does this enable us to 'trace' God in his creation?

One obvious multiple application of the idea might run as follows: as the lion is to other beasts, as the king is to his subjects, as the head is to the body, as the artist to the work, so God is to the world. Thus stated the idea seems evidently illustrative rather than demonstrative of God's existence. The fact that hierarchy is observable *within* the known universe does not oblige us to infer that the universe as a whole is itself subject to a governor. If, however, this objection were waived and we were to concede that the principle of hierarchy may be thus extended analogically, we find that we have started something which we cannot stop. For, if the human emperor of the world with all his subjects constitutes a whole which must itself be subject to further government, the same applies to the unit consisting of the universe plus God; that, too, must be ruled by a meta-God and so on *ad infinitum*. But in fact the existence of three terms in an organised series does not oblige us to infer a fourth.

It is noteworthy that in Mark Pattison's comment the word 'trace', applied by Pope to the business of finding God in the creation, is applied to the altogether lowlier task of finding the laws of nature. The eighteenth century strove valiantly to maintain the thesis that the laws of nature *were* the laws of God, but the identification must either imply a vast extension of one term or an equally abrupt reduction of the other. If the force of the equation is 'The laws of nature are really part of something infinitely greater, the laws of God', we have extended our thesis beyond what is warranted by observation. If, on the other hand, the equation means 'What used to be called the laws of God are really just the laws of nature', religion collapses. Spinoza was the stock example of the philosopher who reduced God to nature. But it seemed that the Spinozan error could be avoided only by breaking the taboo on making inferences beyond one's information. It was felt by many that (as Leslie Stephen put it) man was intelligible as a fraction but not as an integer, and the world was intelligible as a province of a larger order.[14] But the strains in such a view were obvious. If there are defects in our understanding of what is immediately presented to us, what hope have we of filling the gaps in our knowledge by staring sightlessly at that which is *not* presented to us? Even the analogical generalisation of cause and effect yields little which meets the needs of the devout Christian on his knees in prayer. If the entire universe were, collectively, an effect, the most logically appropriate cause would seem to be some sort of counterpart to this world, something immense mingling of good and bad, rather than the traditional God, infinitely good, infinitely unlike us.

It is a common vice of modern commentators to exaggerate the intellectual unity and coherence of past periods of history. I suspect that the Elizabethan World Picture, so briskly summed up by E. M. W. Tillyard, was in fact little more coherent than the Twentieth Century World Picture. The eighteenth century was similarly confused and divided. Samuel Clarke in his Boyle Lectures delivered in 1704 and 1705 was confident that a future state of rewards and punishments was implied by the observable condition of the world (he assumed, on the basis of other arguments, a just God);[15] Locke, on the other hand, replying to Stillingfleet, conceded that the immortality of the soul was not demonstrable and must rest on Scripture alone.[16] Here it might be said that Locke refused to avail himself of analogical inference. Pope in the present passage seems to imply directly that we can know nothing of any other 'station' of man but this, and to be so far a Lockean. This revives our original feeling that, if anything, Pope is curbing the freedom of analogical inference rather than launching himself upon its wings.

In 1736, a little after *An Essay on Man*, Bishop Joseph Butler published the great work of theology which is commonly referred to simply as the *Analogy* (its full title was *The Analogy of Religion, Natural and Revealed*). Butler observed that if we approach too close to a fire we are burned. This, he suggests, illustrates the fundamental principle of punishment, operating in nature, and an analogical extension of the principle suggests a future life of rewards and punishments. But he is too honest a thinker to pretend that such an argument is demonstrative; he contents himself with the assertion that what we see of the organisation of things here is at least *compatible* with the supposition of a larger organisation, so that, as he puts it, there is 'nothing incredible' in the notion of rewards and punishments after death.[17] In the seventh chapter of the first part, Butler struggles to infer the character of the larger scheme. He is in fact deeply exercised by the difficulty of inferring from our own state, in which justice and injustice coexist, a next world of pure justice, rather than one in which the present mingling of the two is continued. The full stretch of his reasoning is to show that either sort of 'complement' to what we have before our eyes is conceivable. What emerges clearly in Butler is that the essence of analogy lies in proceeding from the part to the whole and that such proceeding is always of itself utterly tenuous. Pope in the present passage echoes Montaigne's observation that man sees only the order of 'this little vault' he lodges under,[18] and at line 34 asks boldly how the part can ever comprehend the whole. Thus, again, analogy would appear to be ruled out.

My hope, in dwelling on the notion of analogy, has been to shed a little darkness where previous commentators have shed a too facile light. 'What Pope really thought' remains elusive. Probably he mentally juggled with both ideas, spent little energy on any attempt to distinguish them and very considerable energy on the production of a smooth and acceptable set of couplets. But the *Essay* is a real philosophical poem and has real philosophical arguments in it. If we are to understand it, we must continue, like ill-bred spaniels, to worry and mangle the lines.

Poetically, the intellectually forbidden matter affords a release. In telling us, in detail, all the things we cannot possibly know about (21–32) Pope can fill his couplets with spinning planets and stars, with wonders. He shows no sense of any obligation to dissemble his enjoyment. In a way, he 'expatiates' yet further (though now the expansion is marked by the argument as proud folly). In the writing one senses that the principal tension is between two literary 'manners': on the one hand, the cool, minimising, 'gentlemanly' style and, on the other hand, a Miltonic/Lucretian grandeur. The first manner may intermittently 'judge' the second, but both equally fertilise the poetry.

At line 35, with the words 'Presumptuous Man!' the theodicy, or vindication of God, begins. The enemy is now not the overambitious philosopher or natural scientist. It is the person who cannot accept God's dispensation, the person who complains to God. In the Bible the man who complains most vociferously about the ways of God is Job. In that strangest and most moving of poems, however, the clamorously indignant Job is the hero, and his soothing, piously prudent comforters, who sometimes reason like eighteenth-century theologians, are implicitly condemned. Job's cries have the dignity of authentic suffering and honesty. God meanwhile is utterly incomprehensible and at the same time blazingly manifest in his creation. The poet of Job never seeks to persuade us of God's governance by pointing to the rationally useful aspects of the world – the alternation of day and night that human beings may work and rest, the sending of rain that crops may grow and sun that they may ripen. In Job, God sends rain 'on the wilderness wherein there is no man' (XXXVIII, 26). But God is visibly magnificent: 'Hast thou given the horse strength? Hast thou clothed his neck with thunder? . . . Where wast thou when I laid the foundations of the earth?' (XXXIX, 19; XXXVIII, 4). David Hume in his *Natural History of Religion* (written before 1757 but not published until 1777) was one of the first to treat religion as a natural cultural phenomenon having a history like other phenomena. He noticed that cultures in their earlier phases tend precisely to locate God in the irregular rather than the regular aspects of nature and quoted Euripides' *Hecuba*, 958–60: 'The gods toss all life into confusion; mix everything with its reverse; that all of us, pay them the more worship and reverence.'[19] Pope, the poet, responds to the Jobian picture of God's splendour in independent action. Here, once more, his imagination leaps up to the 'argent fields'. At I, 157 he writes

> Who knows but he, whose hand the light'ning forms,
> Who heaves old Ocean, and who wings the storms

and at II, 109

> Nor God alone in the still calm we find,
> He mounts the storm, and walks upon the wind.

Unlike the author of Job, however, Pope insinuates the idea of hierarchical order and interdependence. In fact it would have been consistent with a radical 'Presume not God to scan' stance to have adopted a fully Jobian position: that God's action is wholly incomprehensible in its majesty. Instead Pope begins to work within the eighteenth-century version of the cosmic chain of being and at once, as we have seen, he is involved in metaphysics, presumptuously rationalising God's scheme, violating his own prescription of humility. Any reasoned vindication must do all these things. It is thus unsurprising that, if we analyse the components of the opening paragraph on pride, the Miltonic line, 'But vindicate the ways of God to Man', falls on that side of the opening antithesis occupied by versions of pride.

Pope condemns as presumptuous the question 'Why are the satellites of Jupiter smaller than Jupiter itself?' Voltaire very reasonably observed that they would not *be* satellites if they were not smaller (he must have assumed equal density); if one of them were larger, Jupiter and the rest would have revolved around *it*.[20] The question Pope condemns is not so much presumptuous as merely incoherent. Voltaire's comment shows, moreover, how Newtonian physics is essentially a self-contained system. Pope's major argument, however, is deeply traditional. An important if remote source of his thought, both here and at 229–30 below, is Augustine's *De Diversis Quaestionibus*, LXXXIII, xli: 'non essent omnia, aequalia si essent' ['All things would never have been, had all things been equal'].[21] Augustine meant that if all things were equal (God being one of the 'things') all things would be perfect and therefore indistinguishable from God. There would thus have been no creation at all. To assent to creation is to assent to degrees of imperfection. Conversely, to complain of evil in the world is implicitly to require that God should not have created the world at all. In one way this argument may seem very abstract. In another it has a curiously intimate force. It says to the person discontented with his or her human status: 'Do you really want not to exist? God in permitting degrees of imperfection has permitted *you*.' Pope's style, with its frequent use of the second person singular, the challenging aphoristic imperative, tends to bring out the personal factor in the ancient argument. But the stronger versions come later.

Line 45 is almost meaningless to many twentieth-century readers:

> Where all must full or not coherent be. . .

The reference here is to a doctrine which can be traced back as far as Plato's *Timaeus*, that God in creating a hierarchical universe had necessarily to fill out with real existence every stage in the great scheme. Otherwise his act of creation would have been defective. The universe therefore is a *plenum*, that is, it is full. This accounts for the first half of Pope's line, but not for the second. In fact the meaning of 'coherent' is not entirely clear. It seems that it cannot bear the sense 'logically consistent'. The only *logical* consistency involved in the doctrine is the consistency with the perfection of God himself, rather than the consistency of parts of the creation with each other. It seems more likely that Pope's word 'coherent' springs from relatively crude 'picture-thinking'. The word has a quasi-physical sense: 'firmly compacted, stable', as though the universe were conceived as an immense tower, threatened and at the same time strengthened by the force of gravity.

Lines 54 to 60 elaborate the idea without clarifying it. The word 'movements' in the line 'A thousand movements scarce one purpose gain' is beginning to assume the technical sense, 'mechanism', as in the 'movement' of a clock. Pope seems now to be thinking not so much of a building as of a machine, but the thought is still physicalist. Pre-Copernican astronomy had interpreted the movements of the heavenly bodies as a complex system of wheels within and upon wheels, cycles, epicycles, deferents, eccentricities. One has only to provide these majestic wheels with cogs and one has an enormous piece of clockwork. Pope, with his 'thousand movements' (54), 'acts second' (58) and 'Touches some wheel' (59), seems in his imagination to have half-envisaged such a transition to cog-wheels, but the interconnecting elements, weirdly, are degrees of imperfection. The strange idea begins to form that the entire universe is an immense machine, designed for a particular purpose we cannot comprehend.

The more rebellious sort of reader may begin to feel that the argument is unfairly loaded in God's favour. We are allowed to entertain unverifiable hypotheses, so long as they tend to vindicate God. Pope the positivist might be forced to admit that, since we know nothing of God, we do not know *anything* about his purposes; they may, then, be good or bad. But to suppose a good purpose is in practice welcomed and to suppose a bad would be to attract at once the accusing finger and the cry, 'Presumptuous man!' It would of course be absurd to expect Pope in the 1730s to explore neutrally the hypothesis of an evil God. In fact mildly confused pluralism is the opposite of doctrinaire bullying. At line 80 he indeed hints that if we did know more of our situation our discontent would actually be *increased*, presumably because we should be vividly aware of the joys which lay beyond our reach rather than because we should perceive any injustice in the system.

Lines 72–6 introduce the dimension of time. Pope lightly turns inside out the medieval description of God as a circle whose centre is everywhere and circumference nowhere. Man, conversely, is a being whose space is a point. In like manner, time, which seems to man an immense sequence, is to God (how does Pope, on his own terms, know this?) a moment. This is clearly out of line with the preceding emphasis on man's position within a complex system. Instead Pope has reverted to a fiercer rhetoric which, so far from placing man in a middle position, lays him level with the dust. In fact the variations of history are an embarrassment to believers in a universe filled to the brim with the best possible contents consistent with the necessary imperfection implied by the mere fact of a hierarchical creation. If something comes to exist in time which did not exist before, it must be possible and yet, previously, the universe lacked its presence, was not truly 'full'. Are there, then, times when God's creativity is operating at less than full strength? To concede as much is to concede the very principle of the *plenum*, or perfected creation.

In the more rigorously necessitarian versions of the doctrine, the necessary simultaneity of all existents becomes inescapable. Spinoza in his scholium to the seventeenth proposition of the first book of the

Ethics wrestles with the argument that 'if God had created every-thing which is in his intellect he would not be able to create anything more'.[22] It might just be possible to suppose that God is free within a *plenum* to vary in time those existents which are of like value, so that it is a matter of ethical indifference if one replaces another. But traditional Christian teaching locates within historical time certain events of stupendous ethical importance: the fall of man, the incar-nation of God as Jesus Christ, the redemption of the world. Thus, the persistent conflict between the timeless, abstract conception pressed by the Deists and the essentially historical, *narrative* concep-tion of the orthodox is in a mannèr anticipated here. If this is the best possible creation, as would seem to be implied by the existence of an all-good, all-powerful God, the Fall cannot in any serious sense have occurred. The more successful such a theology is in explaining away the imperfections of the world, the more surely it undermines the principal historical 'story' of Christianity. Perhaps Pope's instinct was sure when he chose, in treating time, to avoid the imagery of system and interdependence.

I have suggested that the reason why knowledge of our real cosmic position might plunge us in deeper gloom (80) is likely to lie in the intense joys which would then be visible but beyond our reach. In fact the image which follows, if its immediate implication is accepted, momentarily suggests a much darker reason. Man is com-pared at lines 82 ff. with the lamb who is happy because he does not know he is going to be butchered. Pope may have taken the image from Horace's ode on the spring at Bandusia (XIII, xiii). The Latin poem is light and graceful, but Horace drops into his poem, in the second stanza, the idea of the innocent victim's blood mingling with the cold, clear water of the spring, and the effect is a sort of cun-ningly muted shock (lines 6–7). In Pope the sentiment is moralised, and in a very odd way. Man, too, may be doomed: it is much better that he should know nothing: God observes great events and small dispassionately. The writing, as long as the image of the lamb is sustained, is playful. Yet, if the analogy means anything at all, a shadow, so faint as to be almost imperceptible, of Calvinist predes-tined damnation has passed over the poem. By line 90 this shadow, which is utterly uncharacteristic of the *Essay*, has passed, and the hypothesis becomes that of future *bliss*.

The dizzy alternation of the minute with the immense, atoms with astronomical constellations, bubbles with exploding worlds, fascinated the eighteenth century. Voltaire wrote a piece of early science fiction based on this fascination called *Micromégas*. Swift wrote of Lilliput and Brobdingnag; Sterne, most wildly of all, of the tiny armies within a drop of semen (*Tristram Shandy*, I, i). Perhaps, as Marjorie Nicolson has suggested, it was a natural literary consequence of the startling world revealed to scientists by the use of lenses, both microscopic and telescopic. However novel and modish the imagery, Pope directs it to a firmly traditional end in that it illustrates the universal perception of God

> Who sees with equal eye, as God of all,
> A hero perish, or a sparrow fall,
> Atoms or systems into ruin hurl'd,
> And now a bubble burst, and now a world.
>
> (87–90)

Maynard Mack cites Matthew, X, 29–31, and Montaigne. The biblical passage runs as follows:

> Are not two sparrows sold for a farthing? and one of them shall not fall on the ground without your Father.
> But the very hairs of your head are all numbered.
> Fear ye not therefore, ye are of more value than many sparrows.

The relevant passage in Cotton's translation of Montaigne (1693) reads: 'As if to that *King* of Kings it were more and less to subvert a Kingdom, or to move the Leaf of a Tree; Or as if his *Providence* acted after another manner in enclining the Event of a Battle, than in the leap of a Flea.'[23] Mack cites these passages to rebut the suggestion made by Elwin, the great nineteenth-century editor of Pope, that for the God of the *Essay* men and sparrows are of equal value (EC, II, 354–5).

It may be doubted whether Mack is well served by his examples. One can scarcely maintain that the meaning of Pope's lines, traditional as they are, is exhaustively determined and closed by the meaning of earlier specimens of the same tradition. To use the passages in this way is in effect to deny the very existence of tradition as a live, developing thing, and to substitute an inert, anti-historical reduction. Pope's lines, following as they do the half-facetious imagery of the doomed lamb, have a very different taste from both the biblical passage and the sentence of Montaigne. The verses in Matthew convey God's solicitude for his creatures. The lines of Pope, partly because of the suggestion of equanimity in 'equal eye', imply indifference. Mack notes correctly that Montaigne was writing in express opposition to Cicero's stoic view that the gods concern themselves with large matters only and not with trivial details. Indeed, Montaigne's sentence makes his counter-weighting of values clear: God's full power is engaged in every event in the universe, however small. But Pope's God does not 'lay the hand of the government' on anything; he neither 'moves' nor 'enclines' any object; he 'sees with equal eye', *spectator haud particeps*. So detached a God is hardly a standing affront to the 'business tycoon' God of Cicero; one could argue with equal force that Pope's biblically based lines, so far from Christianising a Stoic conception, have the paradoxical effect of pushing it yet farther from Christianity, towards the unconcerned gods of Epicurus. Elwin was not an ignorant reader, incapable of recognising Christian material when it was under his nose. He was a highly educated scholar who smelled something distinctive in the lines before him. I have already quoted, in connection with Deism, Leslie Stephen's remark that with the expansion of trade-routes the scenery had grown too wide for the central drama of the Crucifixion. With the universe revealed to telescopic observation, the scenery grows wider still, until a fear is started that man himself may be of small interest to God.

Pope in this part of the epistle seems obscurely ill-at-ease. The idea of heavenly bliss lay outside the scope of his poem and was in any case not easily reconciled with his governing philosophic scheme. But here the idea of an after-life presses for admission to the argument, and Pope seems not to know exactly how it should be handled. The sudden firmness of 'Hope humbly then' (91) is authentically and fully Christian; but the subsequent lines, restricted as they are to the subjective sentiment, to the hope in separation from its object, seem to hover dangerously on the edge of irony. After all, readers had learned to expect irony from Pope:

> Hope springs eternal in the human breast:
> Man never Is, but always To be blest. . .
> (95–6)

The very style seems fleetingly to assume a mocking smile. Of course

Pope cannot really be saying in the second line that no one ever attains blessedness. He is referring to our state on earth. But the lines themselves put up only the weakest of resistance to a satirical reading: 'Foolish man is for ever hoping for Heaven, but his hopes always delude him.' Nor is it difficult to imagine the libertine Lord Bolingbroke giving such an impulse to the phrase, over a bottle of Pope's claret. The last two lines of the section

> The soul, uneasy and confin'd from home,
> Rests and expatiates in a life to come.
>
> (97–8)

almost imply, with the dangerous indefinite article 'a' in the second line, a proto-Freudian theory of religion as a compensatory illusion. This time, however, the lines include an element of resistance to so cynical a view, in the curiously powerful phrase 'confin'd from home'. Thus, although Pope virtually excludes from his poem any overt reference to the change in our condition known as the Fall, he does not as thoroughly exclude a prospective change after death. It is noteworthy that the phrase 'from home' did not appear in the poem until the 'Pope–Warburton quarto' of 1743 (previous editions have 'at home'). It is very much on the cards that Warburton, the defender of Pope's orthodoxy, induced him to make the change. It was not by chance, perhaps, that I conjured the spirit of Bolingbroke a moment ago. Warburton may well have smelled the same malign influence and taken steps to get rid of it.

The passage on hope is immediately followed by 'the poor Indian' at line 99. The section is lyrically beautiful and benevolently patronising. There is no Voltairean attempt to smash the habitual assumption of European superiority. Voltaire makes his point not with an Indian but with a Chinaman who is aghast to learn that Europeans consume the flesh and blood of their God in a ceremony known as 'the Mass'.[24] Pope's Indian indeed avoids the barbarous terrors of Hell (how serious is Pope here and how far is 'no fiends torment' a blow against Christianity?) but is nevertheless seen as a lovable simpleton. Yet at the same time there is genuine imaginative sympathy in Pope's attempt to convey the intense familiarity of near horizons, of the small place known the more intimately because it is the only place known, and the kind of religious aspiration which goes with that sense of place.

> Behind the cloud-topt hill, an humbler heav'n;
> Some safer world in depth of woods embrac'd. . .
>
> (104–5)

In these lines the Indian is patronised, commended and obscurely envied all at once. Perhaps memories of Pope's own childhood play a part in them. When the poor Indian crops up again, however, at IV, 177, it is as an object of simple contempt!

> Go, like the Indian, in another life
> Expect thy dog, thy bottle, and thy wife. . .

At line 113, Pope turns from the Indian to his well-heeled reader and rallies him with an ironic challenge, 'Go, wiser thou!' Pope invites his reader to see how well *he* does in weighing Providence in his 'scale of sense'. This is the only appearance in the poem of the idea of sense-perception, erected into the foundation of all knowledge by Locke, eagerly adopted by Pope's supposed mentor, Bolingbroke.[25] Because Pope's lines assert only the *theological* insufficiency of sense, they do not formally contradict Locke, who founded natural knowledge alone on sense perception; but, for all that, Pope's tone is notably scornful. To judge God is to make oneself the God of God (unless, presumably, we judge him superior to ourselves). The image of rebellion evokes for a moment the great Miltonic story, usually so firmly repressed in the *Essay*. But it is not Adam who is evoked, but Lucifer, the rebel angel who rose up against God. Man, who in the scheme of the *Essay* has not clearly fallen, may yet by overweening intellectual ambition repeat the original error of Satan himself.

The argument of lines 131–64 is less commonplace than many suppose. The case put by pride was in fact a mainstay of purportedly pious theologians, and Pope in scorning it is not attacking an obvious absurdity as commonly but is casting doubt on something which many eighteenth-century theologians relied on as a mainstay of faith. This is the idea that God has rationally and benevolently ordered the entire universe in such a way as to serve the needs of man, the crown of creation, formed on the sixth day. Pope correctly perceives that this teleological method of vindicating God is implicitly opposed to his own preferred reliance on the great chain of being. A. O. Lovejoy notes the opposition between the two theologies.[26] As Bishop King wrote:

Those . . . who urge the Unfitness of certain Parts of the Earth for the Sustenance of Man, as a Fault or Defect of The Divine Skill in making them, are oblig'd to prove that the Earth was made for the sake of Mankind only, and not of the Universe. . . But this is absurd, and what no one would object, who is not blinded with Pride and Ignorance.[27]

King's words make it clear that upholders of the opposite view had run into difficulties. God sent rain and ripened the crops, certainly, but then sometimes he sent drought, and meanwhile, as we were told in Job, it rains in the wilderness where no one lives. Pope's party, on the other hand, could welcome the rain falling in the wilderness, but unlike the author of Job they were not content to acquiesce in its incomprehensibility. Rather, they rationalised it, but in a modest, open manner which differed sharply from the man-centred rationalisation of the teleologists. The rain is part of *God's* plan, in which many may play a relatively minor part. Thus, the suggestion is that the majestic movements of nature exist for the sake of the whole, regardless of man's interests. In lines 131–40 the anthropocentrist celebrates a universe constructed for his delight. Pope then counters with 'livid deaths', fire and pestilence. The implication must be that these things embarrass the anthropocentrist but do not embarrass *him*, Pope, presumably because they can always be attributed to unknown factors in the Incomprehensible Design.

Lines 145–64 are the most difficult in the entire poem:

> 'No ('tis reply'd) the first Almighty Cause
> 'Acts not by partial, but by gen'ral laws;
> 'Th' exceptions few; some change since all began,
> 'And what created perfect?' – Why then Man?
> If the great end be human Happiness,
> Then Nature deviates; and can Man do less?
> As much that end a constant course requires
> Of show'rs and sun-shine, as of Man's desires;
> As much eternal springs and cloudless skies,
> As Men for ever temp'rate, calm, and wise.
> If plagues or earthquakes break not Heav'n's design,
> Why then a Borgia, or a Catiline?
> Who knows but he, whose hand the light'ning forms,
> Who heaves old Ocean, and who wings the storms,
> Pours fierce Ambition in a Cæsar's mind,

Or turns young Ammon loose to scourge mankind?
From pride, from pride, our very reas'ning springs;
Account for moral as for nat'ral things:
Why charge we Heav'n in those, in these acquit?
In both, to reason right is to submit.

Pope has just pointed out to the anthropocentric theologian that
nature does not always serve human happiness: earthquakes and
plagues consume whole cities. This is an interesting historical
moment in the argument since Pope uses as ammunition for his
cause the very phenomena which Voltaire in *Candide* and his poem
on the Lisbon earthquake was later to use against those very Leibnizian optimists whom one would assume to be of Pope's party. Had
Pope lived long enough to read *Candide* he would presumably have
said that its author confused the cosmic and the anthropocentric
view. 'The best of all possible worlds' does not mean 'that which
gives man the most comfortable ride' but, rather, that which is
absolutely best, in the eyes of God. At line 145 the anthropocentrist
attempts a stumbling defence: the laws according to which God
promotes human happiness are highly general and admit of occasional minor exceptions; after all, nothing is created perfect. It is not
so much a defence as a capitulation. The reader is puzzled for a
moment to find the doctrine that God works by general laws treated
by Pope with implicit scorn. The same thesis, after all, is advanced
as serious wisdom at IV, 35. But the *anthropocentric* appeal to 'general
laws' is vulnerable to falsification, while the use of the same concept by the 'cosmic' party with reference to the inscrutable plan of
God is not. Pope is under no obligation to grant occasional minor
exceptions.

Pope seizes on his opponent's concession that nothing is created
perfect to round on him with the challenge: why, then, should you
expect human behaviour to be perfect? The argument which follows
is *ad hominem*, that is, it is deliberately posed in the terms of his
opponent's philosophy. The normal use of this stratagem is to show
how the opponent's view generates absurdities. Pope's antagonist
has granted that nature does not conform constantly to one single
law but, in detail at least, is variable. By the same token human
behaviour can be expected to vary. Changing skies above may well
be answered by changing attitudes in those who walk beneath them.
If the anthropocentrist grants exceptions to the felicific laws of

nature, he may as well grant that similar exceptions occur amongst human beings. A murdering Borgia is rather like an earthquake in his effect on human happiness. Why, then, says Pope, should we convict God of breaking (or permitting the breaking of) his rule in the case of earthquakes and acquit him in the case of Cesare Borgia? Thus, Pope tries to edge his opponent, inch by inch, from praising God to condemning him.

It is evident, however, that Pope is running into trouble. The anthropocentrist may be persuaded that, if the exceptions to God's great rules (as he construes them) are so numerous and palpable, his theology courts impiety and must be reformed. A less docile mind might draw a somewhat different conclusion: both earthquakes and human villainy are ultimately the work of God and are unforgivable. Pope, one senses, was trying to insinuate his own theodicy within the *ad hominem* argument. But the logic of the *ad hominem* argument is necessarily dominant, and the reader is therefore tempted to infer that, even though the anthropocentrist may have been forced to concede that by a true theology earthquakes, Borgias and Catilines must all somehow be right and acceptable, the rest of us are under no such obligation. In effect, Pope has used the *ad hominem* approach not to disclose an absurdity in his opponent's position but, rather, to elicit an area of agreement (that God's benevolence works in all things). Meanwhile, though we may infer that in Pope's view such horrors must be ascribed to an inscrutable yet good divine purpose, the very fact that the despised opponent has at last lent his support (implicitly) to the extent of acknowledging that such things must be acceptable infects the whole case with uncertainty. Pope seems to have nothing left but a gigantic *petitio principii*: these things must be reconcilable with divine benevolence because they must. Rhetoric and logic are not working in perfect unison here. At the same time one senses that Pope is half-frightened by his own picture of the pain and violence of the world. The section ends with an almost neurotic conceit, attached to the word 'reason':

> In both, to reason right is to submit.
>
> (164)

The principal sense of the line is: 'The reasonable course, since we cannot know God's purposes, is resignation.' But the tempo of the phrasing suggests a half-formed epigram. To bring out the latent paradox we might substitute the words, 'To reason right is to refrain from reasoning', which is of course, like many epigrams, formally self-contradictory. In the *Essay*, however, even the half-presence of such a paradox, lurking behind the line, is dangerous, for the contradiction of thinking the unthinkable permeates the entire work.

Pope is hard-pressed, and the pressure produces the astonishing section, 165–72, in which the common eighteenth-century conception of a harmonious universe is thrown away, and instead a world of Heraclitean strife is embraced. For a brief space the thought seems fully Romantic; rough seas are better *in themselves* than calm. But then the conception of order is simply reasserted. A world of dynamic conflict may still be an organised world. A cosmos need not be mechanical and inert; it may be organic and live.

At 189, Pope returns to his running theme of small thoughts and low ambitions:

> The bliss of Man (could Pride that blessing find)
> Is not to act or think beyond mankind . . .

Yet what has Pope just done, in the magnificent explosion of the preceding section, if not to conceive a supra-human dynamic order and tremble at the conception? Nevertheless, he pushes on with the argument that man could not have larger powers without ceasing to be himself:

> Why has not Man a microscopic eye?
> For this plain reason, Man is not a Fly.
> (193–4)

Pope may have had in mind a passage from Locke's *Essay Concerning Human Understanding*:

> . . . if that most instructive of our senses, seeing, were in any man a thousand or a hundred thousand times more acute than it is by the best microscope, things several millions of times less than the smallest object of his sight now would then be visible to his naked eyes . . . but then he would be in quite a different world from other people . . . And perhaps such a quickness and tenderness of sight could not endure bright sunshine . . . if by the help of such *microscopical eyes* . . . a man could penetrate further than ordinary

into the secret composition and radical texture of bodies, he would not make any great advantage by the change.[28]

Pope, however, in bringing out the question of identity is perhaps more philosophically radical than Locke, though Locke moves towards this idea when he suggests that our very world of ordinary objects, on which all our words and concepts are founded, is threatened by such a change. But the energy of Pope's poetic genius perhaps works against the bias of his intellect. The images of exaggerated sensitivity which follow are the objects of a delighted (if terrified) empathy on the part of the poet who is ostensibly recommending contentment with the human lot. To smart and agonise at every pore, to die of roses in aromatic pain, to be stunned with the music of the spheres, all this is nothing if not exciting and at the same time carries a potent charge of reference to Pope himself, that wretched, magnificent, shivering bundle of intelligent hypersensitivity.

This marvellous empathy is sustained in the jolly Augustan bestiary which comes next. The 'hound sagacious on the tainted green' is especially effective in its use of the faintly odd word, 'tainted'. The immediately relevant sense here is 'imbued with the scent of a (hunted) animal'. The word is so used by Addison in his *Campaign* (line 122):

> So the staunch Hound the trembling deer pursues,
> And smells his footsteps in the tainted dews.[29]

Addison supplies more explanatory information than Pope. The ordinary sense of *tainted*, then as now, was 'contaminated'. Addison makes quite sure that his reader is not confused. Pope is less officiously helpful. He gives, very barely, what the dog receives through its senses and no more. The alien quality of the word 'tainted' in its less familiar sense marks the difference between our world and the dog's, visually impressionistic (mere 'green') and yet keenly perceived through the sense of smell.

In the mood of good-humour generated by the grovelling swine and the half-reasoning elephant, Pope tells us again it takes all sorts to make a world, that a single missing existent would overthrow the entire structure. Moreover, that structure is clearly living, not dead. One still hears the claim that Pope's theology is mechanistic. It is as if, as long as the couplets are strongly pointed in the Augustan manner, no one will believe that they can be celebrating something as Romantic as an organic universe. Yet the meaning is plain:

> All are but parts of one stupendous whole,
> Whose body Nature is, and God the soul;
> That, chang'd thro' all, and yet in all the same,
> Great in the earth, as in th'ætherial frame,
> Warms in the sun, refreshes in the breeze,
> Glows in the stars, and blossoms in the trees,
> Lives thro' all life, extends thro' all extent,
> Spreads undivided, operates unspent,
> Breathes in our soul, informs our mortal part,
> As full, as perfect, in a hair as heart;
> As full, as perfect, in vile Man that mourns,
> As the rapt Seraph that adores and burns;
> To him no high, no low, no great, no small;
> He fills, he bounds, connects, and equals all.
>
> (267–80)

The eighteenth century is conventionally despised for want of strong religious feeling connected with natural beauty. But it is hard to think of a living writer who could match the cumulative impetus of these lines. Pope himself remains for once magnificently unironic, almost rapt. The pantheistic vision of Spinoza seems within his imaginative grasp, but his God remains unequivocally divine. Nature is transfigured; God is not reduced.

The end of the epistle is now not far off. Pope drops his voice once more to the low note, 'Submit', in line 285. Then, as he sums up, he mounts again to a last, swift climax. All nature is art, but art unknown (how, then, did Pope know it?). All chance is really direction (the modest word 'direction' avoids the embarrassment of a Calvinist determinism). All discord is harmony, not understood (the Heraclitean universe of glorious strife now firmly brought to order). (All partial evil is universal good.

> And, spite of Pride, in erring Reason's spite,
> One truth is clear, 'Whatever IS, is RIGHT'
>
> (293–4)

It is all very dexterous, yet Pope has overreached himself. His jaunty style has undone him. That 'whatever is' is really and ultimately 'right' might have been made to emerge gradually, as a difficult yet credible idea, requiring the utmost stretch of faith and imagination. But what the poet must not do – and what Pope has now done – is to bring it forward with an air of briskly complacent confidence. In a chairman of a committee it would be rank bad timing and would cost him the vote he sought. In a poet it is almost unforgivable. But we have not yet finished with the vindication of God.

(iii) EPISTLE II: MAN ALONE

Know then thyself, presume not God to scan. . .

The first three words of the second epistle come loaded with a weight of history which Pope proceeds to ignore. The phrase, a favourite of the Stoics, is traceable beyond them to the half-legendary beginnings of European philosophy. Diogenes Laertius attributes it to Thales of Miletus.[30] Thales was one of the Seven Sages of Greece, which sounds like pure mythology, but he seems nevertheless to have enjoyed a fully historical existence near the beginning of the sixth century BC. He is said to have predicted the solar eclipse of 585 BC. Diogenes adds, however, that Chilon, another of the Seven Sages, used to claim that the phrase was his. Later Ausonius dramatised this claim in his 'Masque of the Seven Sages'.[31] There Chilon recommends curious persons to visit Delphi, where the words might still be seen inscribed on a column. Others attribute the saying to Solon.

Laird, commenting on Pope, observes that the classical adage is severely introspective, inviting us to turn away from the world and look within, where we may find truth, principle and 'perhaps a spark of deity'.[32] Thus, Cicero says that when Apollo told us to know ourselves he meant that we ought to know our own souls.[33] This is the standard interpretation of the saying, which is predictably cited by Robert Burton in his *Anatomy of Melancholy*.[34] That the contrast normally implied in antiquity was with external affairs rather than with theology (which is *Pope's* contrast) appears clearly from a line in a surviving fragment of Menander's *Thrasyleon*: 'The saying "Know thyself" is wrong; it would be more to the point to say, "know other people".'[35]

In 1599, Sir John Davies, the Solicitor-General of Ireland under James I, wrote a long didactic poem which takes this adage, in its

Latin form, as its title, *Nosce Teipsum*. The strong similarity, in terms of aim and scope, between Davies's poem and Pope's makes comparison of them appropriate, and such comparison, not surprisingly, yields in its turn more differences than affinities. The distance between them is nowhere so marked as in the interpretation of this phrase, which plays a fundamental part in either poem. For Davies, knowledge of the soul is hardly to be set *against* knowledge of eternity, since it is through contemplation of the soul that we attain our surest insight into the next world:

> . . . whoso makes a mirror of his mind,
> And doth with patience view himself therein,
> His Soul's eternity shall clearly find,
> Though the other beauties be defaced with sin.[36]
>
> (1301–4)

Davies is able to argue thus because of a doctrinal presupposition that the soul, as he explains at line 121, was at its creation imprinted with the image of God.[37] This is partly a matter of its nature and origin, as disclosed in scripture. At the same time, however, Davies seems to feel, somewhat mysteriously, that the eternity of the soul is directly available to introspection.

It almost seems as if the very *practice* of introspection underwent a fundamental change in the seventeenth century. Descartes, in his celebrated historic effort to investigate his own mind, supposed himself to be discovering the ground of a rational religion. But the phrase of Descartes which is most often quoted, *cogito, ergo sum*, 'I think, therefore I am',[38] suggests meanwhile that not even the *ego*, the *self*, is directly available in introspection but must rather be deduced from it. Instead of the concentric scheme, 'I think, and find therein myself, and, in myself, God', we find in Descartes a venturing out into something like darkness from a given centre: 'I think, therefore I must exist to be doing the thinking.' Spinoza observes that the mind cannot know itself except in so far as it perceives modifications in the body,[39] but seems at the same time to have retained the older concrete intuition of an internal eternity, *sentimus experimurque nos aeternos esse*: 'We feel and know by experience that we are eternal.'[40] Yet Spinoza has no sooner made this thundering assertion than he guards it with a hint that perception itself may be conditioned by conception: 'The mind feels those things that it conceives by understanding, no less than those things that it remembers.'

As time passed, it seemed less and less easy to find *oneself* by introspection, still less to find God. Hume could see nothing when he strove to look within his soul but fugitive, evanescent impressions of the external world.[41] Yet in the Middle Ages the severe exclusion of such external reference had been regarded as a prerequisite of spiritually profitable introspection. Some four hundred years before Hume, Walter Hilton in his *Ladder of Perfection* had also found a terminal darkness in the soul, calling this darkness the image of the first Adam, fallen man, but then found, beyond that, the image of the second Adam, itself an image of Christ.[42] There is some evidence that Pope, as he drew near to death, searched his soul in the manner of his great predecessors. He told Spence in 1744: 'I am so certain of the soul's being immortal that I seem to feel it within me, as it were by intuition' (Spence, 654).

But Pope's *Essay on Man* has no place in this story, itself so important a part of the history of European thought. Here he neither loses his image of God nor is he plunged into that narrower abyss in which self also is lost, because he makes no serious effort to 'introspect' at all. Although he wrote in the argument to the second epistle that he would concern himself with man 'as an Individual' and postpones to a later epistle the consideration of man in society, it is really the species rather than the subjective soul which engrosses his attention. His treatment of the theme is genial, social, public. The second half of the line, 'presume not God to scan', need not mean 'forget God', for 'scan', contrary to popular belief, does not mean 'glance at', but rather implies minute and scrupulous attention. Nevertheless, the broad contrast between futile and unverifiable theology on the one hand and finding out about one's own kind on the other seems inescapable. Pope in effect takes Menander's advice, 'Know other people', and perceives no discrepancy between such a course and the injunction 'Know thyself'. At no point in the poem do we feel the poet straining to understand the recesses of his subjective consciousness. To know oneself is to know (another) human being.

Here one may suspect the influence of Bolingbroke, who was all for sensory knowledge as opposed to metaphysics. Pope may have allowed this favourite contrast of his mentor to colour his interpretation of the classical adage.

I have implied, perhaps, that Pope in taking this course avoided the severer challenge and opted for the superficial. It could, however, be claimed with equal force that Pope merely avoided what could never have been presented in his kind of verse. Our notion even of ourselves is to a very considerable extent socially constituted, and Pope's emphasis on the public sphere is neither extravagant nor stupid.

The great set-piece description of man follows. The general thesis is that man occupies an intermediate position, about halfway up the chain of being. Such a state of affairs might be expected to allay all excitement and to silence poetry. In fact Pope turns it into an amazing display of tight-rope walking. Man balances precariously between immensities, and the poet in his description re-enacts the original feat of balance.

The passage taken as a whole celebrates the ancient conception of an ordered, hierarchically stratified creation. This conception is less uniform than many people think. According to one version, it is argued that man is simply stuck in the middle, a little above dogs, a fair way below the nearest angel. On the other hand, Pico della Mirandola and some of the Hermetists held an almost existentialist conception, in which man is essentially unstable: God created the ordered universe and filled each gradation until the whole blazed before him with complete existence. But then he paused, and determined to make something different. Accordingly he made a creature which had no definite character at all, something dark, insubstantial and fundamentally free. This he called 'man'. He set this creature in the middle of his system not as his fixed place, but merely in order that he might look round him before he ranged through the entire hierarchy; God gave man the negative capacity to become like any of his creatures, a brute or an angel.[43]

Pope's version, which is in all essentials taken from Pascal, is a brilliant compromise between these two philosophies. His primary position is the first: man belongs in a middle state; this is *naturally* his. But all the giddy possibilities of the second conception forthwith appear – relegated, however, to man's *consciousness* of his own nature. Instead of 'able to become a god or beast' we have 'in doubt to *deem himself* a God, or Beast' (8). Pascal wrote in his *Pensées*: 'Que fera donc l'homme en cet état? doutera t'il de tout, doutera t'il s'il veille, si on le pince, si on le brûle . . . doutera t'il s'il doute, doutera t'il s'il est.'[44] The last two doubts, notice, go a little too far for Pope's purpose.

Meanwhile other forms of compromise between the stable and unstable conception of man's place in the hierarchy are lurking in the background. For example, many who would flinch from the Hermetical idea that man, here and now, can make himself god or devil would feel that in a future state such extremities may indeed be thrust upon us, as a consequence of our behaviour in this world. The crucial chronological distinction between such a view and the Hermetical view can be blurred if we consider that the future state, *sub specie aeternitatis*, is more real than our present situation and is in truth not so much 'future' as part of the fabric of that transcendent reality which alone veritably exists.

For Pascal the thought of a real ultimate violence seems to have determined to a considerable extent his conception of our vertiginous imaginings. With Pope this thought is less strong and the imaginings themselves become a degree wilder, a degree more absurd, as a result. The only hints of an ultimate realisation are 'created half to rise' in line 15 and the marvellous word 'isthmus' in line 3:

> Plac'd on this isthmus of a middle state. . .

An isthmus is a narrow neck of ground joining two land-masses. Pope would not have known Sophocles' fragment 146, which contains the phrase 'the short isthmus of life', but he would surely have known Cowley's 'Life and Fame', 10–11:

> Vain weak-built *Isthmus*, which does proudly rise
> Up betwixt *two Eternities*.[45]

But Pope says nothing about eternities before and after. The phrase 'born but to die' at line 10, though formally an antithesis, asserts mortality. The antithesis of death is not immortality but (ordinary) life. Cowley's image of the isthmus operates more obscurely in Pope, suggesting that the intermediate position of man is somehow precarious, but without the poet's explaining clearly why. Doubtless it is one of the words which helped to suggest my own coarser image of the tight-rope.

However, the following line

> A being darkly wise, and rudely great

does not, as one might expect, preserve a nice balance between knowledge and ignorance, greatness and rusticity, but tends distinctly to magnify man: dark wisdom is still a kind of wisdom (perhaps the deepest kind); 'rude greatness' implies more power than 'polished greatness' ever could. The grandeur Pope evokes at this point has a purely formal purpose. He does not want to bias his philosophical presentation of the middle state of man. But he does want the music to swell at this point, an inchoate sense of grandeur to seize the reader's mind before he is explicitly aware whether the grandeur is man's, God's or Pope's. At line 23 below Pope makes his contempt for Neo-platonic Hermetists clear (and makes a similar point in the fourth epistle at line 162). The idea that man might soar to a divine rank is wholly absurd to him. It is absurd because man's position is fixed. Yet Pope's admission of a Hermetic extremism at the level of man's bewildered subjective conception of himself begins to infect the major assumption of his real stability. What man thinks begins to condition, subliminally, what he is. Thus, Pope writes in line 7, not 'he stands between', but 'he hangs between'. The word 'hangs' suggests oscillation, instability. Similarly, the word 'doubtful' can be used in a subjective or an objective sense. If a person is said to be doubtful about a proposition, the term is used in its subjective sense. If the proposition itself is then declared to be inherently doubtful, the term is now being used in the objective sense. Pope's 'man' passes, in this verse paragraph, from a subjective dubiety to an objective. Perhaps because he cannot tell what he should be, he becomes

> The glory, jest, and riddle of the world!

Here, too, Pope has followed Pascal, but with an interesting difference. Where Pascal wrote 'gloire et rebut de l'univers', Pope wrote 'the glory, jest and riddle'. It is possible that to Pope's English eye (if he looked over the original French) Pascal's 'rebut' suggested 'butt' (in fact *rebut* means 'trash' or 'rubbish'). What Pope has done is clear enough. He has introduced a note of deliberate levity, with 'jest'. He is anxious, as Pascal is not, to contain this fiery material, and the best vessel for his purpose is an urbane amusement.

And, indeed, he succeeds. The fire is real and the control is there. Even those who feel that Pope should never have attempted a philosophical poem must confess that here the poet is at the height of his powers. Almost every line of this opening sequence sticks in the memory of literate people. Memorability is no universal criterion of poetic merit but, for all that, lines which everyone remembers must possess a certain power or virtue. Part of this virtue lies in Pope's mere command of the verse form. The idea in the line

> The proper study of Mankind is Man
>
> (2)

is wholly unoriginal. Charron had already written: 'la vraye science et le vray estude de l'homme, c'est l'homme'.[46] But Charron's words are limp beside Pope's; 'et le vray estude' adds almost nothing to the thought while breaking the impetus of the sentence. The echoing of 'l'homme' with 'l'homme' is inert and mechanical compared with Pope's minor variation from the bland 'Mankind' to the conclusive, monosyllabic 'Man'. Here, as so often, Pope shows how the thing should be done. Matthew Arnold said that Pope was a classic of our prose rather than of our poetry.[47] Yet again and again we see sentiments which scarcely stir the emotions raised to a quite different sort of power when transposed into verse by Pope. So transfigured, they are certainly no longer prose. Should we not agree, then, that this is one kind of poetry?

Pope ironically bids man indulge his vaulting intellectual ambition, in order that he may thereupon relapse into his proper station. It is hard to be sure how silly the various projects Pope sketches seemed when the poem first appeared. Measuring the earth and weighing the air may be intended as manifest absurdities, yet even in Pope's time these were serious science. Pope's attack on the scientists, here as elsewhere, ill becomes him. He proceeds to 'jack up' the mockery by pretending that astronomers actually seek, not just to reinterpret the motions of the heavenly bodies but actually to change the motions themselves. The rhetorical movement of thought here reproduces the shift from subjective to objective dubiety in the previous paragraph.

The literary practice of referring to changes in astronomical theory as if they were physical changes in the heavens has its own literary history. We may call it (by a loose analogy with Ruskin's pathetic fallacy) the Kinetic Fallacy. John Donne made brilliant use of it in his *First Anniversary*:

> . . . new Philosophy calls all in doubt,
> The Element of fire is quite put out,
> The Sun is lost, and th' earth, and no mans wit
> Can well direct him where to look for it.[48]
>
> (205–8)

Donne wrote when the old Ptolemaic universe, centred on the earth, was newly threatened by the Copernican hypothesis that the earth and the other planets revolved round the sun. The new hypothesis was not yet confirmed by the physics of Newton, and the state of science was confused. Donne represents this state of *conceptual* confusion by suggesting that the heavenly bodies are themselves lost. He is of course in no sense deluded by the Kinetic Fallacy. For real delusion we may turn to Samuel Johnson's immensely subtle portrait in *Rasselas* of the mad astronomer. When Pope writes

> Instruct the planets in what orbs to run
>
> (21)

he knows, and knows that his reader will know, that astronomers do not really do any such thing.

But, for all that, I suspect that he would not have us be quite as clear-headed as this analysis is forcing us to be. After all, if the gravamen of Pope's attack lies wholly in the absurdity of trying to influence the physical motions of planets, the entire attack collapses as soon as it is confessed that no one except the occasional lunatic really does anything of the sort. The argument of the passage ruefully confesses its own vacuousness with a learned play on the Greek sense of *planet* (*planetes*: 'wandering') as its sole justification for inclusion. This is the sort of thing that gets poets a bad name with philosophers. In fact, however, the situation is not quite so cut and dried. The absurdity Pope is mocking is not wholly confined to the lunatic astronomer. Behind the admitted exaggeration of 'instruct the planets' is an intuition of a real absurdity, a real presumptuousness in seeking to apply the 'laws' of science to such majestic and mysterious things. Shakespeare's Berowne in *Love's Labour's Lost* makes no use of the Kinetic Fallacy but manages to convey his scorn of

> Those earthly godfathers of heaven's lights
> That give a name to every fixed star.
>
> (I, i, 88–9)

The Shakespearian sentiment is disarmingly straightforward. When the astronomers have finished all their talk the stars are exactly as they were and just as beautiful for ordinary folk walking home on a clear night. In Pope, under the flawed but still very civilised rhetoric, there is the ghost of a feeling which is in its essence religious: the heavenly bodies are holy and there is a certain blasphemous brutality in the brisk assumption that they can be brought to order. There is awe and also a kind of tenderness in the passage. Yet astronomy is in fact different from most sciences in that it can set up no controlled experiment and can never modify (so far, at least) the phenomena it studies. Thus, the 'laws' of Newton are very far from being prescriptive. Indeed, to suppose that they are so is to fall victim to the Kinetic Fallacy.

Pope proceeds to undermine intellectual pride with the (for him) somewhat confused image of the eastern priests:

> As Eastern priests in giddy circles run,
> And turn their heads to imitate the Sun.
>
> (27–8)

If the commentators are right, Pope is thinking simultaneously of Dervishes and certain 'Mahometan monks' described by Lady Mary Wortley Montagu. The ordinary reader, prompted by the word 'giddy', thinks most naturally of Dervishes. But Dervishes neither run in circles nor turn their heads as that phrase is normally understood, but spin on a fixed point. Secondly, even if we assume that by 'turn their heads' Pope really intended the spinning motion (with a further subaudition of giddiness) this can hardly be construed as a way of imitating the sun, since, even if one assumes that the earth is still, one does not then have to assume that the sun rotates on its axis but, rather, that it moves round the earth. Pope may have intended that the idea of *running* in circles should provide the point of comparison with the sun but, if so, the whole sentence is ill-formed, obstinately urging us to find some way of understanding how the sun can be said to 'turn' its head. If, on the other hand, we postulate a reader who is well informed enough to infer that various sorts of priest are referred to, the whole passage becomes even more unmanageably vague. Does Pope really wish us to think in sequence of all these separate phenomena and then to work out for ourselves acceptable combinations of meaning?

At this stage of the epistle, after the splendours of the opening, Pope is writing in a kind of mist. Perhaps he felt a certain unclarity might provide protection as he proceeded to undermine the greatest scientific intelligence the world had so far seen, Sir Isaac Newton. One senses that Pope is in part undone by a real admiration for Newton, running against the bias of his chosen stance (pro-Ancient) in the 'war' between the Ancients and the Moderns. The general form of his argument is that the angels, looking down on human-kind, marvel at the best of us (Newton) only as we marvel at a performing ape. Thus far the reasoning is unexceptionable and rhetorically clear. It is suitably complimentary to Sir Isaac and suitably pious in its contention that the highest human wisdom is nothing in comparison with the wisdom of angels. But then Pope backs up his remark with a thoroughly sublunary observation: the great Sir Isaac, who reduced to order the motions of the comet (so astronomy after all *is* possible!), could not understand the first thing about his own mind. The presumption seems to be that Newton and human science are reduced to absurdity since, having leaped the high fence, science falls headlong at the low one. The argument depends on our tacitly agreeing that the human mind is much easier to understand than a comet, presumably because it is not far away and is constantly available for inspection. Since in fact the human mind is quite obviously much harder to understand than the motion of a comet, it is difficult to give Pope the sort of excited assent he seems to be asking for. The failure of cogency in these lines casts doubt on Pope's major project; perhaps heavenly knowledge (in the astronomical sense, at least) is actually *easier* than knowledge of human nature; perhaps the attempt to know oneself is not, after all, a modest enterprise.

Milton in Book VIII of *Paradise Lost* adopted a position with regard to astronomy which broadly resembles Pope's: that it is better not to inquire into that which cannot affect our moral lives. But Milton, perhaps because of his intellectual pride, could not help pursuing at length the various hypotheses which were at last to be judged futile by the angel. His obvious engagement with real scientific argument contrasts strongly with Pope's slick yet intellectually inept dismissal.

In Newton the Augustan Age had found its cosmologist. They were still looking for the great psychologist. The term *psychology*, though it existed in Pope's time, was not in common currency. Yet the term is appropriate. The task which Locke essayed in his great work on human understanding, the burden which Pope himself lightly assumes at line 53, is that of discerning the fundamental laws of human nature. Their attempts form part of a story which extends after them through the Utilitarians to the Freudians.

Pope opens the question with a brisk distinction:

> Two Principles in human nature reign;
> Self-love, to urge, and Reason, to restrain. . .
>
> (53–4)

What Pope offers here is a fashionably up-dated version of the old picture of man as a battlefield of Reason and Passion. In the course of the eighteenth century reason was to be increasingly restricted to mere deduction, which, as Hume loved to point out, is always governed by premisses and can never of itself either instigate or check any particular action.[49] Reason, thus construed, is morally neutral, a mere instrument. The older conception of reason included a cognitive element and a moral corollary: reason was not only the faculty which deduces; it was also the faculty which rightly discerns what is truly the case and discriminates between a disastrous and a useful, a just and an unjust course of action. It therefore had some of the functions of what Freud was later to call the 'Reality Principle'. Where Passion said 'Steal that jewel!' Reason said 'You have no right to that jewel and you may be caught if you try to steal it'. This conception of reason is retained by Pope. But for the other term of the antithesis, 'Passion', Pope substitutes the then fashionable notion of 'self-love'. He does not 'come clean' that he is dealing with the passions until line 93: 'Modes of Self-love the Passions we may call.'

Self-love is correctly explained by John Laird as 'an unfortunate name, dominant in Pope's time, for self-maintenance or self-fulfilment. It was meant to describe the fact that each natural being strives to keep going with its own particular go'.[50] Laird's account, however, leaves one wondering why it was that this particular form of words was chosen to express the idea. *The Oxford English Dictionary* sheds a certain light with its admirable definition, 'Regard for one's own well-being or happiness, considered as a natural and proper relation of a man to himself', but this in its turn omits the dynamic element rightly stressed by Laird.

Although passion had long been seen as the instigator of action and reason as an inhibitor, there was always a certain discomfort in the terminology. The etymology of *passion* makes it the direct opposite of *action* (as is still clear in the adjective, 'passive'). 'Passion' originally meant 'what happens to one' as opposed to 'what one does'. Pope's effort to make passion the source of action is thus against the natural bias of etymology and the history of the words involved. Even if one is careful to explain that action is not identical with the instigating passion but is consequent upon it, 'passion' remains an uncomfortable term for what is seen summarily as the active principle in human behaviour.

'Self-love' becomes an acceptable substitute among those who in the early years of the eighteenth century were struggling to find a natural basis in given human psychology for human institutions without any appeal to theological or metaphysical sanctions. Butler, in his 1729 preface to *Fifteen Sermons Preached at the Rolls Chapel*, in effect, takes two Stoic formulas, 'Know thyself' and 'Follow nature', and merges the second with the first. 'Follow nature', for Butler, no longer means, as it had for the Stoics, 'Conform to the laws of the universe', but, rather, means 'Conform to the laws of your own nature'. This might look to modern eyes like an amoral permission to do exactly as one pleases, but Butler sees human nature as an ethically ordered system, in which conscience and self-love exercise a natural rule over the lower passions.[51] At the same time, in the third sermon the system is enforced with the positive sanction of happiness; thus self-love naturally co-operates with conscience: 'Conscience and self-love, if we understand our true happiness, always lead in the same way.'[52] In Pierre Charron's *De la sagesse* (1607), the Stoic credentials of the concept are much more evident:

Tout homme doibt estre et vouloir estre homme de bien . . . Je veux donc qu'il soit bon et aye sa volonté ferme et resolue à la droiture et preud'hommie, pour l'amour de soymesme, et à cause qu'il est homme, sçachant qu'il ne peust estre autre sans se renoncer et destruire, et ainsi sa preud'hommie luy sera propre, intime, essentielle, comme luy est son estre, et comme il est à soy mesme.

[Everyone ought to be and to wish to be, an honest man . . . I would therefore have him be virtuous and keep his will firm and resolute for uprightness and probity, for love of himself and because he is human, knowing that he cannot be otherwise without renouncing himself and destroying himself; in this way his probity will be intimately his own, essential to him, as his very being, as he is to himself.][53]

The context of Charron's remarks is the Stoic injunction, 'Follow nature'.

Nevertheless, the term 'self-love' remained consciously paradoxical. Then, as now, an implication of mere selfishness was immediately present in the phrase. Pope succumbed to this implication in a letter he wrote to Bethel on 24 June 1727: 'Those very disappointments of a virtuous man are greater pleasures than the utmost gratifications and successes of a mere self-lover' (*Corr.*, II, 437). But it was a mark of enlightenment to transcend the implication of selfishness and show, often with great ingenuity, how a seemingly individualist, self-seeking infrastructure could generate a luminously benevolent superstructure.

At the same time the notion of egoism was itself stretched, sometimes to the point where all free action was seen as necessarily egoistic in character: if I act freely, I do what pleases me; if I do what pleases me, I act egoistically. Bernard de Mandeville did not hesitate to say that a person who saves a child from a fire behaves egoistically, since he would have been so much more uncomfortable had he held back.[54] This is the cynical egoism which Butler, the leading exponent of enlightened self-love, hated and fought. But his opponents (as he did not fail to notice) played into his hands. By reasoning such as theirs the common-sense distinction between selfish and unselfish actions is merely obliterated. All voluntary actions are *ex hypothesi* egoistic. 'No Person can commit or set about an Action, which at that then present time seems not to be the best to him,' says Mandeville.[55] The first effect, indeed, is one of harsh cynicism: human beings, where they are not externally coerced, are wholly selfish organisms. But then a different feeling comes through. If interested behaviour includes things like loving self-sacrifice, then interested behaviour, as Butler points out, is a larger, a more generous, more potentially moral quality than it was thought to be.[56] Certainly it is often socially useful. It was as if, with the new conception of egoism, it was not so much human nature which was cynically reduced as egoism which was optimistically expanded. Both Shaftesbury and

Butler laboured to blur the distinction between private interest and public virtue.[57]

The ferocious Mandeville both violates and complies with this picture. Irwin Primer rightly observes that Mandeville saw those who said that self-love and social were the same as prime targets.[58] Yet this very phrase, with a change in the shading, can be made to express Mandeville's own ostentatiously cynical doctrine, 'private vices, public benefits'. Mandeville detested the rosily harmonious, gentlemanly universe of Shaftesbury, in which virtue and happiness went arm in arm. He always insisted that real virtue (which perhaps never existed) must involve the sacrifice of self and gratification. Thus, for him 'private vices, public benefits' implies not a reconciliation but a collision. With regard to the public consequences of actions he was indeed a kind of early Utilitarian, but his conception of private morality remained ascetic. Otherwise the element of fierce paradox would vanish from his work and his running irritation at the complacency of Shaftesbury would be unintelligible. He could have underwritten 'Self-love and social are the same' only if he could first secure from all present an agreement that 'self-love' meant neither more nor less than rank selfishness.

The term 'self-love' partly rests on an illicit but very natural transition from the idea of pleasure to the idea of egoism. The most extreme example of this transition remains that of Mandeville, for all his scorn of the proponents of self-love. The person who saved the child from the fire followed a calculus of pleasure in so far as he chose the course of action which would cause him the least pain. The real weakness of this proposition is not hard to identify. What he did *not* do was propose to himself the diminution of pain as the *object* of his action. Similarly, the fact that Jane is happy when she gives to the poor does not of itself make her charity egoistic, since she does not give *in order to* secure her happiness but, rather, in order to help the poor. Her happiness is a by-product. Any reasonably skilful novelist could easily show us the difference between two figures of happy charity, the one selfish, the other not. But this distinction, by which alone the ordinary use of 'selfish' can be sustained, is rarely made in the eighteenth century, and the strange moral promotion of egoism is the result. Certainly, any thinker who is seeking the fundamental, natural constituents of humanity, in contradistinction from the various impositions of culture, will look for appropriate spontaneous impulses. These are commonly pleasurable; even when they are not pleasurable, they are certainly free (that, after all, is what 'spontaneous' *means*). In 1734 all this seemed *ipso facto* to imply egoism, though in an exhilaratingly novel form.

We are now in a position to discern a further motive in Pope's rejection of the old 'reason–passion' dichotomy. In the traditional scheme reason had been good and passion had been bad. Pope, as will become clearer later, disliked the harsh rejection of the instinctual side of human nature. Accordingly he begins to rig the case in a contrary direction. Under the old scheme reason had been capable of urging as well as repressing (where the Passion of Greed says, 'Keep hold of your money!', Reason says, 'That man is your creditor, and you must pay him'). Pope contrives to lose this aspect of reason, while remaining in other respects traditional, so that reason becomes merely negative, an inhibitor of action. At the same time the passions, renamed 'self-love', are the source of all energy.

The renaming proved unfortunate in the long run. When the *Essay on Man* first appeared the term would have commanded excited and immediate assent from many of those who took a pride in being up-to-date. They would congratulate themselves on their ability to disregard, as persons who knew better, the adverse implication of selfishness, much as Oxford philosophers in the 1950s took pride in a professed inability to introspect. But the fashion did not last long; the phrase survives in Pope's poetry as a piece of eighteenth-century philosophical bric-à-brac. It is so powerfully of its period that it is hard for us to see what is really going on in Pope's redaction of the old antithesis between reason and passion, namely a highly significant move in the direction of Romanticism. By the time the move was completed (long after Pope's death) the old terms were used again but now passion was *candidly* preferred to reason. When that time came, Pope's 'self-love', instead of being seen as a forerunner, was rejected out of hand as a sorry compromise.

In much the same manner, Pope avoids a direct reversal of ethical values. Instead he gives us a majestically unhelpful *petitio principii*:

> And to their proper operation still,
> Ascribe all Good; to their improper, Ill.
> (57–8)

Since self-love and reason between them cover the whole of human behaviour, it is not very surprising to learn that, when they are well ordered, all is well. At the same time, however, the passage is histor-ically significant. Although Pope retains a cognitive element, he has in these lines made reason morally neutral. He directly implies that reason may misdirect and still be reason. This change, though inex-plicit, is enough to have made contemporary readers of Pope experi-ence a sort of shifting of the ground under their feet. Probably for many of them the experience was faintly exciting.

As Pope's argument unfolds one sees various tensions of Utilitarian theory anticipated.

> Self-love and Reason to one end aspire,
> Pain their aversion, Pleasure their desire;
> But greedy that its object would devour,
> This taste the honey, and not wound the flow'r . . .
>   (87–90)

The use of 'that' and 'this' in lines 89 and 90 is a good example of eighteenth-century Latinate English, although, because the Latinity inheres in the sentence-structure rather than in an obviously learned vocabulary, it is noticed by few readers. It corresponds to the Latin idiom, 'illud . . . hoc', meaning 'the former . . . the latter'. What Pope makes clear here is that what the Utilitarians were to call the principle of the greatest happiness and what Freud was to call the Pleasure Principle apply universally and are not confined to mere appetite. Even when Reason says no, and restrains Appetite, it does so in order to secure happiness or avoid pain in the long term. For, while self-love 'sees immediate good by present sense', reason sees 'the future and the consequence' (73–4). Thus, the difference be-tween self-love and reason is not the difference between hedonism and morality, but between an impulsive and a prudent hedonism. Exactly the same analysis is applicable to Freud's *Civilisation and Its Discontents*, where the Reality Principle, which seems at first to be the simple enemy of pleasure, emerges as governed wholly by long-term prudence and avoidance of pain and is thus wholly subject to the pleasure–pain calculus.

So far Pope has given us self-love both in its naked, immediate form and as it may be enlightened by rational prudence. The crucial step from selfishness to anything resembling ordinary, virtuous action seems as far away as ever. In this Pope is once more facing a difficulty later encountered by those Utilitarians who held that every individual seeks to maximise his happiness and, at the same time, that we ought all to promote the greatest happiness of the greatest number. The second proposition is certainly not deducible from the first and may even be incompatible with it, but this must never be confessed. Pope likewise labours to join the two propositions, but his principal attempt is made not here but in the third epistle. In lines 91–2 he suggests that pleasure enlightened by reason constitutes our greatest good and perhaps thought that he had made the necessary transition to morality. But he has really not advanced at all. Getting drunk is an evil only in the sense that it can ruin one's health. Piling up a healthy bank-balance is, on the contrary, good. Where in all this is morality? Where is the evil of gratuitous cruelty and the good of charity?

In lines 101–22, Pope declares his preference for a live, dynamic conception of humanity, with active passions variously tempered, over the frigid apathy of the Stoics. This thumbnail sketch of Stoicism is less than fair. In the first place, Stoic philosophers granted that certain emotional states were conformable to reason and essential to the well-balanced personality. Hence their occasional use of the term 'eupathy' ('well-emotioned-ness') rather than 'apathy' ('emotionlessness').[59] But the attitude of Stoicism even to passion is itself ambiguous. Stoicism presents two models of ideal humanity, one simple and the other dynamic. The simple model commends *apathy* in its radical sense, a complete absence of passion. Thus, Cicero says the philosopher is 'exempt from all perturbation of mind'.[60] According to the dynamic model, on the other hand, the philosopher is the person who by an exercise of will triumphs over his emotion. Clearly, a man with no emotions would have no need at all to exercise his will in this way. The heroically strong-willed philosopher, however, actually needs passions, if only as the material of moral conquest. Thus, the idea of the passionless philosopher gradually gives place – one cannot say to a warmer ideal of humanity – but at least to a view in which coldness is temporarily contested by warmth. Passion once more figures in the picture. Seneca in the *De Constantia Sapientis* first praises constancy, then an achieved constancy and then the achieving of constancy. He writes of the wise man: 'We do not ascribe to him the hardness of stone or iron; there is no virtue but is conscious of its own endurance.'[61]

Thus, real Stoicism is more like Pope's own scheme than he allows. One can forgive him for forgetting Seneca, but surely he might have remembered the great Stoic picture of Aeneas, shuddering with grief at leaving Dido yet steadfast in his inmost mind, in the fourth book of Virgil's *Aeneid* (437–49). But an important difference remains. Passions may be welcomed by the Stoic but they are welcomed as stern enemies, adversaries worth fighting. The passions in Pope are not only welcomed but also hospitably entertained. At line 106, Pope seems to repose a strange degree of trust in the passions, to such an extent that it leads him to say that, though they are like a great gale, such gales preserve the vessel they harrass. This is an odd thing to say either about a gale or about the passions. Mack in his commentary cites as parallel a passage from St-Evremond, but St-Evremond differs crucially from Pope in making reason the preservative agent, as one would normally expect. Pope obscurely senses that our life and our salvation lie in the passions. It is not what we expect him to say, but it is what he says.

The relation between reason and passion continues to shimmer before our eyes. Is reason the master or the servant? At line 116, Reason 'subjects' and 'compounds' the passions, but it does so in deference to *Nature*. The august word 'nature' is notoriously slippery, but one possible inference is that Pope dimly intended that reason, in all its inhibiting operations, should always follow natural need in the sense already explained, of increasing pleasure and avoiding pain. Nature is an exalted term, susceptible of occasional deification, and yet obstinately assists the values of flesh against the values of spirit.

Lines 121–2

> The lights and shades, whose well accorded strife
> Gives all the strength and colour of our life

are interesting in that they apply to human personality (as if the mind were some great painting) the kind of aesthetic conception which is traditionally applied to the universe in order to account for the existence of evil. Shaftesbury was even willing to extend this explanation in terms of the tonal effects necessary to beauty to account for such things as monstrous births.[62] Here in Pope's couplet the idea is less hard-pressed, as if the poet has momentarily forgotten the need to account for evil, either inside or outside the human breast.

But at line 133 he suddenly remembers. His picture of the soul as a dynamic balance of reason and passion is Arcadian, and he abruptly realises that it is so. Accordingly he endeavours to supply a half-mythical account of the rise of evil, just as in the third epistle he will find himself constrained to supply a similarly mythical account of the corruption of human society. It is as if the Doctrine of the Fall of Man refuses to be banished utterly from the poem but makes its way in, by various back doors, in various disguises. Just as he later 'explains' the corruption of a balanced social order by telling us that 'Force' arose (III, 245), so here we are told that one passion, like a seed of death, grows stronger than the rest and destroys the balance of the mind.

This is the celebrated doctrine of the Ruling Passion. Ben Jonson and countless others a hundred years before had elaborated the theory of 'humours', or fluid secretions holding the key to temperament and character. Virtually everything Pope says is anticipated in the theory of humours. At the same time, the picture Pope presents, though it seems very 'knowing', is not especially true. Sometimes a single passion dominates a personality, sometimes it does not. Laurence Sterne, with his less portentous mock-theory of 'hobby horses', or eccentric obsessions, manages matters with far greater skill. Where Pope attempts and fails to achieve the demonstration of a law of human nature, Sterne shows how some people may be mildly crazy in ways which other people, even people living two hundred years afterwards, can recognise as human. At lines 131–2, Pope refers to the story of Aaron's serpent in Exodus:

> And hence one master Passion in the breast,
> Like Aaron's serpent, swallows up the rest.

Mack, inferring too much, says that the Ruling Passion is therefore a manifestation of God's power (MM, 71). Since the Ruling Passion is forthwith described as the 'mind's disease' (138) this is at least odd, though conceivable in a developed theodicy. One may suspect, however, that an altogether looser form of biblical association is operating here, that behind the serpent of Exodus, in Pope's mind, there lies that other serpent of Genesis, the original 'lurking principle of death' (134).

The doctrine of the Ruling Passion leads Pope to weaken still further the role of reason. It is not surprising to be told that imagination dangerously inflames the workings of a distempered mind (143), but it is a little surprising to be told, not that reason corrects such extravagance (which line 54, 'Self-love, to urge, and Reason, to restrain', might have led us to expect) but that reason may in fact side with the enemy. For now we are informed, consistently with the later assertion of reason's moral neutrality, that it may give 'edge and pow'r' (147) to the vicious Ruling Passion. Here Pope rebuts the Stoics as Augustine rebutted the Manichaeans. The Manichaeans claimed that flesh was inherently bad, spirit inherently good; Augustine asserted that both principles were inherently good, but that both were liable to corruption. The Stoics said that reason was divine and passion brutish. Pope replies that passions nicely balanced are a good (he will soon be arguing that instinct is divine) and that reason may be an agent of corruption. The great anti-Manichaean age in literature is that of the Romantics and the post-Romantics; these exalted flesh over spirit, passion over reason. The position chosen by Pope, the poet of the Augustan enlightenment, is manifestly closer to that of the Romantics than to that of the rationalists.

At the same time, Pope somewhat inconsistently retains the notion of Reason as Queen (at line 150). She is, however, a 'weak Queen' who may at any point relinquish her properly judicial role and turn advocate (155). Here one is reminded of Butler's conception of conscience in his *Fifteen Sermons*: conscience rules *de jure* but not always *de facto*; that is, conscience is manifestly a regulative organ of the personality, even if it cannot always in fact regulate.[63] But to compare Pope thus with Butler is to introduce a sharpness of definition which is not wholly appropriate to the lines before us. It is more important that we should register, imaginatively, the way reason is gradually weakened before our eyes, as Dr Jekyll in Stevenson's fable was gradually drained of strength.

Pope's manner of expressing himself in this passage is partly allegorical. The mind is conceived as a kingdom, or battlefield, or law-court. When Prudentius virtually invented psychic allegory in the fourth century AD he austerely restricted the persons of his *Psychomachia* to the contending elements within the mind. When Guillaume de Lorris wrote *Le Roman de la Rose* he included both figures representing internal elements and a figure from the ordinary, macroscopic world, the lover himself in whose soul the allegorical action takes place. Pope's allegory, unlike Prudentius', like Lorris', is mixed. In a 'pure' allegory, the subjects of Queen Reason would have been the passions. Pope instead says, switching to the macroscopic level, that *we* are the subjects, with the unintended consequence that *we* are other than our reason, for all that reason may sometimes turn corrupt. At the same time, the moral incapacity of Reason, who can do no more than tell us we are fools (152), strangely reflects the moral incapacity of Pope, who can himself do little more than tell us that man is the 'jest' of the world (II, 18). Indeed, in a curious fashion, Pope's disparagement of Reason is here half-admiring, for surely he agrees with her.

Lines 161–202 develop the hint given at line 115 that Reason must be subject to Nature. Pope still grants that the role of Reason is to 'rectify' passions but swiftly adds that it cannot overthrow them (163). Meanwhile Nature, the 'mightier Pow'r' which actually gives us 'strong direction', is contrasted with Reason and begins to look more and more as if it belongs with the party of the passions! At line 115 we suspected that Nature might prove to be merely an august form of the Pleasure Principle. It now becomes clear that, as Passion is the gale which drives and preserves the ship (105–8) and Nature is the 'mightier Pow'r' which 'strong direction sends' (165), so Nature and Passion are in fact one and the same thing. Pope interposes a weak distinction at line 167 when he says that, while other 'passions' may blow variably, the wind of Nature blows constantly in one direction. The word 'other' concedes that Nature is a passion, perhaps the supreme passion, even before the distinction is drawn. Moreover, the examples which follow have a strangely double function. The merchant's toil and the sage's indolence are both ridiculous in Pope's eyes and yet illustrative of a common quest for happiness. It is as if below an absurd variation we may discern a significant unity, and this unity, variously assisted by Reason yet in itself appetitive, is Nature. At line 175, Pope personifies Nature as founding virtue on this central passion. By 183 the rule of Nature is finally confessed to lie in the growth of virtue from passion:

> The surest Virtues thus from Passions shoot,
> Wild Nature's vigor working at the root.

The blurred picture of lines 115–16 has now turned clear. There he said that reason subjected passion but did so in deference to nature. Now he tells us that nature builds virtue on passion. The vestigial claim that reason subjects passion is now presumably jettisoned.

When Pope tells us that virtue will grow from pride, his theory of passion as the proper soil of virtue produces a strangely muffled effect. The proposition is traceable to the notorious Mandeville. In

The Fable of the Bees, Mandeville had said, with profound scorn, that the moral virtues were the political offspring which flattery begot upon pride.[64] In Pope the scorn is removed by the theory, which is now optimistic. Passions produce real, not bogus virtues. Yet Pope's dapper *style* somehow sides with Mandeville and hints an element of unsubdued cynicism.

At line 197 reason, most oddly, begins to make a comeback. To start with, it is given a small but crucial power of deflection: 'Reason the byass turns to good from ill' (197). Then at line 204 we have the full Stoic conception of reason as 'The God within the mind'. There is nothing one can say of this except that, given the preceding argument, it is stark inconsistency.

The real boundaries of vice and virtue are often elusive, Pope grants (210). But it would be a foolish error to infer from this that there is no such thing as virtue or vice. In fact nothing is plainer than that virtue and vice exist (215). For all that, a person might easily have concluded that vice, at least, is an illusion from the proposition, roundly affirmed by Pope, that 'Whatever IS, is RIGHT' (I, 294; IV, 394). Of course, the elaborate defence of God in the first epistle is really there to forestall just such an objection, and Pope's nicely judged allusion to a composition of blacks, whites and greys (213–14) evokes the scheme according to which partial ill is universal good in so far as it is necessary to the grand design. But one senses that Pope's theodicy is beginning to break up through neglect. Pope's talk of black and white at this point naturally recalls the reference at line 121 to

> The lights and shades, whose well accorded strife
> Gives all the strength and colour of our life.

But these lines describe the well-tempered personality and are immediately followed by the fierce description of the way human beings are in fact thrown off balance by the ruling passion. Thus, in our fallen condition, the admixture of white and black, light and shade, is, precisely, *not* well accorded. Can we, then, any longer account for the evil of parts by the perfection of the whole? With a superhuman effort of imagination, one might suppose a higher scheme, truly divine, in which both evil impulses and a generally ill-constituted human nature together figure as shadows in some larger design of ultimate perfection, but Pope does not help us with any such saving explanation.

The Deist intuition that God's goodness must be demonstrable in general terms of universal application seems to have commanded enough of Pope's assent to make him think it proper to vindicate the ways of God to man with little overt reference to the Fall of Man and his Redemption. This leads to the thesis that everything is really perfect, and this proposition in its turn naturally provokes a reaction. The reaction, however, is half-repressed because it smacks of blasphemy. Curiously, it is just at this point that various versions of the Fall tend to intrude, no longer, as in Milton, providing the rationale of a pious justification, but unassimilated by the major argument and therefore implicitly subversive. We capriciously embrace vice (220), our well-tempered personalities suddenly lurch into the most violent distemper (234), and the nice adjustments of human society inexplicably break up into tyranny and oppression (III, 245).

Although Pope does not defend his concession of a disordered human nature by supposing a meta-design in which God makes all good, he does make one attempt to save the day by suggesting that various human frailties always tend to produce happy results within the natural order:

> That Virtue's ends from Vanity can raise . . .
> (245)

Here again he, so to speak, whitewashes Mandeville, who had claimed in *The Fable of the Bees* that private vices were public benefits, since without greed, lechery and ostentation the economy would collapse. In the present passage the cutting edge of Mandeville's economic argument is not present. For that we must go to the *Epistle to Burlington*, where Pope, having described the ludicrous excesses of bad taste committed by Timon in constructing his villa, adds these lines:

> Yet hence the Poor are cloath'd, the Hungry fed;
> Health to himself, and to his Infants bread
> The Lab'rer bears: What his hard Heart denies,
> His charitable Vanity supplies.
> (169–72)

Pope's own note on the passage reads as follows: 'The *Moral* of the whole, where PROVIDENCE is justified in giving Wealth to those who squander it in this manner. A bad Taste employs more hands and diffuses Expence more than a good one.' Pope then refers the reader to lines 230–7 of the second epistle of the *Essay on Man*. In the present passage, soaring clear of the economic argument, Pope contrives to turn Mandeville's slogan into a sort of hymn:

> And build on wants, and on defects of mind,
> The joy, the peace, the glory of Mankind.

>   (247–8)

The trouble with 'saving' the theodicy in this naturalistic manner, that is, by finding good consequences within the natural order rather than imputing them to some vast but humanly inaccessible design of God, is that they are immediately vulnerable to empirical objections. Such a justification manifestly cannot be said to have cancelled or blotted out the picture of depravity and oppression which Pope has occasionally allowed to emerge. A string of particular terrestrial examples of felicity can always be countered by an equally long string of evils. Pope's choice of ground immediately provokes the rejoinder, 'Oh, if *that's* the sort of thing you mean by the great Design of things, then indeed it is well within our view and we are in an excellent position to judge whether it really is as excellent as you say it is'.

Pope, having thus stumbled into the mire of naturalism, plunges desperately on. Everyone is really tremendously happy, he tells us; no one would willingly change places with his neighbour (262). What, not even those whose ruling passion is envy? The learned man is happy exploring nature, the fool is happy because he does not know he is foolish, the rich man is happy because he is so rich, the poor man is happy because Heaven looks after him. This is the very nadir of Augustan poetry, a bland sequence of pseudo-universals. Any hack versifier of the time could in some five minutes supply a set of lines, directly opposed to Pope's, just as true and just as false as his, something, perhaps, like this:

> The learn'd, unhappy, breaks his Wit in vain,
> Th' unhappy Fool both Whips and Fears restrain.
> The rich unhappy, having, yet seeks more,
> The poor Man weeps and shivers at his Door.

It may be said that Pope knows what he is doing: that he shrewdly bases his optimistic conclusion on a far from idealistic view of human nature, which he sees as either fortunate where highly gifted, or smug where not. But complacency will hardly serve as a *guarantor* of happiness.

Pope proceeds from bad to worse. The blind and crippled, he points out, dance about and sing and must therefore be very happy. Starving geniuses, meanwhile, go mad and become megalomaniacs, so they are all right. We have the right to expect from a great poet a more than ordinary acuteness of perception. Pope was marvellously equipped to see more, and more sharply, than others. Here he has nothing to give but a studied obtuseness.

Such optimism is profoundly depressing. There are signs that Pope himself found it so. The epistle ends with acquiescence in the sheer folly of humankind. Line 275 seems to promise an Augustan version of Jaques's Seven Ages of Man speech in *As You Like It* (II, vii, 139–66). But in Pope's version infancy is succeeded by infancy and then by still more infancy. Each age has its toys, and there is nothing to choose between them. Even the prayer-book is seen as an idiot's bauble (280–1). The promised progression collapses into a mere unmeaning series. At line 285, Pope suggests that, wherever happiness is lacking, hope rises to fill the gap, but one senses that he knows the argument's weakness (for hope does not always arise, and when it does it sometimes proves a source of anxiety). One feels the confidence draining from the argument, until the claim at line 289 that each prospect lost is succeeded by another reads not as a trumpet call to awake and rejoice but as more dreary evidence of human futility. Human happiness, with a backwash of cynicism far deeper than anything in Mandeville, is seen as the giggling of a lunatic. Self-love, Pope lets slip, is 'mean' (291). The final line, with a desperate shrug, consigns creation to absurdity and, with a piety now supported only by shreds of natural theology, roundly yet hollowly affirms the wisdom of the creator:

> Tho' Man's a fool, yet GOD IS WISE.
> (294)

(iv) EPISTLE III: MAN AND SOCIETY

The third epistle begins in stillness, in quiescence: 'Here then we rest.' The anodyne truth in which we are to find repose reads like something agreed by a committee:

> 'The Universal Cause
> 'Acts to one end, but acts by various laws.'

But Pope's skill has not deserted him. What seems like a flat conclusion is really only a preliminary pause, cunningly placed before the
true, rising exordium, which begins at line 7: 'Look round our
World.' Here Pope's verse quickens, and the inert opening formula
is magically transformed into a principle of cosmic life. The ancient
idea that love makes the world go round is set going once more, with
a show of corroborative science and a dash of epigram, but also with
serious power.

It may be thought that the combination of 'the chain of love' with
the idea of physical atoms (line 10) is a simple mismatch of ancient
vitalism and recent science, but Lucretius, Pope's principal model in
the ancient world, was himself an atomist and yet began his *De
Rerum Natura* with a great invocation of Venus, the goddess of love
who moves in the rutting beasts and in the winds of heaven. Pope
rises from atomic attraction to the purposive energies of matter
(11–13), but it is not clear that we should see this as a vitalist
superstructure resting on a mechanistic base. The word 'attract' may
be less neutral, more coloured by its use in human contexts, than we
at first suppose. The force of gravity itself still appeared 'unscien-
tific' to some: action mediated by cog-wheels was mechanically intelligible; action at a distance looked almost mystical, obstinately
retained the flavour of vitalism. Elwin in his nineteenth-century
commentary on these lines jibbed at the idea that atoms could be said
to 'embrace' (12) and observed: 'The particles of matter do not clasp.
They are not even in contact, but only contiguous.'[65] But for Pope
the word may have had a double appropriateness. He could read in
Lucretius that the atoms of highly coherent physical bodies might be
'hooked' and therefore entangled with one another (*De Rerum Natura*, II, 394, 445) and he may have half-believed that the attraction
which operated among atoms was a kind of love. Elwin's note
(unusually, for him) is historically ignorant.

Thus, atoms, matter and living organisms are all set in motion by
love, and their movements, cycling but ever changing, work to the
good of the whole. Pope sees all this as carried forward by 'plastic
Nature' (line 9). 'Plastic' means 'moulding' or 'giving shape' and

suggests a semi-divine conception of Nature, existing outside the world and operating upon it. Indeed, if we press this conception we shall find increasingly that 'Nature' is awkwardly 'low' as a word and that 'God' is more appropriate. The underlying question may be brought out if we ask: 'What does the loving which sustains the chain of nature?' Dante, at the end of the *Divine Comedy*, speaks of the love which moves the sun and the other stars, and is thinking of God. But it is the stars which are doing the loving. God moves them, as Aristotle says, 'by being loved'.[66] Dante almost certainly had in mind the Aristotelian doctrine of final causes. Ordinary mechanical motion can be understood in terms of one physical body pushing another; this is called 'efficient causality'. But we see other ways in which one body can move another without contact ('action at a distance'). A beautiful woman at a party may draw men across the room or stir them to complex movements of adoration. Their behaviour is purposive, directed to a certain end, and therefore the causality involved is that which is technically called 'final causality'. God's manner of moving the creation is of the latter kind. But it is likely that Dante's conception extends farther than this. For the love which the creation feels for God is itself God working in his creation, so that, at last, it is God's love which moves all things (so much, at least, is suggested by the strange words of Justinian: 'I was Caesar and am Justinian, who, by will of the Primal Love which moves me, removed from the laws what was superfluous and vain').[67]

In Pope things are much less clear. In so far as Nature is the name of an individual who actually operates upon the universe, Nature ceases to be natural and becomes divine. In so far as 'Nature' remains a way of summing the myriad activities of the visible world, so that the love exerted by Nature is no more and no less than all the loves of the world, from the atom to the angel, conceived as flowing in one direction for the good of the whole, the word 'Nature' remains entirely fitting, and 'plastic' suffers a corresponding loss of force. Pope probably intends the second conception a little more strongly than the first. We may reconcile them by saying that the creative ability of the natural world is endlessly sustained, in another dimension, by God; but to ascribe God's action, or part of his action, to the 'this-worldly' term 'Nature' tends to blur rather than to clarify this account. Pope is here caught in difficulties which had entangled earlier attempts to exploit the idea of *Natura naturans*, nature as an active forming principle (as, for example, in Spenser's Mutability

Cantos). But he betrays no unease. His verse moves with confidence
and shows an easy tolerance of metaphysical ambiguity which we
would never find in Dante.

It is always hard to know how literally one should take poetic
vitalism, that is, the idea that the whole creation is instinct with life.
The usual presumption is that in ancient or medieval sources the
idea is seriously asserted, in the seventeenth and eighteenth centuries it becomes a toy for the imagination to play with (so that talk
of 'amorous winds' is firmly and unequivocally metaphorical), but
that with the Romantics the possibility of a seriously asserted vitalism returns. Wordsworth's mysterious 'presences' in the mountains
are not metaphorical. But in fact one of the most ancient and highly
developed celebrations of a vitalist universe is artfully ironic: the
speech of the pedantic physician Eryximachus in Plato's *Symposium*.
In Pope's day the idea of the medieval schoolmen that a stone fell
because it loved the earth or desired to reach its true place of rest had
become the common object of philosophical ridicule. Hobbes's pen
fairly rasped over the paper when he wrote of it: '. . . as if stones and
metals had a desire, or could discern the place they would be at, as a
man does; or loved rest, as man does not; or that a piece of glass were
less safe in the window, than falling into the street'.[68] Hobbes still
wrote, however, as if the doctrine were in some quarters a serious
candidate for belief. By 1730 it had become an antiquarian curiosity.
Yet Pope, with all his instinct never to make a fool of himself, with
all his vigilance in finding a form of words which would pass in the
most polite society, seems utterly at ease. It is true, of course, that
vitalism never finally dies. David Hume himself has one of the
characters in his *Dialogues Concerning Natural Religion* say: 'The
world . . . I infer, is an animal.'[69] The context of the remark is
philosophically radical, and the words seem audaciously challenging
rather than merely silly. But Pope, one suspects, is not sustained by
a secret consciousness of philosophic power. His strength is of
another order, more magical than rational. He has found a way of
writing which we have seen at other high moments of the *Essay*: a
pre-Romantic manner in which Augustan control remains but ideas
and emotions begin to break into a kind of rapture. The renewed
metaphysical seriousness of Wordsworth is still far off. Pope's writing is jubilant as the music of Handel can be jubilant. The iron gate,
which for the metaphysician always divides metaphorical from literal
assertion, swings open in the wind.

It remains possible, of course, to pick holes in Pope's picture of commutual harmony. The Soul of the Universe, he says, 'Made Beast in aid of Man, and Man of Beast' (24). One may agree perhaps that horses did well in Darwinian terms out of their association with human beings, but in general one feels that the arrangements between human beings and their animals are less than symmetrical. Men eat cows and cows do not eat men. One senses (especially in view of line 45, which probably alludes to the force-feeding of geese for pâté de foie gras) that if Pope were shown a battery chicken farm he would at once explain, in perfect couplets, that the chickens had at last achieved their dearest wish, warmth, total idleness and human beings to minister to their slightest need.

But the idea of an intricate economy of mutual help is transcended by an emotion which is disinterested, a joy in the very uselessness, for every human purpose short of joy itself, of the linnet's voice. It is significant that at this point the language bursts the ordinary constraints of usage with the marvellous 'pours his throat' (33). Pope may be suspected of sentimentalism in his contention that the horse shares in the pleasure and pride of his rider, but it is hard to be sure. People who work closely with animals habitually think of them in these terms.

When the poetry is as strong as it is here, minor factual criticisms seem merely inept. One's mind may fret, but one's legs want to join the dance. Pope's metaphysical altruism, his vision of the glorious independence of nine-tenths of nature from human concerns, almost breaks out in sheer, joyous laughter. Line 38 is both beautiful and disarming:

> The birds of heav'n shall vindicate their grain. . .

The grand word 'vindicate' recalls the original Miltonic design, to 'vindicate the ways of God to Man' (I, 16); but, because birds are so much less solemn than men like Milton or Archbishop King, an ironic light is shed on Pope's own irremediably anthropocentric schemes to justify God. He laughs at himself and rejoices in that which is other than himself.

But Pope is the least innocent of writers. In the section beginning at line 49 he becomes conscious that the human capacity for disinterested wonder can be made into a ground of self-congratulation. Man alone can appreciate the universe. Pope spoils the picture of self-forgetful benevolence by appreciating the fact that he appreciates the world. The tone is altered, and within a few lines celebration is laced with satire (complacency now combated not by mere oblivion of self but by a certain cynical asperity). The thought moves through unnoticed gradations from disinterested delight to the quasi-aesthetic pleasure which the sporting gentleman takes in the beasts and fishes of his estate. But all still tends to good, even though it is not only the pleasure of the master which starts the cycle but also, on occasion, 'pride' (60). Here once more Pope's pointed style almost awakes the familiar ghost of Mandeville, for by a minor shift of emphasis and reference the thesis that pride may be benevolent in practice would be made to echo 'Private vices, public benefits'. But Pope is still thinking of the animals rather than of the national economy. Although one senses incipient irony in the brilliantly subdued oxymoron 'learned hunger' (63), the passage taken as a whole is not cynical.

Nevertheless, the playing down of death in this part of the epistle remains slightly weird. The whole is written in implicit defiance of the classical adage, 'Call no man happy until he is dead'. The felicity of the feasted animal is in fact terminated by butchery – a fact which Pope does not suppress but, rather neutralises with faint writing That this is indeed the stylistic tenor of the lines is shown by the strange expression, 'touch etherial', at line 68. One has to shake oneself in order to realise that what is intended here is death by lightning. The style reflects, with great art, the deliberate anaesthesia of the argument.

It may be said that 'touch etherial' carries a subaudition of divine providence. This is correct, but does not lead to any transfusion of blood (or substance) into the conception. The section ends, at lines 71–8, with the assertion that, as man alone appreciates beauty, man alone understands death, so that it is both an object of dread and a source of hope to him. Pope may have been 'a Deist, believing in a future state',[70] but nothing so strong as belief comes through here. The thought is held in a sort of muffled suspense at the level of subjective natural presentiment. The good literary critic will continue to respond to nuances of style. Pope did not write 'God's' or even 'heavenly'; he wrote 'etherial', and the polysyllabic weightlessness of the word exerts its natural poetic force; it etherialises the sentiment. We find no confident assertion of another world. If this is 'knowledge of its ends', it is strangely unlike other forms of knowledge but oddly akin to guesswork mixed with fear. As in the closing section of the previous epistle, hope is left unsupported. Where the style, formed in the school of Augustan satire, everywhere suggests the possibility of irony, the first thought which arises in connection with hope is that hope is commonly delusive.

The argument of this passage is vulnerable to a brutal summary. Animals are happy because they do not know they are going to die; human beings are happy because they do know or, rather, because they can hope everything will be all right. In any case, they are usually deluded and think death is farther away than it really is. Pope's style keeps the thought relatively indistinct. If he had not done so, the plain import of the passage would have been that, beneath all this great dance of beneficence, there lurks the unassimilable horror of death, the very thought of which is so dreadful that one's best course is to repress it.

In the second section (79–146) Pope carries the demotion of reason, uncertainly begun in the second epistle, a stage farther by subordinating it to instinct. Maynard Mack in his Twickenham commentary stresses the traditional continuity of Pope's thought with medieval scholastic philosophy (MM, 100). In particular the notion that instinct is divinely planted and in a manner infallible (commonly represented by the scholastic tag *Deus est anima brutorum*, 'God is the soul of brute animals') is indeed technically orthodox. It stems from the careful rejection by the Church of the Manichaean belief in the inherent evil of matter and goodness of spirit. The Church maintained on the contrary that matter as made by God was good, though liable to corruption. In like manner human passions were inherently good but since the fall of Adam had been corruptly discharged. None of this, however, should blind us to the fact that Pope, in his express exaltation of instinct above reason, is expressing a paradoxical view. The normal position, without doubt, was that it was good to be rational and bad to be governed by instinct alone. The Church judiciously corrected the more extreme tendencies of Manichaeism. Pope, as we have had occasion to remark before, almost succeeds in standing Manichaeism on its head ('Instinct wholly good, reason bad').

The Fall of Man is a shifting factor in the debate over reason and instinct. Milton in *Paradise Lost* had given a strong impulse to the view that not only man fell but nature also, in a manner, fell with him. God had his angels tilt the axis of the earth, and the perpetual

spring of Eden was replaced by the harsh alternation of the seasons
(X, 670 ff.). But other poets in the seventeenth century, notably
Marvell and Vaughan, had conveyed a very different feeling, namely
that on this beautiful earth only man is vile. Nature remains unfallen.
Moreover, they presented this intuition with a kind of famished
tenderness, with a sensitive deference to the green, inhuman world,
which seems quite foreign to earlier discussions. Their poems thus
strike the literary historian as pivotal, echoing the scholastics but
also, still more potently, pre-echoing the Romantics. In the eighteenth century, to be sure, the tone tends to be light. In *The Logi-
cians Refuted*, formerly thought to be Swift's but now attributed to
Goldsmith, we read:

> I must in spite of them, maintain
> That man and all his ways are vain,
> And that this boasted lord of nature
> Is both a weak and erring creature;
> That instinct is a surer guide
> Than reason, boasting mortals' pride;
> And that brute beasts are far before 'em.
> *Deus est anima brutorum.*[71]

The tone of these lines makes it clear that the exaltation of instinct is
paradoxical. Goldsmith uses a technical element in traditional
orthodoxy to work against the main weight of tradition. But there is
no sign whatever of the excited deference to nature which stamps
Marvell, Vaughan and, yes, Pope, too, as truly 'pivotal' poets. One
senses that, although Goldsmith's lines formally allow that human
instinct is good, the principal contrast there as in book IV of Swift's
Gulliver's Travels is simply between the vileness of man and the
relative innocuousness of brutes. The natural world is not seen as
Paradisal, but man is certainly seen as fallen. Swift may be said to
have darkened rather than clarified the whole subject. He was an
intricately ironic writer who delighted in crossing the wires of ordinary discourse. In *Gulliver's Travels* he made horses rational and
men irrational. But his rational horses are not especially *ratiocinative*.
They rarely reason because they rarely disagree. The most powerful
difference between the (equine) Houyhnhnms and the (human)
Yahoos is that the horses are clean and the human beings filthy.
Swift, although he despised human reason and professed a preference for brutes, remains closer to the Manichaean end of the spec-

trum: ratiocination is bad because it is insufficiently rational; the brutes are good because they are so much less bestial than man. In Pope, on the other hand, there is as usual little sense of a fall. Man is unified by his instincts with nature, and nature in its turn (see I, 268–80) is interpenetrated by God. The sexual instinct which to Swift was manifestly corrupt is happily included by Pope in the general felicity of nature at line 122.

Pope is not only concerned to argue for the moral innocence of instinct, however, but also to stress that it does not make mistakes. This thesis, it might be said, is either trivially non-significant or else false. It would be merely trivial if Pope were simply pointing out that instinct consists simply of appetites and aversions. A desire cannot be erroneous, not because it is immensely shrewd but simply because it is not the sort of thing that we can apply the adjective 'erroneous' to. It cannot be erroneous as a chimney pot cannot be erroneous. It simply advances no claim, makes no factual assertion. If, on the other hand, one wishes to say that instincts, while they do not directly propound truths, nevertheless imply them, the thesis becomes vulnerable at once to a direct refutation. Pope seems to have taken the second course when he says in line 100 that instinct teaches animals that certain foods are poisonous to them. Here he enters the realm of the empirically testable. Instinct usually warns animals pretty efficiently, but it is by no means infallible. Here the implacable Elwin is in his element, bombarding the luckless poet with counter-examples:

> Misled by the odour of the African carrion flower, the flesh-flies lay their eggs in it, and the progeny, not being vegetable feeders, are starved . . . a jackdaw drops cartloads of sticks down a chimney, in the vain endeavour to obtain a basis for its nest. (EC, II, 407–8)

But, when Elwin has done his worst, Pope's broad contrast between the relative sureness of instinct and the continual aberrancy of reason remains strong. It is important to remember that he wrote before Darwin had supplied a naturalist account of instinctive 'sagacity'. Creatures with self-endangering instincts are presumably eliminated by natural selection. It is not surprising that those which remain have the other sort of instinctual apparatus. But Pope cannot be expected to have seen this. For him the sagacity of instinct

implied a sagacious creator just as for Paley the manner in which the
human eye is minutely adapted to the needs of the organism implied
a purposive, benevolent God.[72] Given these premisses, the inference
in either case was wholly rational. Even in these post-Darwinian
times scientists like C. F. E. Pantin and Sir Alister Hardy can marvel
at the amazing 'geodetic' structures of silicious 'scaffolding' set up
by the simplest cellular animals very much as Pope marvels at the
faultless parallels of the spider's web (103).[73]

Maynard Mack comments here that by 'parallels' we must understand concentric circles (MM, 102). One suspects that he has not
looked hard at a spider's web. The 'circles' in a web are not concentric, nor, strictly speaking, are they circles. Rather, a single line is
drawn from radius to radius. The form of the operation is that of a
spiral rather than of concentric circles, save that the course followed
is not curving but a continuous sequence of progressively deflected
straight lines, which gives the impression of a curve if viewed care-
lessly or from a distance. Moreover, the 'spiralling' method is consistent with parallel rather than progressively diverging lines (as a little
reflection will show) if one varies the angle of deflection of the
'spiralling' thread. Today it is not fashionable to press so hard on
mere facts in a literary study, but that is because the habit of combin-
ing minute observation with wonder has fallen into disuse. Pope
marvelled at the spider and would have us do the same. But we
cannot share his emotion if we will not look for ourselves. Even the
unsympathetic Elwin with his counter-examples is in a way closer to
the spirit of Pope than the modern critic who assumes that such
details cannot be relevant to the study of poetry. Biologists may still
be heard speculating how it is that migrating birds successfully
'navigate' in order to reach a certain group of islands in the ocean,
very much as Pope speculated (in lines 105–8) on the manner in
which birds congregate and then set off in a certain necessary direction, but such things are no longer the normal matter of verse. This
is sad, because what Pope does here is certainly poetry. Such poetry
of natural observation has a special 'taste', much relished by those
who understand it.

Lines 109–46 apply the principle of self-love to society. Pope
turns with alacrity to the task of showing how social benevolence
may be derived from an egotistical set of natural impulses. One way
of doing this is to show how the mass of weaker individuals may
combine to curb the destructive pleasures of the strong individual,

so that through the application of sanctions even the most powerful find their interest lies more in co-operation than oppression. Pope here chooses a different course. He suggests that self-love *naturally* expands into benevolence, through an involuntary extension of the notion of self to include more and more of the surrounding world. Thus, the love of a parent for his or her child is really an extended self-love, and the love of man for his own species is likewise self-love. When Pope returns to this theme in Epistle IV with the image of the circles spreading on the surface of a lake (IV, 364 ff.) he carries the principle even farther than love of species, to

Take ev'ry creature in, of ev'ry kind. . .
(IV, 370)

The process, so to speak, propels itself. The very same psychological pressure which makes the child cram food into its mouth makes the adult give money to OXFAM, makes the conservationist defend the countryside. Pope does not consider the possible conflicts which might arise between undeveloped and developed versions of the impulse: the mother who goes hungry to feed her children is not normally thought of as self-loving; the thief who steals the charity-box is not normally blamed for having an insufficiently developed love of self. Yet Pope's argument asks us to think in just this way. It would seem that the natural process he presents could equally be called 'the auto-distruction of self-love', since, by the time the process is extended to cover the whole of creation, the prefix 'self' no longer retains any distinguishing force; 'self-love' has gone, and has been replaced by 'love'. The retention of the prefix 'self-' merely suggests a wholly unfounded mystique of continued identity, the 'genetic fallacy' whereby a thing is presumed to be always what it was at the beginning (thus Freud would have it that because most energies began in a sexual form their later manifestations were really distorted sexuality – as if oak-trees were cunningly disguised acorns).

Moreover, where the full range of supposedly moral behaviour is so effectively covered by wholly natural impulse, there would seem to be no room left (because no need) for ethical exhortation. Virtue grows like an oak-tree, and no one tells an oak-tree how to grow.

At one point, however, Pope leaves a chink in his massively naturalistic scheme. At line 133 he suggests that reflection and reason assist in the extension of familial love to social. If 'reason' here bears its ancient sense of 'just perception', Pope may be said to have surrendered the naturalism of his scheme. It is as if he flinches momentarily from the idea that mere self-love, however inflated or extended, can ever produce, without some infusion from elsewhere, something so thoroughly opposite in its nature as altruism. But the passage is elliptical, and we cannot be sure of the sense. By 'reason' Pope may mean only that a shrewd estimation of long-term interest will accelerate the natural process, and this more modest interpretation leaves the major thesis essentially unimpaired and, moreover, sits more easily with Pope's picture of the property instinct later in the epistle (at line 278).

We come now to Pope's account of the State of Nature. There are, we have seen, two ways of explaining how, under God, evil enters the world. One way – Milton's way – is to tell a story. The other way – the way of the philosophers – is to explain that seeming evil may really be good. The writings of Locke, Toland, Tindal, King and others had made the tension between these two methods more and more inescapably evident. This is the place where it comes to a head in Pope's poem. For this is the place where, having opted for the static theodicy of the philosophers, Pope is driven back upon the old method of myth. By the end of the first epistle he had made the radical, necessary claim of every philosophical theodicy: 'Whatever IS, is RIGHT.' In other words, this *is* the Golden Age, this *is* Paradise, nor are we out of it. The Fall of Man, if that means a catastrophic rupture and the end of God's law, never happened. The matter of that story, the darkness and the pain, must be lifted from the assertive order of history and reclassified as a tissue of human misconceptions. This is the path Pope chose and valiantly maintained (though he occasionally flinched). At this point in the third epistle, however, his resolution failed. The pressure to acknowledge that something has gone wrong, at least to some extent, at last forces Pope to surrender his static postulate of a God-filled world for a dynamic, changing picture, a world which has, in some degree at least, fallen from a better state.

Pope does not fly straight to the Miltonic, biblical story. He remains silent on Adam and Christ. But he can use the remoter myths of Hesiod and Virgil, updating them freely as a very British, Lockean state of nature. The myth of decline has broken in, once more. In all the intricacies which follow, a simple principle of economy holds: the thought of God obliges the poet to embrace a static scheme (for God is unchanging); the thought of the world obliges the poet to confess its otherness from God and makes the notion of descent in time both acceptable and necessary. Pope has given a picture of social morality which accords seamlessly with the beneficence of God and the new worship of natural impulse. But it fails to accord with the behaviour of real human beings (for love of self does not always grow into love of all). It is certainly very doubtful whether we can distinguish Pope's account of the loss of the state of nature from the story in Genesis by saying that the first is history and the second myth. Pope's adversary, Crousaz, admittedly, read the lines as bad history (he marvelled at Pope's confidence in undertaking to supply a detailed account of so remote a time).[74] But in fact Pope's narrative is determined less by the pressure of real historical evidence than by the exigencies of explanation. In other words, it is aetiological.

Pope's state of nature, unlike that of the philosopher Hobbes, is Arcadian or Paradisal.

> Nor think, in NATURE'S STATE they blindly trod;
> The state of Nature was the reign of God:
> Self-love and Social at her birth began,
> Union the bond of all things, and of Man.
> Pride then was not; nor Arts, that Pride to aid;
> Man walk'd with beast, joint tenant of the shade...
>   (147–52)

It is said that people can be divided roughly into two classes. The first class consists of those who believe that human nature is naturally good, but is variously warped and distorted by tyranny, oppression and restrictive rules. The second class consists of those who believe that human nature is naturally vicious, and can be made tolerably virtuous only by the imposition of rules. The Romantic movement, as a movement, clearly inclines to the first view. But it is impossible to arrive at any clear historical partitioning of opinion. Hobbes belongs to the second class but, then, so do Freud and the author of *Lord of the Flies*. Pope, on the other hand, belongs to the first group. Hobbes's state of nature is a place of violent egoistic collision, *homo homini lupus*. Pope's is the world dictated by his naturalist theodicy; the birth of nature is coeval with the rise of that self-love which is also social love (149). But the story he tells has the

effect of banishing the world picture normally presented by the
optimists to a remote, lost time. Once, self-love and social were the
same. Once, whatever was, was right.

At the same time it is clear that certain aspects of the economy of
commutual bliss envisaged by Pope elsewhere do not yet apply. Man
does not give the beast free board and lodging in return for his
carcass. Man and beast walk together in friendship. The moral
atmosphere is so heightened that even the killing of an animal would
be a kind of murder, and no animals are killed (154). Pope's primal
man, like Milton's Adam, is vegetarian (Milton's Adam also
abstained from alcohol, but the more genial Pope does not make a
point of this). It is curious how thoroughly Pope is freed by his myth
to say all the things which opponents naturally bring up to refute
optimists like Pope.

> Ah! how unlike the man of time to come!
> Of half that live the butcher and the tomb. . .
>
> (161–2)

The butcher's trade is here no longer presented as a means of ensur-
ing a luxurious existence for cows. Butchery is butchery once more.
Pope sketches primal religion as celebratory rather than petitionary.
The priest is simply dressed, sacrifice is unknown (157–8). Here, it
might be said, Pope deliberately flouts such historical evidence as
was available to him.

From this state of happiness man, by a process of natural imita-
tion, developed his arts, learning from the bee how to build, from
the little nautilus how to sail (175–7). Pope even contrives, at line
188, a very British defence of small-scale private property; it is
directly founded on nature, for man had only to look at the cells of
the bee-hive. He notes the presence of laws (189–90), but these seem
like the descriptive or predictive laws of science rather than the
restrictive laws imposed by government. Yet the one sort of law,
he sees at 191, may gradually be contracted by reason (here, once
again, the villain of the piece) into the other, the descriptive into the
restrictive.

Pope always writes well when he thinks of small animals or
insects. So here the writing becomes luminous.

> Learn each small People's genius, policies,
> The Ant's republic, and the realm of Bees;

How those in common all their wealth bestow,
And Anarchy without confusion know;
And these for ever, tho' a Monarch reign,
Their sep'rate cells and properties maintain.
Mark what unvary'd laws preserve each state,
Laws wise as Nature, and as fix'd as Fate.
In vain thy Reason finer webs shall draw,
Entangle Justice in her net of Law,
And right, too rigid, harden into wrong;
Still for the strong too weak, the weak too strong.
(183–94)

The ant and the bee are presented as models of happy ingenuity. But then, at the level of metaphor, the spider reappears as reason, drawing ever finer webs (191); it is here that we meet the brilliant line,

And right, too rigid, harden into wrong. . .
(193)

Thus cities rose, and states joined by love or else (now a darker note) fear. Some lands were richer than others, and so war broke out. The Arcadian scheme seems to be broken, but Pope's writing remains calm. The ship lurches to one side and then rights herself to sail smoothly on. Rising war was magically dispelled by the supervening strategy of commerce, so that 'he return'd a friend, who came a foe' (206). Thus still, 'Love was Liberty, and Nature Law' (208). This is indeed the Arcadia of the pastoral poets, the world of the famous chorus in Tasso's *Aminta*, 656–723, which Samuel Daniel translated in his 'A Pastorall'. In that happy time, honour

Was not yet vainly found
Nor yet sad griefes imparts
Amidst the sweet delights
Of joyfull amorous wights.
Nor were his hard lawes known to free-borne hearts.
But golden lawes like these
Which Nature wrote. *That's lawfull which doth please.*[75]

Pope had used the line on love's liberty once before, with only one minor variation, in *Eloisa to Abelard* (92). There the context is one of frank erotic longing. Eloisa yearns to be Abelard's mistress, or indeed something yet freer than a mistress. The two contexts taken together strongly imply that Pope intended to suggest that 'free love' was practised in the state of nature. It was a thoroughly earthly heaven in which indeed there was no marrying or giving in marriage but meanwhile plenty of sexual bliss.

But Pope's Arcadian state of nature is not exempt from historical change and development. We have seen the hint of war and the rise of commerce. Now we watch the growth of patriarchal monarchy. Pope found what he wanted in Locke's second *Treatise on Government* (1714): 'Thus the natural *Fathers of Families*, by an insensible change, became the politick Monarchs of them too . . .'[76] Pope's scheme obviously resembles Locke's, in that the rise of human institutions is seen, not as an extrinsic curbing of anarchic appetite, but as the gradual codification of impulses already present and 'naturally governed' by the law of human nature. 'The *State of Nature*', says Locke, 'has a Law of Nature to govern it, which obliges everyone.'[27] But why bother to codify that which is already spontaneously effective? An answer might run on these lines: either the principal, inherently social impulses of human nature are contested by other darker impulses, or else parts of human nature are susceptible of being perverted or dislodged by external pressure, unless periodically returned to their proper, normal course by a set of rules which is now distinct – but only just – from scientific description. This answer would allow us to go on saying that all is happening naturally, though it involves the concession that, even in the remote, happy time, not *everything* was right. Moreover, it might be thought that the natural agent of codification is reason, hitherto seen as the source of perversion from nature. Pope avoids making any of these difficulties explicit, but the question about reason is probably lurking at the back of his mind, for it surfaces a few moments later, when he reverts to the subject of primal religion.

Pope explains that the original monotheistic religion was formed when people extrapolated the idea of a universal, ruling father from the given image of a human patriarch. Once again the theory is naturalist and, because naturalist, implicitly reductive, but Pope seems not to realise the fact. Just as morality is implicitly reduced by being derived from a mere extension of self-love, so religion (rather more clearly) is reduced if it is explained as the projection upon the skies of merely human conceptions and concerns. God in such a theory is simply a father-image. For Pope, of course, the picture is rather of primitive human beings coming ever closer to the real truth of things by merely natural light; their imaginative extrapolation from benevolent patriarchy happened to show them a profound truth. But Pope's method of explanation is dangerous in a work which deliberately disclaims any reliance on Revelation. The more persuasive the account, the greater the risk that it will be taken to be complete, in which case the whole of religion can be classed as a psychological construct, a mere projection.

The passage is doubly puzzling because Pope writes as if he were describing the beginning of religion. But what, in that case, had the 'vocal beings' and 'the blameless priest' been doing in the green temple (155–8)? It is as if an intuitive primal monotheism were succeeded by a secondary projective monotheism. The only thing that is clear is Pope's strong claim that, somehow, monotheism preceded polytheism. Hume, within a few years, was to argue the contrary thesis in his *Natural History of Religion*:

> As far as writing or history reaches, mankind, in antient times, appear universally to have been polytheists. Shall we assert, that, in more antient times, before the knowledge of letters, or the discovery of any art of science, men entertained the principles of pure theism? That is, while they were ignorant and barbarous, they discovered truth: But fell into error, as soon as they acquired learning and politeness.
>
> But in all this assertion you not only contradict all appearance of probability, but also our present experience concerning the principles and opinions of barbarous nations. The savage tribes of *America, Africa* and *Asia* are all idolators. Not a single exception to this rule.[78]

Regarded as an answer to Pope, this may be in one respect ill-judged. For surely Pope would not be at all put out by the suggestion that learning and politeness produced error, while simple nature led mankind in the ways of truth. This, after all, has been a running theme of the *Essay*.

Nevertheless, as we have seen, there is a difficulty in supposing that simple *nature* can herself produce *supernatural* truth. Even if we allow that this may perhaps be done by analogy (as the prince to his people, so God to the world) we need, if not polite learning, at least a non-corruptive faculty of reason to work out the analogy. This finally breaks through at lines 229–34, where Pope writes:

> The worker from the work distinct was known,
> And simple Reason never sought but one:
> Ere Wit oblique had broke that steddy light,
> Man, like his Maker, saw that all was right,
> To Virtue, in the paths of Pleasure, trod,
> And own'd a Father when he own'd a God.

He has dealt with his difficulty by splitting reason in two. On the one hand we have 'simple Reason' in profound and natural accord with nature, and on the other we have 'Wit oblique'. 'Wit', now beginning to move from the sense 'intelligence' towards the sense 'frivolous ingenuity', is here chosen by Pope, with his usual sure sense of semantic drift, to convey the pejorative implication.

What, then, went wrong? The question is growing urgent. This is supposed to be an aetiological myth, and we have not yet clearly reached the phenomenon it is designed to explain, the manifest depravity of human institutions. Pope at last asks – and, almost in the same breath, answers – this question in lines 241–5:

> Who first taught souls enslav'd, and realms undone,
> Th' enormous faith of many made for one;
> That proud exception to all Nature's laws,
> T'invert the world, and counter-work its Cause?
> Force first made Conquest and that conquest, Law. . .

It is an answer which explains nothing.

Pope, having dropped back into the old mythical method of theodicy, now discovers how difficult it is to bring off. One may see the third epistle as standing roughly halfway between the aetiological myth of *Paradise Lost* on the one hand and Freud's *Civilisation and Its Discontents* on the other. Milton employed the story given in Genesis, fenced about with a theory of creaturely freedom. Man fell because the Devil tempted him. The Devil was himself a fallen angel, Lucifer, and *he* fell because in his pride he resented the position assigned to him in Heaven. Lucifer was able to rebel and Adam to yield to Lucifer's temptation because both were created free. 'Freedom' means that either could divagate from the will of God. It is a scheme which satisfies only at a distance. Milton found when he subjected it to the harsh imaginative test of close narrative that things were less straightforward than they had seemed. In particular, the 'because' in 'because they were free' is inwardly weak. If Adam had been created all-good, he would have chosen spontaneously to love and serve God. Freedom is indeed a necessary condition of his choosing otherwise, but it is not of itself a cause. It does not account for a choice which is seemingly in flat contradiction of the moral nature of the subject. The same arguments apply to Lucifer. We sense that for Adam to have assented to temptation as he did, he must already have been corrupted. Augustine had the same feeling, for he wrote: 'Our first parents fell into open disobedience because already they were secretly corrupted; for the evil act had never been done had not an evil will preceded it.'[79] But, if Adam was already corrupt, *this* story obviously will not serve to account for his first corruption. Milton's myth presupposes the phenomenon it was supposed to explain.

It is likely that Milton became aware of the difficulty as he composed the poem. Hence, perhaps, his systematic blurring of the crucial moment of corruption, most brilliantly through the device of having Satan approach Eve by way of her unconscious, toad-like at her ear as she slept (IV, 799–809), but also in the shimmering multiplicity of Book IX (did evil enter when Adam bit the apple, when Eve tempted him or even when she disobeyed him by going off alone into the garden?). In Pope's myth of the perversion of society the crucial originating moment is similarly blurred and multiplied. Was nature first overthrown when man learned arts (169), with private property (188), with envy and impending war (203–4) or with the rise of 'Force' (245)? The last, like the eating of the apple in Milton, must bear the main weight. And there is no shadow of explanation. Everything was pretty wonderful until, suddenly, everything was not wonderful. Pope cannot even contrive an appearance of postponing his problem by assuming that some outside agency disturbed the harmony of the state of nature. He has no Satan to fly from the other side of Chaos and creep into the green and happy place. 'Force' is not an explanation but, rather, a description of what occurred: 'Why did that rich, happy and well-adjusted young man murder his sister?' 'Well, because he used violence.'

It might be thought that such difficulties are peculiar to religious philosophies. When once the hypothesis of an all-powerful, wholly good creator is dropped, there need be no difficulty in simply accepting that some things are ill ordered. But very similar difficulties can arise in a naturalistic scheme such as that of Darwin. Darwin seemed to some to imply that any creature not well ordered must somehow be breaking the laws of nature; such a creature should have been eliminated long ago by natural selection. The inference, to be sure, is loose and is not firmly attested by Darwinian theory, which allows considerable latitude even for degeneration, but it was nevertheless made.

Thus, imperfections of design do not only embarrass the theologian. Conversely, accounting for the structure of morality from a non-moral base is not only a problem for modern positivists but also assails Pope, whose theory of self-love is, after all, thoroughly naturalist.

For Freud, writing some two hundred years after Pope, the problem was to account, not for the origin of morality as such (though, with a little care, he might easily have argued that, as property is theft, so morality itself was the first 'sin' against nature) but, rather, for the origin of guilt. A mind consisting of appetite occasionally curbed by self-regarding prudence is not going to feel guilty. It may curse its own errors and resolve to be more careful in future, but it will not feel guilty. Freud, like all the others, drops evasively into myth. Once upon a time, the sons, needing women, rose against the old father and killed him in order to gain possession of his females. The consequent conflict of emotions crystallised as guilt.[80] Yet again, the story fails to explain. The sons may well, on Freud's terms, have experienced a mingling of triumph, unexorcised fear of the father and a sense that they might have made a mistake. But add or multiply these elements in any way you like – you will never obtain the answer 'guilt'. Once again the conclusion is tacitly presupposed. The missing factor is indeed morality itself.

Thus, the difficulties of supernatural theism are strangely reflected in the difficulties of naturalism. From the ethical point of view both Milton's and Freud's theories are forms of naturalism in that they strive to account for an 'ought' situation with a series of 'is' or 'was' propositions, in the indicative mood – to derive an 'ought not' from a 'was'. Myth is the ancient way of dealing with such questions, yet it is really ill-adapted for the purpose because it is so firmly committed to the indicative mood. Although we may think of myth as congenial to the old religious culture and philosophic theodicy as belonging to a more sceptical age, at the deepest level naturalism is implicit in the very narrative method of myth, and theodicy, conversely, can be viewed as the last convulsive effort of religion to be true to itself.

Pope is in some ways nearer to Darwin, or even to Freud, than to Milton. He is struggling to understand, not how God's creature could choose wrong, but how nature could go wrong. The categories of his thought in this part of the poem are (pseudo-) historical and psychological rather than theological; even when he explicitly considers religion, he comes close to a theory of psychological projection. The Miltonic scheme is thoroughly naturalised. At the same time, however, we must not forget that the state of nature was 'the Reign of God'.

The universalism of 'Whatever IS, is RIGHT' is indeed subjected to a strange series of retrenchments in this epistle. 'Whatever is' is implicitly restricted to 'Nature' – itself a term at first universal in scope but progressively opposed to human artifice and so restricted. Moreover, nature has suffered in the course of time. Human interference, corrupt civilisation and the like have not kept still but have grown monstrously. Thus, 'Whatever IS, is RIGHT' moves (with the help of an allusion to Genesis) into the past tense and we read, at line 232:

> Man, like his Maker, saw that all was right.

Something very strange has happened to Pope's optimistic theodicy. He had formerly chosen to show that the universe was conceivably – and perhaps even visibly – compatible with an all-powerful, all-good creator. In the last analysis, *everything* must be compatible with such a good, and 'everything' obviously includes the entire universe, as we know it *now*. That is why explanations in terms of the Fall were rejected as insufficient. Archbishop King, from whom Pope borrowed freely, explicitly rejects the idea that all evil can be said to proceed from Adam's sin:

> The Scripture nowhere teaches that there would have been no manner of natural Evil, if Man had not sinned. God indeed made all things good and perfect in their kind, that is, he created and still preserves everything, in a state and condition suitable to the whole System of Beings. . .[81]

For King and for Pope (most of the time) what we call 'evil' is inherent in the very fact of creation. If we could apprehend the whole, we should cease to speak of 'evil'. In essence, the implied contradiction between a bad creation and a good creator was resolved by denying that the creation was bad. To say that at some remote point in the past all went wrong is to imply that God became the sustainer of a universe which had become in some respects less than the best possible. King in the passage quoted speaks of 'natural evil'. When he turns to moral evil, he submits to the same obligation to supply a *general* account. He grants that freedom is a good, but holds that erroneous or ignorant choices are simply natural evils, inherent in the fact of creation.[82] The theological optimists of the eighteenth century have been endlessly abused by modern critics, who take their cue, with small reflection, from Voltaire. In fact we may discern both honesty and philosophic courage in the refusal of such as King to adopt the easy explanations of myth.

But the denial of evil is hard for natural man to sustain, and especially hard for a poet who delights in pointed, concrete illustration. The seeming deficiencies of the visible are corrected by a pious conception of the invisible and, as Dr Johnson said in another context, immateriality supplies no images.[83] Pope had begun increasingly to conduct his vindication in terms of visible goods, but merely visible goods, as we saw, can always be countered by merely visible evils. The great vindication had a certain formal power as long as the realm of perfection was the universe itself, infinitely outstripping our powers of perception. In this way local 'evils' were incorporated and transcended by the argument. Pope, finding that to his irremediably concrete imagination the local evils presented an increasingly formidable opposing front to God, decided that they might be permitted to stand, as a corruption or falling away from God's scheme. But, if God is the upholder of a scheme flawed by corruption, the ground so laboriously gained by King and Leibniz is simply surrendered. They had, on philosophic principle, rejected mythic narratives of decline; but Pope, having majestically (and very fashionably) banished Genesis from his poem, simply drops back into a mode identical in its logical form with Milton's. It is not really surprising that his story fails to produce an *explanation*. Pope's myth of the lost state of nature is simply a confession that evil is, after all, to be admitted. He preserves the God-filled universe affirmed as present in the first epistle as a pastoral, reminiscent dream. It can now assume the concrete, Arcadian form Pope must always have half-wished to give it, because it has ceased to operate as a philosophic conception. God's goodness is no longer a matter of vast, unimaginable design, but inheres in things like trees, sex, friendship and hymn-singing, and was simply succeeded, in a latter age, by blood and cruelty. Because, forsooth, Force arose.

As Pope conducts us into the second phase, the state of nature now destroyed, he can use to the full his powers of pungent summary and judgement. We see yet another rise of religion (the first was 'the blameless priest', the second the extension upwards of patriarchy). This time, because he is treating the fallen phase, the projectionist theory of religion can be explicit:

> Fear made her Devils, and weak Hope her Gods. . .
>
> (256)

Formally, the contrast with the earlier phase is clear: it is the difference between spiritual inference to truth in accordance with the light of nature and reified fantasy. But Pope's recurrent naturalism is always there in the background, eroding the foundations of this distinction. Here hope is frankly described as weak, which Pope can afford to do because his subject is pagan superstition. But three times before in this poem we have encountered the notion of hope (I, 95; II, 274; III, 74); in each it was made by the poet to play a crucial role in orthodox piety, and, though its weakness was not confessed, it was not difficult to discern. Pope has now moved within the purview of ascertainable history. His corrupted, polytheistic second phase is essentially identical with what Hume (with more historical conscience) laid down as the first phase in his *Natural History of Religion*.

By the time he reaches line 269, Pope has thoroughly darkened his picture of society. But the darkening permits, he suddenly realises, a fresh application of the idea of self-love. Earlier in the poem, Pope, explaining the transformation of self-love into social benevolence, had faced a choice. He could either suppose that self-love *naturally* extended itself to include first family, then nation, then all mankind, or else he could suppose that self-love would lead the weak to combine in order to protect themselves against the strong, imposing such sanctions on the now isolated tyrant as would lead *his* self-love to direct him to a course of social conformity. At III, 124, Pope opted for the first version. Its relatively rosy view of human nature accorded closely with the optimistic world picture hitherto adopted in the poem. But as the scene changes to one of conflict the alternative scheme comes into play. The original idea of a naturally extending self-love seemed at first to be based on a timeless conception of universal human nature. Now one senses that Pope has relegated this conception, as he relegated his general optimism, to the Arcadian period. In a time of running conflict self-interest may conceivably produce irenic institutions, but only through a tense series of negotiations, involving pain or the threat of pain:

> All join to guard what each desires to gain.
> Forc'd into virtue thus by Self-defence,
> Ev'n Kings learn'd justice and benevolence:
> Self-love forsook the path it first pursu'd,
> And found the private in the public good.
>
> (278–82)

Pope, in making this move, had adopted, without noticing it, a profoundly different position. He has left the class of those who see human rules as harsh distortions of nature for the class of those who see rules as a necessary curb. At line 192 he had drawn a contrast between the 'laws' of nature and the fatal entanglements which stem from the laws laid down by reason. Now (at line 272) law becomes the indispensable restraint of power and lust. It may be said that the earlier conception is entirely appropriate to an uncorrupted nature and the second is likewise appropriate to a corrupted nature; that Pope quite properly finds in self-love a double capacity, first to grow by natural degrees and secondly to preserve the species from destruction (once harmony has been broken) through enlightened self-interest. But at each stage of his argument Pope has appealed for corroboration to currently observable facts of psychology. The reader was implicitly invited *to look about him* for evidence of the self-extending powers of self-love or the harsh rigidity of imposed laws. Perhaps, nevertheless, this is one cake which Pope can both have and eat.

Aetiological myths of a great Fall, so far from providing a justification of God's ways, can be made to do so only by being turned inside out: that is, by being turned at last into stories of a great Promotion. Thus, Milton in *Paradise Lost*, in order to reconcile the entire melancholy sequence with divine love, was drawn at the end of his poem to make use of the old idea of the *felix culpa*, or Happy Fall, whereby the expulsion of Adam from Eden was really his promotion to a moral arena from which he might at last win through to a happiness far greater than anything Eden could offer. It is no good trying to retreat from 'Whatever IS, is RIGHT' into explanatory narrative, since narrative alone explains nothing. It is evident that the Fall considered as the great primal disaster actually embarrasses theology, just like any other apparent evil. The transformation of the entire sequence is subtly done by Milton, who knows that if this second conception is trumpeted too loud it will be seen to be violently at odds with the common, traditional image of the Fall. In Pope the same pressures can be seen at work. He has so far defected from his scheme of vindication as to concede the corruption of human institutions and has forthwith slipped back into the ancient method of myth in order to account for the corruption. The myth, as ever, has failed to supply the much-needed *theological* justification and, in consequence, we find Pope (rather feebly) twisting the tail of his myth, in order to show that the entire process led, after all, to a great good, in that self-love was able to produce social institutions. Of course, the institutions thus produced are the very ones whose corruption seemed before so inescapable that some explanatory myth of loss was required. Thus, there is an element of circular futility in Pope's version which is absent from Milton's.

The final conception of self-love is indeed bleak. We noted earlier (at line 133) a possible softening in Pope towards the idea that moral reason might be needed to turn the mere impulse of self-love into true benevolence.[84] In the final section of the epistle this possibility seems to be forgotten (if it was ever really there). Once more the satiric edge of Pope's style, which no philosophy or piety can long keep sheathed, assists the cynical reading of phrases like 'Forc'd into virtue' and 'Ev'n Kings learn'd justice' (279, 280). To find 'the private in the public good' (282) is simply to find that 'altruism' pays dividends.

Yet Pope would think, and would have us think, that the benevolence thus extorted from man can be, in its own way, real benevolence. Lines 283–302 are a celebration of this benevolence, but the celebration requires, we sense, an effort of will on the writer's part. Poet and patriot (not, notice, saint and martyr) arise to rekindle the ancient light of nature. The theodicy is again secured for most readers, though there will always be an ill-conditioned remnant who fretfully complain of the chaotic interval between the state of nature and the recovered 'well-mixt State' (294) – especially since it is the interval, and not the time before or after, which most faithfully mirrors our experience. By far the finest line in the sequence is 288

> If not God's image, yet his shadow drew

and it betrays, momentarily yet unmistakably, the sense that nature's light has not really been relit, that a love thus reconstituted is a kind of ghost.

To conclude the epistle, Pope drops into a minor key. After all the trumpets (triumphantly majestic yet hushed, at moments, in a dying fall) of lines 283 to 302, he suddenly reverts to an ordinary speaking voice. He grows confidential and confesses that, between us and him, it does not really matter what form of government one has (despite the commendation of a mixed form of government, possibly constitutional monarchy, at lines 289–94):

> For Forms of Government let fools contest;
> Whate'er is best administer'd is best. . .
>
> (303–4)

Pope of course never saw a well-run concentration-camp, but he had access to records of highly efficient tyrannies. Contemporaries of Pope were shocked by what they took to be an immoral indifference to the wickedness of certain forms of government. Pope in reaction scribbled in the margin of one of the pamphlets pressing this view,

> The author of these lines was far from meaning that no one Form of Government is, in itself, better [than] another . . . but that no form of Government, however excellent or preferable in itself, can be sufficient to make a People happy, unless it be administer'd with Integrity. On [the] contrary, the Best sort of Governm't, when [the] Form of it is preserved, and [the] *administration* corrupt, is most dangerous. (MM, 124)

Such self-defensive interpretations, written in response to criticism, are seldom entirely trustworthy. Pope wrote quite clearly in the *Essay* that dispute over which form of government is best is futile, and that the really important factor is the manner in which whatever system prevails is administered. This is not the same thing as saying that some forms of government are inherently better than others but that the best can be ruined if it is not well administered. Pope has over-reacted and strained our credulity farther than he needed to. For in fact the original lines taken in their proper context do not suggest that, when Pope writes 'best administer'd', he is thinking solely of smooth-running efficiency. In view of his insistence a few lines later on charity, it is overwhelmingly likely that he was thinking of a *kindly* efficiency. The real danger of this kind of talk is not cynicism but vacuousness. Pope comes very near to saying that things will not be far wrong as long as they are done right, and that virtue is a Good Thing. But, in truth, most readers can see what Pope means and many find it perfectly reasonable.

The last line sums up the epistle:

> And bade Self-love and Social be the same.
> (318)

Pope introduces this assertion of identity with an elaborately astronomical metaphor (313–14). Planets rotate upon their axes and at the same time revolve round the sun. Mack cites *Spectator* 588, where the same metaphor is employed:

> Is it [benevolence] inconsistent with self-love? Are their Motions contrary? No more than the diurnal rotation of the earth is opposed to its annual; or its motion round its own center, which might be improved as an illustration of self-love, to that which whirls it about the common center of the world, answering to universal benevolence. (MM, 126)

But it is one thing to say that two motions are compatible and another to say (as Pope does) that they are identical. Pope, indeed, seems so far swayed by this thought as to grant for a moment that he *is* after all dealing with two distinct faculties:

> And one regards Itself, and one the Whole.
> (316)

But then he pulls his verse together for the final grand identification of the two. Pope's metaphor, to be sure, is majestically Newtonian, which is as much as to say that it implies throughout the unifying operation of gravity. But this does not mean that annual motion is the same thing as diurnal motion, nor, strictly speaking, that annual motion is diurnal motion writ large; it means only that the same force operates in either case, and this force is, in itself, not 'diurnal'. Thus, if we apply the analogy, we shall find that there is no longer any special reason to call the fundamental power which moves in individuals and in societies '*self*-love'. Rather it is, as in the most ancient sources, simply 'love'. When it appears in an introverted form within a single individual it is 'self-love' and when it appears on a larger scale it is merely love. The metaphor does not support but, rather, tends to dislodge the original reductive, naturalistic enterprise of the epistle whereby a fundamentally selfish instinct was made to 'yield' the higher forms of institutional altruism. Meanwhile the mildly combative tone of the passage in the *Spectator* makes it perfectly clear that, as we suggested earlier, a flavour of improbable paradox continued to hang about the term. Fashionable philosophers gave it excited assent but other people could not help thinking that selfishness was selfishness. To say this is not to deny that in the work of a great thinker like Butler the concept assumed considerable power. In Pope it produced some surprisingly acute analysis of the evolution of social institutions, but never came of age philosophically.

(v)   EPISTLE IV: HAPPINESS

In the third epistle, self-love became social by ceasing (in effect) to be self-directed, by turning into mere love, as the circles gradually extended across the pool of creation. Yet Pope showed every sign of wishing to keep hold of the notion of an original, self-regarding instinct as still, in some sense, lying at the heart of social institutions, and therefore contrived a second picture, in which the many combined to safeguard their gains, so that even the powerful were

> Forc'd into virtue thus by Self-defence. . .
> (III, 279)

At the beginning of the fourth epistle, Pope tells us why we are on earth, what our end or purpose is. Our end is happiness.

The reaction of Elwin is profoundly Victorian and not without force:

> Happiness is with Pope the sole end of life, and virtue is only a means. The means cannot be more binding than the end, and happiness is not obligatory and virtue is. A certain contempt, again, for pain and privation is heroic, but indifference to moral worth is degradation. Thus virtue is plainly an end in itself, and is superior, not subordinate, to happiness. (E & C, II, 429)

Pope's choice of happiness as the end of life is in fact utterly traditional. But the mere fact that it is traditional cannot of itself allay the fears of those who perceive in the poem a constant drift towards mere sunny selfishness (those who would show how altruism may be derived from egoism may end by showing that altruism is reducible to egoism). 'Happiness', as it stands, does not naturally imply either altruism or charity. Pope might have chosen 'love of God' or 'to help one another'. But he chose happiness.

Already, to be sure, we are deep in unresolved ambiguities. The notion of our 'being's end' (line 1) is equivocal. Our 'end' may be that which God intended as our proper function. The first conception is merely descriptive, the second retains a prescriptive, moral dimension. As often in this poem, much depends on the question, is man fallen from his original state? If the Fall really happened, then our two conceptions may indeed be light-years apart; what man in his depravity struggles for will be quite unlike that for which he first drew breath in Eden. If, on the other hand, there was no Fall, then what we do, here and now, must be what God would have us do. Therefore that for which we all strive *is* that for which we ought to strive; the one melts into the other.

If one removes all theological reference, that is, all reference to God, Eden and the like, one finds that the two meanings of 'end' are, quite simply, 'usual purpose' and 'moral purpose'. The first is merely non-ethical. As we have seen, the tendency of eighteenth-century Deism was to play down the Fall and to insist that everything we see, here and now, must be compatible with the wishes of an all-powerful, benevolent creator; this produces, ineluctably, the thesis 'Whatever IS, is RIGHT'. But if whatever is is right there is no need to exhort anyone to behave differently; there is no need for the word 'ought'. And if there is no 'ought' the ethical dimension has vanished. Thus, the great attempt to pull the universe up, in an act of religious love and celebration, to the level of divine goodness can result in a gigantic, inadvertent reduction, not only of God to the level of his creation, but also of the ethical to the non-ethical. This precisely mirrors the danger we noted earlier, whereby those who derive altruism from egoism may end by reducing altruism to egoism. The running conception behind all of this is naturalism, in the sense it bears in ethical philosophy. Naturalism in ethics consists in providing an account of the ethical in non-ethical terms. If one says that actions are virtuous in so far as they promote pleasure and that is all that 'virtuous' means, one is guilty of naturalism. To charge the Utilitarians, say, with naturalism is not to deny that pleasure is good but, rather, to deny that it exhausts the meaning of 'good'. If 'pleasant' were the dictionary meaning of 'good', a person who in opposition to the Utilitarians held that truth-telling and self-sacrifice were terminal goods would not be a serious philosophical opponent; such a person would simply have betrayed his ignorance of the meaning of the terms. In fact, as we all know very well, ethical debates are not like that at all. Rather, the Utilitarian who believes in the greatest happiness of the greatest number feels an obligation to *argue* that happiness measures up to the standards implied by 'good', which means in turn that 'good' remains conceptually distinct from 'pleasant'. The person who is alert to the danger of naturalism will again and again feel obliged to drive home, like a wedge into a tree-trunk, the fundamental distinction between 'is' and 'ought': 'Happiness is desirable, yes, but "desirable" can mean "such that we desire it" or "such that it ought to be desired".' This, notice, parallels our initial distinction between two senses of 'our being's end'.

The notion of ethical naturalism, once grasped, is both fundamental and very simple. But one form of it will always give trouble. That is the mode of ethical naturalism which says that 'good' means 'what God wishes'. The difficulty arises from a mere confusion. The proposition is clearly naturalist in the technical sense: it translates the ethical into non-ethical terms. But the non-ethical terms are themselves (in quite another sense) *supernatural*. A 'supernatural naturalism' looks like a contradiction in terms, and people simply shy away from the conception. But the contradiction is easily removed. What we are confronted with is a metaphysical supernaturalism which involves, at the level of ethics, naturalism in the technical sense of the term. Pope's mentor Bolingbroke held that 'good' could be translated without remainder into 'what God wants'. God does not desire things because they are good; they are 'good' because he desires them.[85] The appearance of inverted commas round *good* in the second clause betrays the fact that a reduction of the ethical has occurred. For Bolingbroke is, quite clearly, an ethical naturalist.

With Deism and eighteenth-century theodicy the element of naturalism is not always as explicit as it is in the writings of Bolingbroke. To say that the universe is a great dance fulfilling the will of God certainly did not 'feel like' a draining away of the ethical, at first. That was because the notion of God was already instinct with value. But the very notion of value, of 'good', depends on there being some palpable difference, locally, here and now, between the way things are and the way they ought to be. The philosophic lifting up, with trumpets and jubilation, of the universe to match God's mind was equally a bringing low of God. The apotheosis of the world led to a mundane God. Here is incarnation with a vengeance: God crammed within the fleshly limits of his ruinous work. If whatever is is right, right is whatever is. In the terrible words of Hume, 'The whole presents nothing but the idea of a blind nature, impregnated by a great vivifying principle, and pouring forth from her lap, without discernment or parental care, her maimed and abortive children'.[86]

It will be seen that the great project of justifying God by justifying the universe amounts in the end, not merely to ethical naturalism, but to ethical naturalism of a peculiarly absolute and fundamental kind. The 'hard' Utilitarian who reduces 'good' to 'pleasant' at least allows *some*, practical, specifying force to the word 'good'; though it fails now to distinguish 'ought' from 'is', at least it is not freely applicable to anything at all. But the identification of 'good' with God's will and of God's will with everything that happens means that good has suffered just this fate.

The dangers surrounding Pope should now be a little clearer. With his conception of happiness as the End of Man he stands on the edge of a particular form of ethical reductionism. Meanwhile his overarching doctrine, 'Whatever IS, is RIGHT', intermittently threatens a reduction more fundamental still. But we need not jump before we are pushed. Traditionally the reductive implications of 'happiness' as a term have been kept at bay in various ways. The Greeks did it with their conception of *eudaimonia*, which is roughly speaking intermediate between the two modern concepts, 'happi-

ness' and 'blessedness'.[87] According to the classic argument Socrates
discontented is *happier* (that is, more *eudaimon*) than a contented pig.
Socrates in Plato's *Philebus* (21c) speaks contemptuously of 'the life,
not of a man, but of an oyster'.[88] This was the conception by means
of which John Stuart Mill hoped to 'elevate' Utilitarianism, to lift it
clear of its gross, Benthamite origins.[89] When we say Socrates,
though discontented, is 'happier' we mean that we would rather be
Socrates than the pig. But this is only because there are elements in
the discontent of Socrates (such as intelligence, for example) on
which we set a (separate) high value. Socrates is therefore more
enviable than the pig, and his *eudaimonia* or 'happiness' (one senses
at once that the English word is being strained) consists solely in that
fact. It is, of course, a fact which, so far from elevating Utilitarianism, rather subverts it, for it shows very clearly that we value other
things besides pleasure. But as long as the word 'happiness' is
stretched to cover such a generous area one may indeed feel that the
doctrine is not reductive. But, by the same token, it is now much less
novel, much less fundamentally explanatory than it first seemed to
be. As usual, the choice seems to be between falsehood ('Pleasure is
identical with good') and tautology ('The good is what we value').

Another method is to locate true happiness in Heaven. Since there
is a presumption that Heaven is restricted to the virtuous, the danger
of immoralist hedonism appears to recede. The atmosphere of sanctity
works against the implications of selfishness. Yet, even if the happiness for which we strive is Heavenly, in so far as it really governs
and determines all our actions, it must infect those actions with
self-interest. The eighteenth-century author in whom this became
inescapably clear was Paley. His definition of virtue is notorious:
'The doing good to mankind, in obedience to the will of God, and for
the sake of ever-lasting happiness.'[90] This is eschatological
Utilitarianism of the most obvious sort. Plain Utilitarianism asserts
that human beings strive to maximise their pleasure, and struggles to
build an ethical theory on this inertly descriptive foundation. Fancy
Utilitarianism, on the other hand, leaps over all difficulties by de-
claring that 'the greatest happiness of the greatest number' constitutes
our proper, moral purpose. The step from plain to fancy
Utilitarianism is, like the step from self-love to social, seven leagues
wide.

It is partly to Pope's credit that in the opening sections of Epistle
IV he makes little use of either of these palliatives. By 'happiness' he

means, not some elevated condition of the soul, but 'Pleasure, ease, content' (line 2). True, I have omitted 'good', but the word is a blank cheque, and is at once cashed by the unpretentious synonyms which follow. The notion of Heavenly bliss, admittedly, gets in in lines 3–4:

> That something still which prompts th'eternal sigh,
> For which we bear to live, or dare to die. . .

The second line of the couplet in particular is tensely paradoxical; a happiness for the sake of which death itself is ventured hardly looks like an easy option. Yet, if we take Paley seriously, it is certainly easier than everlasting torment. Pope, indeed, is not Paley. The later writer would have spelled out, in heavily objective language, the felicity of the life to come. In Pope, as we may by now have learned to expect, the next world is restricted to its glimmering half-existence in the *hopes* of pious Christians. The couplet easily receives – almost invites – a thoroughly sceptical interpretation: 'Even when people refuse, for all their wretchedness, to commit suicide, even when they die like martyrs, the reason they do it will turn out to be *happiness*.' So far from expanding the concept of happiness to include altruistic tendencies, Pope's expert couplet implicitly reduces the self-devotion of the saint to a species of self-interested calculation. Love of God becomes another instance of the quest for happiness. Yet, as the epistle continues, it is made clear that happiness is in fact readily available for all in this world (16–17).

Pope, in opting for the common-sense conception, has created a problem for himself which is partly a technical difficulty of rhetoric. Although in the long run pleasure is pleasure, he could have built his opening paragraph round the idea that all earthly pleasures are vain and true happiness exists only in the world to come. This would have accorded easily with his talent for urbane disparagement (never far below the surface of his verse). Before Pope even starts to think, his *style* begins to minimise and deflate. The traditional way to harness these energies is to channel all the mockery towards this world and its vanity. Various snatches of English poetry, as usual, are half-quoted in the lines, and the tendency of all of them is firmly to divide the Heavenly from the merely human. In 'Lycidas' Milton wrote:

> *Fame* is no plant that grows on mortal soil,
> Nor in the glistering foil

> Set off to th' world, nor in broad rumour lies,
> But lives and spreds aloft by those pure eyes,
> And perfet witness of all judging *Jove*;
> As he pronounces lastly on each deed,
> Of so much fame in Heav'n expect thy meed
>   (78–84)

In Pope, Milton's 'fame' becomes 'happiness' and weighty assertion turns into a conditional clause, followed by a curiously open-ended question:

> Plant of celestial seed! if dropt below,
> Say, in what mortal soil thou deign'st to grow?
>   (7–8)

It is as if Pope, still trembling slightly from the mere echo of the Miltonic thunder, hastily composes himself to ask, with a mixture of trepidation and mild greed: 'Yes, but if it *were* here, where do you suppose one ought to start looking?' Even the dapper Dryden (also echoed here) is unequivocally (if conventionally) hostile to this world, in *Absalom and Achitophel*:

> Desire of Power, on Earth a Vitious Weed,
> Yet, sprung from High, is of Caelestial Seed,
>   (I, 305–6)[91]

The lines, indeed, go on to argue that the divine origin of roistering ambition renders its wild excesses forgivable, but this argument (since it concerns the bastard Duke of Monmouth) is of course partly ironic. The initially planted contrast between vile worldly ambition and divine glory is intended to stick in the mind and to exert its condemnatory force on the figure Dryden pretends to excuse.

This firm division of human and divine is preserved (but with a difference) in Andrew Marvell's 'The Garden':

> Fair quiet, have I found thee here,
> And Innocence thy Sister dear!
> Mistaken long, I sought you then
> In busie Companies of Men.
> Your sacred Plants, if here below,
> Only among the Plants will grow.
> Society is all but rude,
> To this delicious Solitude.
>   (9–16)[92]

Marvell, though he rejects the busy vanity of human affairs, makes one strange exception to the rule that only Heavenly happiness is real. He exempts the plants, the green world of solitary contemplation, from corruption. It would be easy to be drawn into a lengthy exploration of Marvell's meaning, for these lines occur in a poem of dazzling imaginative and conceptual brilliance, so dazzling that the sifting of ironic and unironic senses is far harder than in the case of Dryden. Marvell ascetically prefers the society of plants to the society of women with their white skin and rosy cheeks and lips, but for the most un-ascetic reason: plants are sexier.

> No white nor red was ever seen
> So am'rous as this lovely green
> (17–18)[93]

He blasphemously suggests that Eden was half-spoiled by the arrival of Eve, but then he also suggests that Apollo pursued Daphne *because* she would turn into a reed; both are jokes, and so is the blasphemy lessened? These questions beget others, and we have no leisure to pursue them here. The fundamental convention, the thing that is merely given, before great Wits begin to play, is perfectly clear: the happiness valued by the world is vain.

Pope sets out along this path but cannot follow it to its natural rhetorical conclusion.

> Say, in what mortal soil thou deign'st to grow?
> Fair op'ning to some Court's propitious shine,
> Or deep with di'monds in the flaming mine?
> Twin'd with the wreaths Parnassian lawrels yield,
> Or reap'd in iron harvests of the field?
> (8–12)

It is impossible to be certain that Pope is making conscious use of Marvell (whose lyric works fell into obscurity after his death), but these lines look very like a brilliant fusion of two passages in Marvell. First, the opening lines of 'The Garden':

> How vainly men themselves amaze
> To win the Palm, the Oke, or Bayes;
> And their uncessant Labours see
> Crown'd from some single Herb or Tree.

> Whose short and narrow verged Shade
> Does prudently their Toyls upbraid;
> While all Flow'rs and all Trees do close
> To weave the Garlands of repose.[94]

The second passage is from 'The Coronet':

> And now when I have summ'd up all my store,
>   Thinking (so I myself deceive)
>   So rich a Chaplet thence to weave
> As never yet the king of Glory wore:
>   Alas I find the Serpent old
>   That, twining in his speckled breast,
>   About the flow'rs disguis'd does fold,
>   With wreaths of Fame and Interest.
>   (9–16)[95]

The second is much more powerfully Christian, less Roman, than
the first and may therefore be thought more remote from the Augustan Pope. But Pope's use of the word 'twin'd' cannot but suggest the
serpent to anyone who knows Marvell's lines. This creates a subaudition of something stronger than the usual contempt of the world, a
Calvinist intuition that worldly success is not merely futile but evil,
the Kingdom of Satan. Certainly complex energies are quickened in
these lines. The courtier, like a gorgeous heliotrope, is transfixed in
the blandly vacuous 'fair op'ning' (notice the admirable placing in
this line of the pompous polysyllable, 'propitious', with its weakly
plosive first consonant, and the unusual use of 'shine' as a noun,
where we might have expected 'shining', giving an effect of tailing
away into nothingness).

The marvellous oxymoron of 'iron harvests' in line 12 seems to be
related to two lines in the *Epistle to Burlington*:

> There Gladiators fight, or die, in flow'rs

and

> Deep Harvests bury all his pride has plann'd. . .
>   (124 and 175)

The *Epistle to Burlington* first appeared in 1731, the fourth epistle of
An Essay on Man early in 1734. The gladiators of the *Epistle to*

Burlington are of course statues, while the 'iron harvest' of the *Essay on Man* reaches back to the *ferrea seges* of Virgil's *Aeneid* (III, 45–6) and refers to real wars. The effect of the 'innocent' image of harvest is to intensify by unasserted contrast the real horror of what is intended. The ferocity rises with each successive line, and we grow hungry for the clinching final condemnation of all these desperate delusions of humankind, but it never comes. Instead we are given the extraordinary couplet

> Where grows? – where grows it not? – If vain our toil,
> We ought to blame the culture, not the soil. . .

> (13–14)

The rhetorical volte-face amounts almost to a dislocation. Pope's breathless punctuation marks the lurching rhythm of the thought.

It could be said that he is here adopting the ancient figure of rhetoric known as *aposiopesis*. This is used by Virgil when in the *Aeneid* he has King Neptune raise his head from the waters, rebuke the winds and then break off without specifying what precisely he will do to them (I, 132–5). But a curtailed threat is entirely natural (schoolteachers do it all the time), while a sudden back-pedalling in the middle of a diatribe on human felicity is simply bizarre. Pope has chosen as the dominant music of his exordium a rhetorical pattern of contempt for human happiness. But his philosophy is in fact not contemptuous of such things. He therefore drops in the line, with extraordinary abruptness, the idea that happiness is to be found everywhere. This means that the dominant contrast between the false bliss of this world and the true bliss of Heaven must be swiftly overlaid by a subtler contrast, that between false and real pleasures, here on earth.

The dislocation of line 13 is not utterly unprepared for. It is foreseen in lines 5–6, describing the happiness

> Which still so near us, yet beyond us lies,
> O'er-look'd, seen double, by the fool, and wise.

But in this couplet Pope, as frequently when he is in some trouble, almost vanishes from view in his own cleverness. The first line of the couplet, following as it does the line about martyrdom, could easily be taken to refer to happiness beyond the grave, but the second line seems (a little late, and a little obscurely) to determine the meaning to the present world. The machinery of the antithesis in the second line is elusive. Elwin glosses the line: 'Overlooked in the things which would yield it, and in other things magnified by the imagination' (E & C, II, 429). This gloss fails to place 'the fool' and the 'wise'. Following the usual rules of Popean antithesis, one gets: 'Overlooked by the fool when it is right in front of his nose and magnified by the "wise" man when it is not really there at all.' This is possible, but far from smooth. To make sense I was forced to put *wise* in inverted commas. Otherwise I might have written, 'magnified by (even) the wise man', trusting to the fact that so elliptical a sense might be successfully conveyed in reading by stressing 'and' in Pope's line. Either way, the formal antithesis between 'fool' and 'wise' collapses into a virtual identity, and the whole line is a little less clever than it seemed to be.

Yet Pope has a way of putting this very elusiveness to work. The manner in which the reader's expectations are half-frustrated and deflected is paralleled by the nature of happiness itself, as Pope presents it. For happiness is both obvious and unobvious, as palpably available to some as bread and butter, yet others find that the harder they look the less they find. It is therefore in a way quite proper that the paragraph itself should shimmer before the reader's mind. Apart from line 13 with its lurching syntax, the poet is in control. He brings the whole exordium to an elegant conclusion in a neat, resolving compliment to his 'Memmius', Bolingbroke, at lines 17–18:

> 'Tis never to be bought, but always free,
> And fled from Monarchs, ST. JOHN! dwells with thee.

The last steps of the figure are faultlessly performed and the reader, formally excluded by the personal pronoun, 'thee', politely applauds from the sidelines.

Formally, indeed, the rounding-off is unexceptionable. But in a philosophic poem matter is endlessly rebellious. Was Bolingbroke really a figure who could, by his mere visible character, cut across and resolve the ambiguities of happiness? Was he in any way like, say, the Man of Ross, described in the *Epistle to Bathurst* (250–82) as relieving the poor and the sick and reconciling enemies, 'thrice-happy' on five hundred pounds a year? Was Bolingbroke to felicity

what the Man of Ross was to benevolence? In short, was Bolingbroke *luminously* happy?

His youth was riotous rather than happy; he outdrank everyone.
Goldsmith met an old man who had once seen Lord Bolingbroke
'run naked through the Park, in a fit of intoxication'.[96] Swift said
that he modelled himself in part on Alcibiades, the notorious profligate genius of Athenian politics at the time of the Peloponnesian
Wars.[97] Bolingbroke was a powerful and effective politician at the
time of the War of the Spanish Succession. The 'Grande Alliance',
consisting of Britain, Austria and the Dutch Republic, was at war
with France. In 1712, Bolingbroke was behind the secret negotiations
with the French which led to the sudden and treacherous abandon-
ment by Britain of her allies. In due course he received the con-
gratulations of the French minister, Torcy, on the occasion of the
French victory over Prince Eugene of Austria at Denain. Doubtless
Bolingbroke's behaviour was defensible, but it certainly was not
luminous. A year later he quarrelled with his fellow-Tory, Harley
(later, the Earl of Oxford). Swift attempted to patch up the quarrel
but could not. Bolingbroke was behind the Schism Bill of 1714,
which effectively repressed the education of Dissenters (no one
could keep a school without a licence from a bishop). When George I
came to the throne Bolingbroke was dismissed, fled to Europe and
helped organise the interests of James, the Pretender. He quarrelled,
however, with his fellow-Jacobites and turned to the English government for pardon. Bolingbroke could with greater justice have
been placed later in the epistle, with Bacon, say, as another example
of flawed genius. Lord Chesterfield called him 'a most mortifying
instance of the violence of human passions and of the weakness of
the most improved and exalted human reason'.[98]

It may be said that such matter is extraneous to the poem. But
Pope's contemporaries would certainly not agree. Many of them
must have snorted with incredulity at the bare-faced flattery of line
18.

At line 19, Pope embarks in earnest on his account of false notions
of happiness. This he does, in his usual manner, by ranging the
current views in two opposite camps, with a running implication that
every assertion is cancelled by its contrary, leaving the mind (so far)
with nothing. The learned are no use, since some of them recommend public service and others a life of seclusion. At least each of
the contending views is touched with morality. A moment later this

impression is strengthened:

> Some sunk to Beasts, find pleasure end in pain;
> Some swell'd to Gods, confess ev'n Virtue vain. . .
> (23–4)

'Ev'n' implies that virtue might normally be expected to supply a surer foundation for happiness than vice. Nevertheless, we do not here see virtue judged by its power to produce happiness (and here the direct implication is that, after all, that power is not very great!).

Once again Pope drops from an artfully contrived confusion into simplicity:

> Who thus define it, say they more or less
> Than this, that Happiness is Happiness?
> (27–8)

But this will hardly do. One almost expects Pope, were he not so courtly, to open with the phrase, 'Well, what I say is, when all is said and done'. Such majestic tautologies may well command sage assent in the bar-parlour; but the Philosophic Poem of the age needs stronger intellectual meat than this. The suggestion that the ethical doctrines of Epicureans, Stoics, Dogmatists and Sceptics all amount to exactly the same thing is simply false. In any case, the preceding work of demolition has been found less than satisfactory. Laird comments: 'The account of false pleasures with which this epistle begins is a clear mistake. A pleasure is just a pleasure when it has its moment and cannot be either true or false. It may be brief and lead to unpleasant consequences. But that is quite another tale.'[99] In Pope's defence we might point out that he does not in fact use the expression 'false pleasure' but, rather (in the argument prefixed to the epistle), speaks of 'false *Notions* of Happiness' (my italics). A notion obviously can be false, where 'false' means 'incorrect'. But Laird's major point may stand. Pope may be suggesting that some forms of happiness are unreal, and this would seem to merit the brusque rejoinder, 'Brief, perhaps, but why unreal?' Common sense, however, suggests that Pope means 'delusive' rather than 'unreal'. One might express the point by drawing a distinction (which Pope admittedly never clearly does) between pleasures (brief, concrete) and long-term happiness. Some people, Pope suggests, are led to believe that certain pleasures will gradually compose full happiness, but in this they are deluded, since the pleasures in question either stop short or else produce consequent pain. Most people understand all this without any trouble. Laird displays the deliberate donnish obtuseness of the academic philosopher.

Nevertheless, a certain discomfort remains. This discomfort arises from the fact that Pope's approach to happiness seems somehow to be inclusive and exclusive at the same time. On the one hand he seems to be saying that happiness is just happiness in the most obvious sense of the word: 'pleasure', 'ease', 'content' are synonyms, and everyone knows what these are. On the other hand, he seems also to be saying that every time anyone tries to explain what happiness is he or she gets it wrong. This is either a contradiction or (more probably) something rather subtle. St Augustine said that he knew what time was so long as no one asked him what it was, but as soon as the question was posed his knowledge vanished.[100] Pope may be struggling with a similar strangeness in the notion of happiness. For example, it is possible to isolate a 'Naturalistic Fallacy' with respect to 'pleasant' in much the same way as we isolate it with respect to 'good'. The hedonic naturalist would be the person who maintained that 'pleasant' is *defined* by the concrete instances usually known as *the* pleasures: friendship, consciousness of virtue, good food and drink, sex, sport, music, poetry – these *are* Pleasure. The non-naturalist in response will point out that one can, without immediate logical contradiction, stand back from any of these and ask: 'But is it *really* pleasant?' (exactly as G. E. Moore loved to point out that one could step back from any concrete instance of goodness and ask 'Is it really good?'). It would therefore appear that the notion of pleasure is not passively derived, in an automatic manner, from determining instances but is, rather, a normative conception, to which various candidates for the title 'pleasant' either measure up or fail to measure up. This normative conception, it might be said, is indeed available with elemental clarity to almost everyone, but it is *so* elementary as to resist intrinsic definition. When they attempt definition people have recourse to the 'candidates', the concrete, objective pleasures, but at this point they run into the fact that there is no necessary relation, no firm determination of the concept by the candidates. The join at first appears to be perfect but the scheme is flawed by an almost invisible logical discontinuity. The hedonic naturalist is like Jack Ketch's victim in the old story. Jack

Ketch could take off a man's head as neatly as you please (as with a razor whetted with oil). After the operation the victim would say, 'My head's still on', and Ketch would answer, 'Try shaking it'.

In this way we might agree that happiness is both immediately available and elusive. Pope's poetry, his instinct for the mysteriously fruitful and persuasive ambiguity, leads him farther in philosophy than his powers of ordinary conceptual analysis could ever have brought him. One suspects that the triumph is only partial and, because largely instinctive, very precarious. But, for all that, for a few moments Pope was writing not versified metaphysics but philosophical poetry. The fastidiousness of the poet and the fastidiousness of the philosophical psychologist became one thing.

The second section of the epistle begins at line 29 with the usual intellectual placebo, prescribed whenever the brains begin to ache: 'Take Nature's path.' Yet again, description masquerades as prescription and 'Be what you are' is offered as a useful solution to the evils of one's present state. As before, Pope, in his anxiety to show that he has thought of everything, virtually concedes that he is not, after all, providing a means of dispelling intellectual difficulties:

> There needs but thinking right and meaning well. . .
> (32)

That is: 'You find you cannot think things out? Follow nature! You'll see, so long as you think things out properly, all will be well.' It could be said that this avoids outright contradiction, since thinking *after* submission to nature may be more fruitful than thinking in arrogant isolation. But now the attempt to 'save' Pope begins to feel strained. All states can reach happiness and all heads can conceive it, he says, in line 30, with bald directness. After nature has proved so generous and human opinion so 'mad' (29) it might seem more prudent to lay aside any ambition of 'right thinking'. Pope has fallen into the role of polished host, and the thought suffers accordingly.

There are two words which have for Pope a 'healing' quality. The first is 'nature'; the second, rather oddly to our ears, is 'equal'. 'Equal' does not in Pope get its warm 'affect' from reference to social equality. Its reference is more primitive: to balance, calmness, repose. We may remember from the first epistle, 'admitted to that equal Sky' (111) and 'Who sees with equal eye on God of all' at line

87. So here, after a draught of sustaining 'nature', he has recourse to the word 'equal' in line 34:

> Equal is Common Sense, and Common Ease.

Pope reassures us: common conceptions of where contentment is to be found match very well with its true sources.

That Pope should appeal, in so thoroughly English a fashion, to the saving sanity of common sense will surprise no one. One should remember, however, that the phrase 'common sense' was not in Pope's day the common coin of thought as it is for us. The history of the phrase is indeed curious. It begins like so many other conceptions, in Aristotle. His koinê aisthesis, or 'common perception', was devised to account for those occasions when we perceive, apparently by a simple act, and yet cannot name with confidence the sense with which we perceived. Thus, Aristotle suggested that we perceive, for example, the passage of time by a common operation of all the senses, that is, by koinê aisthesis. This sense drops out of use and is gradually replaced by the modern sense, 'plain, ordinary wisdom, such as is the common possession of mankind'. The idea of community is transferred from the co-operative senses to their human subjects in society. The modern sense can be traced back to the sixteenth century, but it was in the eighteenth century that it became prominent. When a word is thus newly energised it is likely that it carries rather more argumentative force than it does later, when it is a settled element in unreflective discourse. In particular, the implication of 'common' is pressed hard, to the point where it is suggested that the mere agreement of great numbers of people, without corroborative evidence, constitutes an argument of probability (this clearly reflects the common medieval argument *e consensu gentium*). The eighteenth-century 'Philosophy of Common Sense' which arose after Pope's time, notably in the work of Price, Reid and Beattie, went farther and made common agreement the ultimate criterion of truth.

Clearly such thinking implies a kind of respite, a way out of brain-taxing cogitation, and it is no insult to Pope to say that his lines breathe this same air of relief. As Beattie wrote a generation later:

> *Common Sense* hath in modern times been used by philosophers, both French and British, to signify that power of the mind which perceives truth, or commands belief, not by progressive argumen-

tation, but by an instantaneous, instinctive, and irresistible impulse; derived neither from education nor from habit, but from nature.[101]

'Instinctive', 'impulse', 'nature', all the magic words are there. At the same time, the phrase for Pope was probably coloured by the Latin *sensus communis,* which is more heavily moralised than the modern English 'common sense'. It means roughly 'the moral sense, the common tact and discretion of humanity'. This sense was lightened by Lord Shaftesbury (one of Pope's principal sources) in the direction of 'good-humoured sense of community with one's fellow human beings'.[102] Thus though Pope in referring difficulties to common sense really was taking an easy way out, it is not quite the platitudinous non-answer it would be today. The term was philosophically live as it is not now, and still seemed to many of the best minds of the day to promise a genuine resolution of major problems.

Pope now returns to the theme first canvassed in an exceedingly difficult passage in Epistle I, namely:

> 'No ('tis reply'd) the first Almighty Cause
> 'Acts not by partial, but by gen'ral laws;
> 'Th' exceptions few; some change since all began,
> 'And what created perfect?' – Why then Man?
>
> (I, 145–8)

In the present epistle he writes:

> Remember, Man, 'the Universal Cause
> 'Acts not by partial, but by gen'ral laws'. . .
>
> (IV, 35–6)

The inverted commas in the fourth epistle can hardly be intended to remind us of the fact that these words are in the first epistle placed in the mouth of the despised anthropocentrist. We may suppose that the inverted commas merely mark the important aphorism, as at V, 145 (' "Whatever IS is RIGHT" '). In Epistle I the argument was tensely and elliptically *ad hominem.* Pope chose as his imaginary opponent the person who believed that all creation was for the sake of man. When challenged with the obvious unpleasantness to man of earthquakes and plagues Pope's adversary answered that of course there are a *few* exceptions to the General Laws of God; the main lines of the design, however, hold firm. Pope then pounced: if you allow that the design admits occasional exceptions, why should not man be one of them, or, if not man, the occasional individual, a Borgia or a Catiline? As often with *ad hominem* arguments, it was difficult at that point to tell how far the premises used were genuine common ground between the disputants and how far they were chosen merely because they were believed by the opposition and could nevertheless be made to yield a conclusion favourable to Pope's cause. It is possible that when the anthropocentrist says that God acts by general laws with minor exceptions Pope is drawn into agreement. But this implies that God's design does not incorporate all the details but exists in spite of some of them. The design survives, not because of its transcendent assimilation of all elements, but because those things which break the rule are so few as to be virtually unnoticeable. Pope in Epistle I gleefully seized on the concession of exceptions as a way of showing that the anthropocentrist had implicitly allowed for human evil, as an unimportant accidental blemish. But if Pope seriously adopts this as his own solution he has betrayed his own major theodicy in a fundamental way.

Let us consider two conceptions of the Divine Plan. In the first the plan is infinitely intricate, beautiful and good and is beyond our comprehension. Things which to us seem horrific or inexplicable would instantly become acceptable if we could understand how they in truth contribute to the whole design. According to the second conception the Divine Plan extends to broad categories but not to details; not everything that happens is important enough to figure significantly in the whole; on the contrary, certain things may be from God's point of view negligibly small. Thus, the Plan can tolerate minor divagations, which are indeed wholly independent of the divine will, so long as they do not threaten the major structure. Each of these conceptions implies a different God. The first suggests a God who, while incomprehensibly infinite in wisdom and love, is minutely aware of everything that happens; the second suggests a God who is like the general manager of a vast commercial company, too busy to find time for every detail but in firm command of the situation. There is no doubt whatever which of these two conceptions fits the Christian God; it is the first. But Pope, whose awareness of the fundamental distinction between them seems at best infirm, is in real danger of opting for the second.

At first, indeed, he struggles to suggest that individual pleasures always conduce to the larger design:

> There's not a blessing Individuals find,
> But some way leans and hearkens to the kind.
>
> (39–40)

Here his error is simply to supply an *a posteriori* justification of an *a priori* conception. Although by the major theodicy God's plan is incomprehensible, Pope feels that he must *show* how the plan is in fact served by such details as we can observe (*ex hypothesi* such a demonstration is impossible for man, and in that very impossibility lies such strength as the theodicy may possess). For the examples Pope gives are thoroughly sublunary and immediately invite the raising of counter-examples. For example, the individual pleasure of the rapist seems to do nothing for the human race in general.

Pope's adoption, against the taste and bias of the age, of Donne's beautiful phrase from the 'Valediction: forbidding Mourning', 'leanes, and hearkens',[103] is almost poignant in its very inappropriateness. Donne used the phrase to suggest the movement of souls in separate lovers, each towards the other. It would be a fine thing if individual pleasure always showed a like tenderness and inward movement towards the good of the species, but it obviously does not. Of course, much depends on 'always'. Drop that requirement and the thesis at once becomes both interesting and challenging. It is a fact, rightly emphasised by Shaftesbury in the time of Pope and by such psychologists as McDougall and (in a very different way) Suttie in our own century, that a great deal of human pleasure seems to be fundamentally social; going to the theatre alone is both less fun and somehow unnatural.[104] But to allow that not every case is thus is to allow exceptions to the Divine Plan after all, despite the fact that at line 39 Pope seemed to be going for the other options, according to which individual pleasure serves rather than breaks the great scheme of things. Nevertheless, with a last-minute twitch which is very characteristic, Pope plants at the end of his paragraph one of his smooth concessions, intended to complete the survey of relevant facts but really betraying his argument:

Each has his share; and who would more obtain,
Shall find, the pleasure pays not half the pain.

(47–8)

Thus, though some individual pleasures may not contribute to the happiness of the whole, be assured that in such cases the pleasure is succeeded by pain. A 'bright' order of commutual happiness is supplemented where necessary with a darker order of sanctions; both are conceived *a posteriori* and thus the last, swift recovery of order on Pope's part is just as vulnerable to the well-placed counter-example as his first version (what about the happy, well-adjusted thief?).

There are signs in Pope's manuscript that he was aware of these objections. Immediately after line 40 he wrote in the margin:

The strongest, noblest pleasures of the mind
All hold of mutual converse with the kind.
Can sensual lust, or selfish rapine know
Such as from bounty, love or mercy flow?

A little later he adds:

'Tis not in Self it can begin and end
The bliss of one must with another blend.[105]

These lines are an attempt, which is to be made again and again in the history of Utilitarian thought, to moralise hedonist theory by distinguishing 'higher' from 'lower' pleasures. Of course, if one merely asserts that some pleasures are 'nobler' and leaves it at that, one gives up the original thesis, which was that the concept of happiness alone can be made to yield a satisfying ethical system. It is impossible to maintain that one is *nobler* than another, merely because it maximises – pleasure! The criterion which differentiates, qualitatively, one pleasure from another must be something other than pleasure. But in that case there may after all be many other values, such as generosity, truth and so on. To retain the original framework of the system it is necessary to argue, indeed, that the higher pleasures really are, not just nobler, but *more pleasurable* – that they *taste* better. Pope, to his credit, seems to have seen this and in the manuscript lines he makes a good shot at supplying the required material. It is a good deal more convincing than one would, perhaps, have expected. But the old objections are always there: why, if such things are so much more enjoyable, are they not universally practised? Why (in short) the need for exhortation?

At line 49 Pope returns to the theme of the first epistle: the fact of creation itself implies subordination:

> ORDER is Heav'n's first law; and this confest,
> Some are, and must be, greater than the rest. . .

One expects him to infer that, given such a system of subordination, it is inevitable that degrees of happiness should vary. Surely the rapt Seraph is happier than the guilt-ridden tyrant? But Pope rejects the inference out of hand. The idea that the rich or the wise are happier affronts, he says, all common sense. One could with difficulty imagine an ingenious demonstration that the rich are no happier than the rest of us, but it seems extraordinary to assume that the whole demonstration can be by-passed with a brisk appeal to *common sense*. Common sense, indeed, seems to say the exact opposite.

The more exalted, the more moralised Pope's conception of happiness – that is, the more closely it corresponds to the Greek *eudaimon*, 'blessed' – the more implausible his position here. Socrates discontented is still wise and, because of his wisdom, is happier than the pig. The cancelled lines in the manuscript had urged that 'bounty, love' and 'mercy' gave an *extra* happiness. It would be very easy to add wisdom to that list, but by doing so one would at once imply that 'the wise' at all events *are* happier than the rest of us. *Quod non erat demonstrandum.* Meanwhile the contention that the rich and wise get no more (low-grade) pleasures than the rest seems doubtful. But (since common sense is presumably represented by proverbs) it is only fair to add that there is one proverb which works for Pope: 'What's the use of money? It doesn't buy happiness.'

Pope then claims (53–6) that the sum of happiness, equally distributed as it is, is increased as a whole by the energising system of mutual needs. For a second time he chooses to cast his claim in what might be described as the least persuasive form possible:

> Heav'n to Mankind impartial we confess,
> If all are equal in their Happiness. . .
>
> (53–4)

Pope really is an appalling negotiator. He exposes his flank with that
'if' (a large 'if', surely). To assume, as he does, immediate assent is
at least imprudent. The sheer implausibility of the if-clause, together
with the natural tick-tock impetus of the Augustan couplet, almost
begets an answer, before Pope can stop it:

> But, if they vary, then indeed we must
> (Or so it seems) confess that God's unjust.

The quality is less than Popean but my excuse must be, the lines
wrote themselves.

On the doctrine of commutual happiness Mack cites La Bruyère.
Yet it was La Bruyère who recorded the most terrifying of all
descriptions of rural poverty:

> L'on voit certains animaux farouches, des mâles et des femelles,
> répandus par la campagne, noirs, livides, et tout brûlés du soleil,
> attachés à la terre qu' ils fouillent et qu' ils remuent avec une
> opiniâtreté invincible; ils ont comme une voix articulée, et quand
> ils se lèvent sur leur pieds, ils montrent une face humaine, et en
> effet ils sont humains.

> [Scattered about the countryside are to be seen certain wild ani-
> mals, males and females, black, discoloured and all burned by the
> sun, fastened to the earth in which they root and turn over clods
> with an invincible obstinacy; but they seem to be capable of
> articulate speech and when they get to their feet and stand upright
> they show a human face; and in fact they are men.][106]

These words are a judgement on the *Essay on Man*. Pope could never
conceivably have written anything like this himself, although he had
one friend who could.

The *concordia discors* of line 56

> All Nature's diff'rence keeps all Nature's peace

is perhaps plausible, but only as long as we exclude the preposterous
postulate of equal happiness. One could, in Pope's time, argue with
some show of reason that social inequalities ultimately compose a
stable system, with the implication that even the satisfaction of

certain specific wants might threaten the harmony of the whole. The French Revolution had not yet occurred. Even afterwards some found it possible to reconcile the Revolution with Popean theory by alleging that uprisings are caused as much by improvements as by deterioration in the lot of the oppressed.[107] As a bleak, amoral assessment this line might stand. But Pope does not intend it so. His lower ranks are somehow supposed to perceive that the peace so precariously balanced is in their interest, too, and in consequence to feel a happiness as great as that felt by anyone.

In lines 57 to 66 he begins by arguing that, since happiness is independent of its various circumstances and conditions (in line with his earlier exposure of the 'hedonic naturalistic fallacy'), happiness is everywhere the same, and then adds that if all were equally gifted by fortune they would be bound to fight with one another. The first argument shows only that happiness may be, intrinsically, the same kind of thing in all cases, but not that it is always found in the same quantity. The second argument is not much stronger. Though subordinates may be restrained from competing by a sense of the hopelessness of their position (though this seems not to sit very easily with Pope's later claim that they are buoyed up by Hope at line 70), it may be guessed that the very system of subordination may instil a sense of injury, such that, when opportunity comes, they fight the more fiercely. One is reminded of Huxley's *Brave New World* in which even the Epsilons were happy to be as they were.

The claim that the powerful are handicapped by anxiety (obviously *they* have not perceived the strong stability of the commutual system!) while the poor are compensated with a (presumably delusive) hope follows immediately at lines 67 to 72. The comment of Pope's gad-fly, Crousaz, is entirely in order:

By what Means is the *just Balance of Heaven* made *equal*? Is it not because all Men . . . may equally hope for the Approbation of God? No, says this Writer it is because Men are harassed with Fears in Proportion to their Elevation, and amused with Hopes in a State of Poverty and Distress. But Experience will not inform us that these are certain consequences . . . Nor does God, to make the Happiness of Mankind equal, fill the Heart of one with idle Fears, and of the other with chimerical Hopes.[108]

Pope concludes the section with a grand apostrophe and a mocking ironic challenge:

> Oh sons of earth! attempt ye still to rise,
> By mountains pil'd on mountains, to the skies?
> Heav'n still with laughter the vain toil surveys,
> And buries madmen in the heaps they raise.
>
> (73–6)

He has generalised his thesis in a strange manner. One might have expected, after the crushingly conservative social doctrine of the previous lines, some concluding mockery of proletarian or rustic ambition. Instead, Pope suddenly switches back into the theme of presumption, inaugurated in the first epistle, and berates *man* for cosmic discontent. The transition from social harmony to cosmic is merely elided. 'Sons of earth' certainly does not mean rustics, as in common twentieth-century usage. Pope has cleverly employed a term which works both inside and outside his metaphor of the giants who piled Pelion on Ossa in an attempt to reach Heaven. The giants (like the Titans and the Cyclopes) were the progeny of Gaia, Earth (see Hesiod, *Theogony*, 45–52, 139, 207). Pope's source for the story of the piled-up mountains is likely to have been Dryden's translation of Virgil's third Georgic (lines 374–5 of the English, 280–1 in the Latin) and he would doubtless have known the variant version in Horace's *Odes* (III, iv, 52). It is, of course, a mythological commonplace. But at the same time 'sons of earth' is immediately and naturally applicable to human beings, earthbound, sublunary, locked into their proper station in the cosmic hierarchy. Indeed, Pope manages his image with great skill. As the giants of myth are the human beings of reality, so the Zeus or Jupiter of the myth is the God of Milton and the Christian tradition. Here Pope again makes the division between metaphoric and literal sense momentarily transparent by a cunningly placed echo of Milton:

> Heav'n still with laughter the vain toil surveys. . .
>
> (75)

In the twelfth book of *Paradise Lost* the denizens of Heaven look down on the building of the Tower of Babel and, in Milton's words, 'great laughter was in Heav'n' (XII, 59). This curious episode forms part of a larger movement in *Paradise Lost*. The building of Babel in the last book formally echoes the building of Pandemonium in the first (670–730). The link is made explicit by the allusion to Babel at I, 694. The laughter of Heaven at the building of Babel echoes the laughter of God at Satan's desperate enterprise in making war on Heaven (V, 733–4). Thus, the curious *doubleness* of Milton's epic, in which the Fall of Man is a re-enactment of the Fall of Lucifer and his angels, subtly assists the transition in Pope from the primal Giants to the human race. One senses a certain imprudence in Milton's attempt to share in the divine merriment, to appropriate it for his own poetic and theological purposes. Surely from his, human, point of view Satan is a formidable adversary. Or is the laughter an attempt, rooted in secret fear, artificially to minimise the opposition? Certainly Pope's anxiety to replace direct analytic criticism with urbane ridicule sometimes suggests a similarly dubious motivation.

But Pope's mingling of ancient and Christian motifs is undeniably expert. Milton also excelled, it might be said, at this sort of thing: he linked Eve, threatened in the Garden, with Proserpine gathering flowers in Enna (IV, 269) and Lucifer falling from Heaven with the nine-days fall of Mulciber (I, 740). But there is a difference. Milton keeps ancient myth and Christian story utterly distinct, so that a special pathos of inadvertent truth arises from the coincidence of fable with dreadful reality. Pope works instead with a deliberate, brilliant indistinctness. Yet the further implications remain coherent. The suggestion implicit in the borrowing from Milton is that for man to resent his position in the universe is at bottom diabolical. It is what Lucifer did so long ago. This is the force of the admirable 'still': the laughter still rings because the joke is the same joke. The present passage is thus the last important reference to the principal repressed image of the poem, the Fall. In profound accord with the structural logic of the poem, it is translated from a primal event into a current philosophic error. Yet here, surely, it will prove inexpugnable. For even those who claim that evil is an illusion usually claim at the same time that those who oppose them are (in the old-fashioned sense of the term) wrong, and that error is not a good thing.

The laughter in Heaven is the proper correlative of the spectacle of human presumptuousness laid before us in the first epistle. The presumptuousness, of course, no longer consists in an attempt actually to scale the heights of Heaven but in an over-reaching of the mind. It springs from the failure to realise that one can know nothing but oneself. How, then, can Pope (who has excluded Revelation from his poem) know that Heaven laughs?

Pope opens his third section by telling us that, after all, true pleasure inheres in 'Health, Peace, and Competence' (80). Since health and competence (that is, a sufficient income) are manifestly not universally available, Pope's contention that happiness is everywhere equal would seem to be in ruins. He has thrown away the precarious invulnerability he secured by affirming that happiness is independent of visible (checkable) circumstances. Note that the income of the Man of Ross (*Epistle to Bathurst*, 280) is 'five hundred pounds a year' (about £13,000 a year in 1983 terms). This is regarded by Pope as very small (but it is important to remember that it is to be regarded as a basis for a life of public service and charity). Even so, it is so far above the income of the poorest as to embarrass his argument here. As for health, Pope of all men knew that it was not universally available even to the temperate. In this section, clearly, he is anxious to raise the moral tone. That is why he announces that temperance gives health and virtue peace (81–2). Honesty is the best policy. Vice, on the other hand, is a risky business (85–6). People are kind to the good and despise the vicious. What vice would regard as a triumph is despised, as affording a weak degree of happiness, by virtue (89–90). Felicity is not in these lines fused with virtue. The two are not even allies. Virtue is valued as it *serves* felicity. The moral tone is exactly as it was. Pope rounds off his paragraph with the lines

> And grant the bad what happiness they wou'd,
> One they must want, which is, to pass for good.
>
> (91–2)

With the three words, 'to pass for', the entire structure caves in. What they can never attain, presumably, is real, authentic goodness. 'Passing for good', in this corrupt world, lies well within their scope. Is there no such thing as successful hypocrisy?

In lines 93 to 110, Pope turns to face the fact that sometimes the good die before their time:

> See FALKLAND dies, the virtuous and the just!
> See god-like TURENNE prostrate on the dust!
> See SIDNEY bleeds amid the martial strife!
>
> (99–101)

Pope's strategy is to choose examples which in no way diminish our sense of tragic loss but, rather, invest it with a saving glory. Falkland, once the centre of a brilliant circle at Great Tew, died for the king at the battle of Newbury in 1643. Clarendon describes him, with unusual tenderness, as small in stature and weakly, yet with an 'inimitable sweetness' so that he was loved by all.[109] Turenne, similarly, was weak in body but strong in courage. He, too, was a royalist and died as a result of one of the first shots fired at Sassbach in the summer of 1675. Sir Philip Sidney, who died of wounds at Zutphen in 1586, is still the example everyone gives of the ideal Elizabethan gentleman made flesh. C. S. Lewis wrote of him: 'Even at this distance, Sidney is dazzling'.[110] The list, it will be said, was evidently made by a Tory. But the examples are strong enough to transcend party. When Turenne died his body was taken to St Denis and buried with the kings of France. In 1793, when the bones of the kings were scattered, the revolutionists respected the bones of Turenne and preserved them in the Jardin des Plantes, whence they were removed in 1800, by order of Napoleon, to the Invalides.

Each of these examples is answered by an example of virtue sustained through long life, Digby, Belsunce and Mrs Pope. Though Robert Digby died in 1726, his father, the fifth Lord Digby, lived on to die at last eighteen years after the publication of the fourth epistle of the *Essay on Man*, in 1752. Belsunce, the Bishop of Marseilles, worked indefatigably among the sick and dying in the plague of 1720 but survived. And Pope's mother lived to be 91. The point of these counter-examples is not to match the others statistically, to suggest that despite some aberrations virtue is normally rewarded with long life. Rather, Pope is saying that long life and short are equally possible and, whichever end is given, it will prove to have been brought about not by virtue but by something else. Falkland, Turenne and Sidney were killed not by virtue but by war.

Pope, it might be said, has simply substituted ordinary causality for the divine *moral* ordering of things; the common suggestion was never that virtue should *automatically* produce happiness, but that an all-good, all-powerful God should ensure by special providence that goodness is rewarded with happiness. Moreover, the connection with lines 85–8, where Pope spoke of the risks attendant on vice and the warm approbation which follows virtue, is far from easy. There the most natural interpretation seemed to be that virtue does indeed cause happiness, not by special divine contrivance but by the simple operation of cause and effect. This, however, is merely contradicted by the heroic deaths of lines 99 to 101. There we are told that natural causes will produce their effects independently of virtue and vice. Pope wishes to say that virtue brings happiness, notices in mid-course that sometimes it does not, and forthwith revises his scheme in such a way as to make nonsense of his earlier demonstration. The most obvious way to resolve the difficulty is to locate the reward of virtue in an afterlife, but, as we have seen, Pope (perhaps influenced by Bolingbroke) was not willing to do this. One sees the idea straining for admission at line 109 and, more important, at lines 173–4:

> Weak, foolish man! will Heav'n reward us there
> With the same trash mad mortals wish for here?

But in these lines the point is not that the manifestly unjust distribution of happiness in this world will be corrected in the next, but only that the proper reward of virtue is inherently spiritual, immaterial in nature.

Pope's reaction to a creaking argument is, again and again, that of the expert rhetorician rather than of the philosopher. He is aware of an urgent need to pull out of the hat some formula, reflecting all the tensions but with a tone of reconciliation, to turn incipient contradiction into a pleasing *discordia concors*. In the present passage he contrives a 'saving' effect by suddenly moving laterally; the third-person mode, in which truths are paraded in profile, is beautifully modulated to the face-to-face mode of the first person singular at lines 109–10:

> Or why so long (in life if long can be)
> Lent Heav'n a parent to the poor and me?

The pellucid monosyllables impose a stillness on the whole poem, and few readers are unmoved. The couplet is for Pope unusually simple, yet it seems to be disturbed by a sort of gesturing of the mind towards the idea of immortality, in the barely formulated parenthesis, 'in life if long can be'. The telescopic phrasing of 'to the poor and me' creates a subaudition of a self-pitying 'poor me', but this is kept at the right distance, both by the plain sense of the sentence and by the rising note of interrogation at the end. Pope has used the device of modulation away from the third person before, at line 17:

And fled from Monarchs, ST. JOHN! dwells with thee.

But this time a sense of the reality referred to is less subversive of the sentiment.

But Pope knows that the beast cannot be kept quiet for long with means like this. In lines 111 to 116 he turns and faces, yet again, the fact of evil:

> What makes all physical or moral ill?
> There deviates Nature, and here wanders Will.
> God sends not ill; if rightly understood,
> Or partial Ill is universal Good,
> Or Change admits, or Nature lets it fall,
> Short and but rare, 'till Man improv'd it all.

Metre is faithfully preserved, but the thought stammers woefully. His first answer is to ascribe physical ills to the 'deviation' of nature and moral evils to man's free will. This is the old Miltonic scheme strangely extended so that the Fall of Nature is now not mysteriously entailed in the Fall of Man but is somehow analogous to it, and carries a like burden of explanation. Why did Adam fall? Because he chose to do wrong and so deviated from the will of God. And how did Nature fall? It, too, 'deviated'. But it could deviate from the will of God only if it had in some sense a will of its own. Physical evil is the Primal Sin committed by *Nature*. In 'accounting for' or 'accommodating' the real existence, after all, of evil, Pope has simply inverted his previous scheme. If both man and nature deviate from the will of God, one can very nearly say, 'Whatever is, is wrong'. Yet, at line 114, Pope suddenly swings back to his basic doctrine, 'partial Ill is universal Good'. So, after all, it *is* God's will, and Nature and Man have not deviated? Well, perhaps, says Pope, now thoroughly confused. Or perhaps not. Because Chance may be the villain of the piece (he has entirely forgotten his assertion at I, 290, that all chance is direction) or else (switching back again to his first, bad shot) Nature starts the damage in a minor way and Man merely completes the disastrous masterpiece. The idea of a deviating nature, previously ascribed by Pope to the despised anthropocentrist, who was absurdly thrown by the fact that the world did not always serve his needs, who could not understand that what conflicts with the will of man may nevertheless be in profound accord with the will of God, is now seriously advanced, abruptly withdrawn, and then advanced again as an *explanation* of the fact of physical evil. When such argument is put to explain moral evil, it has at least a little force by virtue of one's awareness that the will is a fluctuating and capricious thing. But we have no such corroborative sense in the case of nature. Indeed, the bias of the whole poem has lain in the other direction. Pope has defined the stable goodness of nature and instinct by stressing the way both are exempt from human folly.

But then Pope settles to the idea that God's purposes are so vast that it is absurd of man to complain, for example, about the way that certain diseases, incurred by the vicious, are then passed on to the virtuous. It is easy to mistake this for the full doctrine that apparent ills really serve a purpose in the inscrutable plan of God. That doctrine, however, asserts *de fide* that there are no accidental oversights or minor deviations from the main design, but that on the contrary all things are divinely governed; at the same time it places the grand design itself firmly outside human comprehension. Doubtless the 'laws' of Newtonian physics are parts of the divine plan, but they, too, are mere details; we should not imagine that in comprehending them we are in any sense comprehending the essence of God's scheme. But Pope falls precisely into this trap. The design of God is naturalistically identified with the laws of nature, as investigated by the scientist. Landslips and avalanches are simple illustrations of the law of gravity, which can hardly be suspended because Bolingbroke happens to be passing below (IV, 127–8). The point is a little more obscure in the case of the asthma which troubled Pope's poor friend Bethel (IV, 126) but presumably it is the same: physical laws operating in certain conditions inevitably produce asthma. The laws of physics may be ineluctable for man but they are not so for God. He has deliberately chosen a scheme which he knew would result in such locally unhappy consequences.

Pope implies that God loves physical law more than human beings. We are not now confronted with the embarrassment of trivial 'exceptions' to the divine plan, for all physical events (setting aside miracles) really do conform to the laws of physics. Pope suggests in lines 121–2 that to ask for a different dispensation is to treat God as if he were a weak prince, who could be flattered into favouritism. The analogy suggests the deflection of justice from its proper, moral application. But a God who loves the law of gravity more than he loves a good man is no figure of justice, austerely avoiding favouritism. The good man is *ex hypothesi* deserving. Meanwhile the law of gravity has no moral content at all. The petitioner in such a case is not so much attempting to corrupt the moral nature of God as striving to introduce him to the mere existence of morality.

Pope in this part of the *Essay* is like a dazed boxer. The spectacle is in a manner touching. For it is his honesty which will not let him rest. Again and again he returns to the recalcitrant matter which a more prudent poet might have preferred to repress. Thus, at line 135 he succinctly states the major objection:

> The good must merit God's peculiar care. . .

He answers, there is no sure way to know who the good are. If that is the *only* answer, the way is now clear: we can conclude *a posteriori* that the manifestly happy are the truly good (supposing that rewards after death are left out of the case); the virtue which earns the reward is not accessible to our inspection, but the reward is plain to see and the virtue may thus be inferred where it cannot be seen! If, on the other hand, happiness, like virtue, is not perfectly visible to us, both are visible to God. This might yield a strained but consistent account: those who are good really are rewarded by God but none of it shows. The strain lies in the curiously complete privacy of the entire argument. If both goodness and happiness are so inaccessible, one begins to wonder how it is that we employ the terms at all in public language, and ascribe the states to our fellow-creatures. Pope does what he can to weaken the cultural basis of moral terms in lines 137 to 144. Some think Calvin a saint, some think him a devil, some are theists, some are not. This, it might be said, is evenhandedness gone mad. Pope's antithetical relativism ends by placing the atheist level with the theist. If such fundamental beliefs are themselves mere 'mad Opinion' (IV, 29), why should we trust any sort of theodicy? If God is thus, and man is thus, why should theology exist at all? How could we even venture the negative proposition, 'God is inscrutable'?

As the fifth section of the epistle comes to an end (lines 149 to 166) Pope's tone becomes almost testy. He treats the complaint that virtue sometimes starves while vice is fed as if it were some querulous importuning by a self-interested petitioner. His immediate, epigrammatic answer is that the proper reward of virtue is hardly likely to be anything so grossly material as food. But doubtless, he continues, you (who would have the virtuous rewarded with wealth) would not stop there; you would be baying for health and power, and these demands in their turn would escalate (the language of twentieth-century negotiation is oddly appropriate) until the final stage is reached, the virtuous man must be a god and earth must be heaven. This passage is ill-judged for two very different reasons. First, the very reasonable complaint of Pope's imaginary opponent is grossly caricatured – so grossly that there seems to be a note of hysteria in its mounting absurdity. One wishes to pluck Pope by the sleeve and calm him, somehow, by explaining that one is asking nothing for oneself but only that the truly good should be granted an appropriate measure of ordinary happiness ('good, pleasure, ease, content'); it is simply untrue that anyone who is shocked by the spectacle of a good man starving thereby proves himself a crass materialist, interested in nothing but food and money. Even granting – to play Pope's strangely technical game for a moment – that the proper pleasure of virtue is inward peace, could not starvation conceivably interfere with that very peace? The second reason why the passage is ill-judged lies in the wholly inadvertent snub it gives to traditional Christianity. The Church may not teach that the virtuous become gods, but it does teach that they are exalted in glory and their earth becomes heaven. The opinion Pope shrilly denounces as excessive is held, it would seem, by God himself.

Maynard Mack cites at this point a eudaemonist passage from the *Nicomachean Ethics* (1100*b*) where Aristotle takes the extreme position that virtuous activity itself *constitutes* happiness. This is the tightest possible version of 'Virtue is its own reward'. So radical a view cannot but modify the meaning of terms. In fact the English word 'happiness' will scarcely stretch so far, though 'blessedness' might. Pope is better understood as following the Stoic view that virtue *produces* a distinct happiness, consisting in a special stability of mind, peace and harmony. In the sixth section, beginning at line 167, Pope presses this conception hard:

> What nothing earthly gives, or can destroy,
> The soul's calm sun-shine, and the heart-felt joy,
> Is Virtue's prize: A better would you fix?
> Then give Humility a coach and six. . .

Is this true? Between Pope and the modern reader stands the austere figure of Kant, with his insistence on the independence of moral action from any extra-moral inducement: an act to be moral must be performed in obedience to the moral law and for no other reason. But none of this need imply that virtuous people need not be – in fact – happy. All that is required is that they should not have performed their acts of virtue for the sake of that happiness. Thus, the question 'Does virtue give happiness?', which seemed so natural in the eighteenth century, may be allowed to stand. The difficulty is to answer it. If I carry out the mildly distasteful task of looking at the people I happen to know and singling out the ones which seem to me the most virtuous, I find (to my own slight surprise) that they do in fact seem a little happier than the rest. One might then seek to account for this connection by assuming that a constitution which produces, say, a constant kindliness is unlikely to be subject to violent disturbance, to dark terrors or irrational depression. But this argument draws what little plausibility it has from the initial choice of *constant* kindliness: naturally, constancy in one quarter may imply constancy in another. This is a very Stoic conception of virtue, and it may well have been Pope's. But there are other kinds of virtue – truthfulness, say, or heroism – which co-exist quite readily with profound unhappiness. One suspects that Pope (or Shaftesbury) would urge that self-congratulation might properly attend on these, but here the obvious strictures of Kant are surely entirely in order: such self-congratulation implicitly erodes the moral purity of the act.

Pope's brief account, in lines 170–1, of Humility in her ostentatious coach and Justice with the conqueror's sword is a neat eighteenth-century allegory of crossed lines (like a Hogarth picture). But Pope's does not sustain the incongruity, when he comes to 'or Truth a gown' (for the gown, whether academic or the Lord Chancellor's as is suggested by the manuscript version,[111] is formally appropriate to Truth). Perhaps he really intended his reader to register a joke within the joke – to be arrested by the apparent tame propriety of the image and then released once more as he realises that this is quite as incongruous as the rest – but it is hard to be confident that Pope is so subtle here. The reader is given none of the usual signals from punctuation and metrical emphasis. The immediately following reference to crowned Public Spirit is almost certainly a satirical allusion to George II, who abandoned Pope's faction when he ascended the throne.

Pope's normal mode of argument is that natural to a satirist. He presents the position of his opponent as grotesquely absurd. It is a way of proceeding which is rarely serviceable in serious philosophical argument, which commonly does not address the manifestly absurd but instead assumes the more difficult task of refuting, by careful demonstration, some really plausible error. Certainly Pope's contemptuous manner (stylistically the exact opposite of Bishop Butler's unfailing intellectual courtesy) seems thin and strained in this part of the poem. At line 189 he writes:

> Oh fool! to think God hates the worthy mind,
> The lover and the love of human-kind,
> Whose life is healthful, and whose conscience clear;
> Because he wants a thousand pounds a year.

This is mere bluster, pathetically open to a cool counter-attack: 'But what about the good man from whom both competence and health are withheld?' Pope began by engaging to justify starving virtue (149) and is reduced to justifying the fact that the virtuous sometimes have less than a thousand a year!

Difference of wealth, Pope tells us, is in any case superficial. The clothes may differ but the wearer, fundamentally, does not. Line 196

> One flaunts in rags, one flutters in brocade

puzzled Dr Johnson, who thought the verbs should be transposed (EC, II, 413) since rags flutter, while stiff brocade may properly be flaunted by the proud. Warburton defended Pope's phrasing by observing that 'the pride of heart is the same in both the flaunter and the flutterer, as it is the poet's intention to insinuate by the use of those terms' (EC, II, 491). This takes us some way towards a better reading but is insufficiently analytic. The line is in fact an example of Pope's use of levelling antithesis, but the antithesis is so faint as to be unnoticeable to some and an unintelligible minor irritant to others (such as Johnson). Pope has deliberately transposed the verbs in order to show that even the beggar in rags may flaunt and even the brocaded gentleman may flutter gaily. The second half of the line, admittedly, fails to supply a satisfyingly pointed and symmetrical contrast. But Johnson's implied revision immediately removes the peculiar Popean life. It is a subtler, less culpable version of the notorious (apocryphal?) revision of Shakespeare's

> Sermons in stones, books in the running brooks

to

> Sermons in books, stones in the running brooks.

Pope is now back on course with the theme, so fitted to his genius, of human folly and outward show. One can sense a sudden access of good spirits in the tongue-twisting, slightly 'dotty' ingenuity of line 204:

> The rest is all but leather or prunella.

The 'Irish' rhyme of 'race' with 'Lucrece' at 207–8 again suggests verve, and the jangling allusion to 'kings, or whores of kings' at 206 evokes the profligate age of Charles II and all those portraits of delicious royal mistresses, already darkening with age. At line 217, Pope turns to scourge 'Greatness'. 'Greatness', like 'happiness', is a term which may be more or less moralised. Earlier uses of the word tend to be restricted to external power. Shakespeare's 'Some are born great, some achieve greatness, and some have greatness thrust upon them' (*Twelfth Night*, II, v, 132–3) almost certainly refers throughout to exalted rank rather than to nobility of mind, for all that moralising schoolteachers may use it as a hortatory text. In Chapman's Jacobean essay in Stoic tragedy, *Bussy D'Ambois*, one can see the term in transition. When Bussy says

> Show me a Great Man (by the people's voice,
> Which is the voice of God) that by his greatness
> Bombasts his private roofs with public riches[112]
>   (III, ii, 25–7)

he is using the word in its old sense, but the heroic egotism of III, ii, 75, marks a crisis in the semantic history of the term:

> His greatness is the people's, mine's mine own[113]

By the end of the play we find 'great mind' used in a fully moral-ised sense (V, iii, 71).[114] In Chapman the old sense is the natural object of satire, the new of an excited admiration. One might have expected that Pope, even as late as the 1730s, might have followed a

similar course, continuing his scorn of crowns and titles with a diatribe on the empty greatness of high office. The conclusion then
virtually writes itself: *true* greatness lies in valour and wisdom.

But this is not what Pope does. It is as if the mere impetus of
tradition carries him into an attack on 'greatness', but as soon as the
term itself enters his verse he slips, and accepts the modern sense
where he should have stuck, for a time, to the old. As it is, he
suddenly finds himself obliged to maintain his satire against real
warriors and sages. But he deals with the difficulty smoothly
enough; the warriors (Alexander the Great and Charles XII of
Sweden) he satirises for want of wisdom, and the wise for want of
courage. One begins to feel that as in Pope's metaphysic one cannot
lose (for whatever is, is right) so in Pope's satire one cannot win. But
at line 233 we find the conclusion we originally predicted:

> Who noble ends by noble means obtains,
> Or failing, smiles in exile or in chains,
> Like good Aurelius let him reign, or bleed
> Like Socrates, that Man is great indeed.

So greatness does after all lie in wisdom. The despised interlocutor
was perfectly correct at 218. But it is ill-natured to complain when
the writing is so marvellously polished. There is the ghost of a
zeugma in line 234, 'smiles in exile or in chains' (compare 'Dost
sometimes Counsel take – and sometimes *Tea*': *Rape of the Lock*, III,
8). The effect of this is exceedingly subtle. By making the iron
chains co-ordinate with the abstract condition of exile Pope contrives
an imaginative correlative to Stoic fortitude, which by contemning
the world renders all its trivial discomforts equally unreal. In the
second couplet the chiastic arrangement (ABBA, Aurelius–reign,
bleed–Socrates) for once rocks the punctuation *against* the line but
terminates in the satisfying end-stopping of line 236. The effect of
this, however, is marred by the fact that Socrates, notoriously, died
by drinking hemlock. It is odd that Pope in this ostentatiously classical, un-Christian list (no saints, no martyrs) should make so elementary a mistake. He could have substituted 'Seneca' for 'Socrates'
without violence to either sense or metre.

The following section on the vanity of fame is similarly threatened
by 'higher' senses of the term Pope seeks to disparage. At 241–2 he
observes that we *feel* the effects of fame only in the small circle

of our immediate acquaintance. It is easy to imagine the poet who celebrated the widening circles of self-love expatiating (were he in a somewhat different mood) on the way a shining reputation can gradually spread outwards from the centre and quicken noble emulation in generations yet unborn. He does no such thing, but the examples he gives (Cicero, Caesar and Prince Eugene of Savoy) remain obstinately impressive figures.

Line 247

> A Wit's a feather, and a Chief a rod

is explained by the commentators as referring to the quill pen of the thinker and the rod of the ruler (compare the *fasces* or 'rods' of Roman authority, from which we derive the word 'fascist'). These emblematic instruments are then, with extreme ingenuity, turned upon their possessors. Metonymy, under our eyes, shifts and changes into satiric metaphor. By calling the pen a 'feather' Pope obtains the sense 'light thing' and can insinuate triviality. The second half of the line is less witty, since Pope does not bring out two senses for 'rod' as he did for 'feather'; the meaning is simply that the tyrant is the scourge of his people, but Pope can perhaps assume that symmetry is satisfied by an antithetical subaudition of 'heaviness' in the idea of the rod, given that 'feather' has just been mentioned.

He rounds off his paragraph on fame with the lines:

> All fame is foreign, but of true desert,
> Plays round the head, but comes not to the heart:
> One self-approving hour whole years out-weighs
> Of stupid starers, and of loud huzzas;
> And more true joy Marcellus exil'd feels,
> Than Cæsar with a senate at his heels.
>
> (253–8)

The first line is elliptical and may be expanded, by way of a gloss, to 'All fame is foreign, but that which comes from true desert'. By 'foreign' Pope probably means 'alien', that is, not truly the property of the subject. This term then covers two conceptions properly distinct; first, that a reputation honestly earned truly belongs to the earner, and, secondly, that because it is truly his it is felt by him as other kinds of reputation are not. The second conception is assumed to follow from the first, but in fact it does not. Undeserved 'loud huzzas' may be vividly felt and enjoyed by the recipient, and a modest man may, conversely, be wholly unconscious of his own high desert. But the poet of rational self-love prefers to present another picture: the just man who rejoices in his own justice. You cannot beat, says Pope, well-grounded complacency. Once more, the satirical side is more persuasive than the unironic 'positive' side. The phrase 'at his heels' at line 258 deftly transforms the Roman Senate into a pack of dogs.

Nevertheless, at line 262, Pope grants that the wise man will be aware of his faults. The concession is there, but is lightly stated. The impression is given that the faults are a minor feature of the general picture. The wise man is 'above life's weakness' (268) in lonely eminence. It is odd to reflect how recently Calvin had dominated the mind of England with a conception of human nature as diabolically, totally depraved. Here it is as if Calvin had never been.

In lines 269 to 308, Pope reverts to his usual mode, which is to 'see through' the apparently splendid, to detect the latent absurdity. The entire poem, we now must realise, is an oscillation between this manner and its opposite, a converse bland refusal to see anything but bliss, where the meanest intelligence can perceive a mixed condition. The second posture is dictated (or so Pope believed) by the programmatic theodicy; the second is admissible when not the works of God but the thoughts of men are the matter of his verse. The satiric mode relieves and quickens the poetry. 'Sir Billy' in line 278 is probably the Whig, Sir William Yonge, Walpole's garrulous, aimiable party worker. 'Lord Umbra', on the other hand, is indistinct, faceless ('Sir Shadow'), though the noble title gives the spectre a strutting presence in the verse. Bacon is transfixed in the famous line

> The wisest, brightest, meanest of mankind. . .
>
> (282)

Bacon, philosopher, essayist and Lord Chancellor of England, was brought down in 1621, when a certain Christopher Aubrey, followed by Edward Egerton and Lady Wharton, laid charges against him of receiving money from litigants while suits were pending. Bacon could show that he had ruled against those who had paid him but could not wipe out the fact that he had accepted the gifts. The Great Seal was taken from him, he was fined forty thousand pounds and sent to the Tower. Soon afterwards the king found means to relieve

him, but Bacon's political career was ruined. Maynard Mack gives
what is almost certainly the direct source of Pope's line, a passage
from the leader in *The London Journal* for 1 July 1732:

> What is call'd Learning . . . is not at all necessary to form a *Great
> Man*: He may be *Great* without any of [the arts and sciences], and
> *Mean* with them all. Lord Bacon, tho' *cover'd with Learning*, so
> cover'd that his *Sense* could not many times be seen thro' it, was
> one of the *meanest* Men in the World; *vicious* in Prosperity, and an
> *abject Coward* in Adversity. (MM, 155)

Although Bacon's fault was receiving bribes, it is most unlikely that
'mean' in Pope's line has the modern sense 'niggardly'; rather, the
sense is more general, 'ignoble', 'small-minded', forming an exact
antithesis to the assertion of Bacon's great intellectual powers. Pope
has deliberately contrived an insult which is so exactly co-extensive
with the preceding praise as to look for a moment like a contradiction, but then it succeeds as the reader acknowledges the difference
between mere intelligence and true greatness of mind. All the raw
materials of Pope's line are there in *The London Journal*, but the
management of them is Pope's alone. The superlatives seem at first
to ascend; 'brightest' is more dazzling than 'wisest', but it also contains an implication of insubstantiality, and so the sudden descent to
'meanest' is subliminally pre-echoed in the line.

Lines 289–90 are a minor miracle of Latinate compression:

> In hearts of Kings, or arms of Queens who lay,
> How happy! those to ruin, these betray. . .

The reference is to men like Marlborough, who insinuated himself
into the favour of the king and carried on an intrigue with the king's
mistress, the Duchess of Cleveland (no queen, but near enough for
Pope's loose purpose), in due course ruining the former and betraying the latter. Pope forces the English pronouns 'those' and 'these' to
behave like the Latin *illos . . . has*, but where the Latin genders
automatically highlight the sex of either party the English is less
helpful and the reader is in consequence made to work harder.

Much less successful is the simile comparing the elevation of the
falsely great with the rise of Venice:

> Mark by what wretched steps their glory grows,
> From dirt and sea-weed as proud Venice rose. . .
>
> (291–2)

One is tempted to borrow the language applied by Macaulay to the wretched Montgomery. Montgomery had written:

> The soul, aspiring, pants its source to mount,
> As streams meander level with their fount.

Macaulay commented: 'In the first place, no stream meanders, or can possibly meander, level with its fount. In the next place, if streams did meander level with their fount, no two motions can be less like than that of meandering level and that of mounting upwards.'[115] Pope's simile, in like manner, gives a sense opposite to that needed. Venice rose from mud to gorgeous splendour, but Pope's exemplary figures plunged deeper in the mud of corruption as their greatness increased. Venice is a fine image for Pope's purpose in so far as it combines vividly the ideas of slime and opulence, but the temporal ordering of those ideas turns out to be fundamentally inapposite.

But the section ends superbly:

> What greater bliss attends their close of life?
> Some greedy minion, or imperious wife,
> The trophy'd arches, story'd halls invade,
> And haunt their slumbers in the pompous shade.
> Alas! not dazzled with their noon-tide ray,
> Compute the morn and ev'ning to the day;
> The whole amount of that enormous fame,
> A Tale, that blends their glory with their shame!
>
> (301–8)

The lines move from darkening architectural magnificence to shadows and nightmares; the threatening figures of wife and minion persist in the dreams of the person lying on the death-bed. The strongly placed word 'Tale' in line 308 is perhaps a remote echo of Shakespeare's 'tale/Told by an idiot, full of sound and fury,/Signifying nothing' (*Macbeth*, V, v, 26–8).

The seventh section (309 to the end) is essentially a recycling of the idea that the greatest happiness lies in virtue (where virtue is identified with benevolence). Once more the image of the Fall of Man recedes from the poem, though it may be touched on in line 312, where we are told that the virtuous man 'tastes the good without the fall to ill'. But the idea has shrunk almost to vanishing-point. The Universal Fall of Man has here become the ordinary observable tendency in most of us to occasional lapses, and from these the virtuous man is in any case free. At 315–16, Pope says that benevolence enjoys its triumphs but feels no pain at its losses. The picture of a personality so securely defended is not wholly attractive, but Pope may have felt that he was stating an important truth. His letter to Bethel of 24 June 1727 registers the difficulties; works of benevolence, he says, 'often afford the highest pleasure . . . At the same time it must be own'd, one meets with cruel disappointment in seeing so often the best endeavours ineffectual to make others happy . . . But still, I affirm, those very disappointments of a virtuous man are greater pleasures than the utmost gratifications and successes of a mere self-lover' (*Corr.*, II, 437). The closing, unguarded contrast between virtue and self-love we have already discussed (p. 89, above). The difference in kind between the satisfaction afforded, even in adversity, by a quiet conscience and the fierce pleasure of the voluptuary is so great that one almost feels that the two cannot be brought together under the same term, 'happiness'. Pope, it might be guessed, is more truly moral, less hedonistic than his philosophic scheme suggests, for here surely he must mean that it is better (that is, *ethically* better) to be disappointed in a just enterprise than gratified in some merely sensual pursuit. In fact, however, the comparative terms in which Pope presents his case make it clear that this is not what he means. He really is saying that actual failure in a moral enterprise is attended by a kind of happiness which is inherently better *as happiness* than anything experienced by the immoral man. One senses that, if this is true, it is a truth which it would be better to leave unsaid. For, by an ethical equivalent of Heisenberg's celebrated principle, one cannot bring such things into the full light of consciousness without altering their nature and destroying the proper context of innocence. The good man who is too explicitly aware of this mode of felicity is so far the less good. Meanwhile the very sharpness of his ordinary disappointment when he fails in some benevolent attempt is itself a symptom of pure altruism.

Pope himself senses the difficulty and trusts to the very Augustan notion of equilibrium to carry him between Scylla (the hollowness of

merely egoistic 'virtue') and Charybdis (virtue fatally separated from
its proper felicity):

> Never elated, while one man's oppress'd;
> Never dejected, while another's bless'd. . .
>
> (323–4)

Taken as it stands, the couplet seems to concede that the good man is
ipso facto neither happy nor unhappy. But Pope likes to have his cake
and eat it. The seemingly even balance of the two conceptions is
covertly rigged, since it is possible to view elation as a rather peculiar, inherently unstable, dangerously hysterical mode of happiness.
In that case the virtuous man is still winning, after all. The man
described, notice, is entirely altruistic. But the reader persuaded to
virtue by Pope's analysis of the attendant happiness could never, for
that very reason, be as purely altruistic as the man Pope describes.
Pope's inference from the seeming equilibrium of lines 323–4 is that
such a man can have no wishes (except the wish for more virtue, and
this wish, because it is in itself meritorious, is automatically self-
gratifying). This inference is mistaken. Varying the terms of Pope's
antithesis inversely we might infer that such a person might be elated
when oppression was lifted from another and dejected when another
was not blessed. In either version, one term of the antithesis supplies
a situation in which the virtuous man would wish things different.

In lines 327 to 330, Pope says that happiness must be greater for
the good than for the bad. This just inequality of distribution might be
held to conflict with the picture given in Epistle II, 261 ff., and even
with lines 69 to 70 of the present epistle. In order to be able to affirm
that the drunken beggar and the learned sage were equally happy,
Pope was constrained to cast his net wide, to include every sort of
gratification, however absurd, in his democracy of pleasures. But
now that moral distinctions have at last broken in he isolates the
'higher' happiness of virtue and so far prefers it that he is almost able
to affirm that the good alone are truly happy. Of course, he can still
say that this exalted happiness is in principle available to everyone.
But that is quite a different doctrine from the one advanced in the
second epistle. His best course might have been to divide pleasure
from happiness as sharply as he could; God in His goodness gives
pleasure to all, and in His justice reserves the highest happiness for
the virtuous.

At line 330, Pope begins to gather together the threads of the whole poem. The good man is he who apprehends and loves the great design set forth in the first epistle. As self-love became social, so now, through understanding of the great chain of being, social love may terminate in love of God (340). Pope turns to the scriptural virtues, faith, hope and charity, but the original clear supernatural reference of these is oddly muffled by some (Bolingbrokian?) impediment. Hope as before seems to issue in vacancy. Faith pours its bliss and fills the mind, but it is 'Faith in bliss unknown' (344–6). Pope understands how *Nature* has planted hope in man; Nature, we are thus told, makes none of her promises in vain (a curious weakening of the ancient *Natura nil agit frustra*) and so we may trust the hope she gives. The theological order of corroboration is very strange. Instead of hope grounded in God we have religious hope somehow guaranteed by, of all things, Nature. Pope has, perhaps injudiciously, endowed the central absurdity of *a posteriori* theology with imaginative life. Lines 349 to 352 are indeed strange. Quoted separately they sound like a traditionally Christian statement of heavenly rewards:

> Wise is her present; she connects in this
> His greatest Virtue with his greatest Bliss,
> At once his own bright prospect to be blest,
> And strongest motive to assist the rest.

But the 'she' of line 352 is Nature. Therefore the 'greatest Bliss' of the next line is not, as we might suppose, Heaven, but earthly happiness which, in line with the argument of the whole epistle, is bound up with earthly virtue. The rhetorical need for a crescendo gives us the high religious language, but the radical meaning of the passage confines that high language to a merely natural frame of reference.

Pope knows that somehow he must raise the moral tone. Predictably he does it by shifting to what we have called 'tight eudaemonism', that is, to the Greek conception that virtue does not *produce* but, rather, *constitutes* happiness (so that happiness can no longer figure as a mercenary motive to virtue). We have seen enough to know by now that if he pushes this idea too hard he will lose his former argument, since 'happiness' so defined is rather blessedness, wholly absorbed by the ethical. Pope asks imperiously whether 'to make thy neighbour's blessing thine' is 'too little for the boundless heart?' (354–5). A stony, unconvinced reader might answer testily: 'Not too *unimportant*, but why should I pretend that it is *pleasurable*?'

The epistle draws towards its end with the curious and beautiful image of the diminishing circles of God's love meeting and crossing, in mutual delight, the widening circles of man's love:

> God loves from Whole to Parts: but human soul
> Must rise from Individual to the Whole.
> Self-love but serves the virtuous mind to wake,
> As the small pebble stirs the peaceful lake;
> The centre mov'd, a circle strait succeeds,
> Another still, and still another spreads,
> Friend, parent, neighbour, first it will embrace,
> His country next, and next all human race,
> Wide and more wide, th' o'erflowings of the mind
> Take ev'ry creature in, of ev'ry kind;
> Earth smiles around, with boundless bounty blest,
> And Heav'n beholds its image in his breast.
>
>   (361–72)

God loves the whole before he loves the individual (line 361). Here one is tempted to observe, unhelpfully, that his clear preference for an unimpeded law of gravity over the interests of the individual crushed by the landslide (IV, 127–8) strongly suggests that God's love has not yet attained its full development but is arrested at the immature stage of generality. Once more the Augustan love of balance produces, subliminally, strange consequences. The very style makes the condition of God balance rather than enclose the condition of man, and the very imperfections of the lower half of the antithesis are reflected in the upper. To us, born after the Romantics, the terms of the antithesis may actually begin to work against God. If one party loves individuals but not the whole (oddly enough, precisely Swift's attitude to the human species), and another party loves the whole but not the individual, which is the more advanced morally? The disquiet is faint, and swiftly abolished by Pope's triumphant imagery of completed movements, but it is not wholly unauthorised, all the same, by the poem which has preceded it. Moreover, circles as they spread on water grow gradually weaker. Crabbe cleverly exploited this when he turned Pope's image against the whole Augustan theory of rational benevolence, in his description of the Laodicean vicar of the Borough:

> Though mild benevolence our priest possess'd,
> 'Twas but by wishes or by words express'd:
> Circles in water, as they wider flow,
> The less conspicuous in their progress grow;
> And when at last they touch upon the shore,
> Distinction ceases, and they're view'd no more.
> His love, like that last circle, all embrac'd,
> But with effect that never could be trac'd.[116]

But the closing of Pope's comparison, in which the pool where the circles spread becomes the earthly mirror in which Heaven may see its own face, even to the momentary overlapping of the image of the mirror with the image of God's breast at line 372, is filled and overflowing with imaginative life. The sky is reflected in the pool; the earth is the breast of God; to speak so of God is to bring him, with infinite tact, closer to Nature. In this way (almost too late) Pope the poet begins to heal the philosophic wounds inflicted earlier. Augustan poets are not supposed to be capable of this sort of thing, but Pope does it.

At line 373 he apostrophises Bolingbroke:

> Come then, my Friend, my Genius, come along,
> Oh master of the poet, and the song!
> And while the Muse now stoops, or now ascends,
> To Man's low passions, or their glorious ends,
> Teach me, like thee, in various nature wise,
> To fall with dignity, with temper rise;
> Form'd by thy converse, happily to steer
> From grave to gay, from lively to severe;
> Correct with spirit, eloquent with ease,
> Intent to reason, or polite to please.

Because this is a philosophical poem, Pope does not address the Muse but his friend. The tradition descends from Lucretius' address to Memmius and will continue to Wordsworth's apostrophe of Coleridge in *The Prelude* and beyond. But the Muse is not absent. Almost unregarded, she has by turns descended and ascended as the poetry rose and fell. But the dominant formal mode is that of social, human discourse. Bolingbroke is an attendant Genius, a tutelary

spirit, but, most firmly of all, he is Bolingbroke. Pope is too fastidi-
ous an artist to conclude his poem with the thunder of lines 361 to
372. He knows that he must cool his poetry before he ends. Thus,
while his retrospect of the *matter* of the poem, God and the universe,
was very properly written at full lyric stretch, he now steps back and
reviews not the matter but the form. He sees his own poem not only
in terms of its subject but also in terms of its manner. In all this he is
deeply unlike Milton, who invoked the highest supernatural aid, not
just a Muse but the Holy Spirit. But, then *Paradise Lost* was an epic
before it was a treatise. At the end of *Lycidas* Milton shows that he,
too, knows how to modulate to a minor key. Pope, in his recovered
quietness, assumes once more the manner of the Augustan man of
letters, critical, urbane, minimising.

Thus, where Milton found his way, in blindness, to a voice greater
than his own, in the *Essay on Man* we are returned to the quotidian
voice of Alexander Pope. Yet at intervals even in this poem the
utterance has seemed larger than life, and sometimes the occasion
was marked by inverted commas (not always the signal of interven-
tion by an imagined interlocutor): ' "Whatever IS, is RIGHT" ' (I,
294; IV, 145), ' "the Universal Cause/Acts not by partial, but by
gen'ral laws" ' (IV, 35–6). At III, 172 (' "Go, from the Creatures thy
instructions take" ') we are told that it is Nature who speaks. Elsewhere the source of this Greater Voice is undisclosed. But now, at
the very end, the Voice returns. This time we have, not inverted
commas, but capitals, and a hint that Nature is indeed the speaker is
given, once more, at line 393:

> For Wit's false mirror held up Nature's light. . .

The substitution of Nature for the Muse is curious; the claims of the
poem are thereby rendered, simultaneously, more modest and more
arrogant. This, the poet implies, was not whispered to me by a
goddess; it is just true. The last four lines do not repeat the imaginative splendours of 361–72 but they do return us to the matter of the
poem, this time to its doctrinal core. They are esemplastic, not as
Coleridge understood that term (with reference to imaginative
fusion) but rhetorically and prophetically esemplastic; they mould
the themes into a single, connected shape: whatever is, is right;
reason, passion answer one great aim; self-love and social are the

same; virtue alone brings happiness in this world; know then thyself.

(vi) CRITICAL RECEPTION

It is commonly believed that Pope's reputation was high in the eighteenth century, fell abruptly in the nineteenth (the century of Matthew Arnold), and gradually recovered in the twentieth. There is some truth in this picture. Voltaire, in so many ways the voice of the eighteenth century, was quick to hail Pope as 'the best poet of England, and at present of all the world'.[117] William Ayre concluded his biography of Pope (1745) with the words: 'It must be confess'd, that not only of this Age, but speaking of all former Ages, in our Language, he was THE GREATEST POET.'[118] But the 'Romantic' view that Pope was deficient in feeling and imagination, for example, was common before the eighteenth century had ended. 'The Sublime and the Pathetic', writes Joseph Warton, 'are the two chief nerves of all genuine poetry. What is there transcendently Sublime or Pathetic in Pope?'[119] Warton is clear that poetry and intelligence are mutually exclusive; thus Donne is placed with Swift and Pope as 'a man of wit' (and here Warton is following Dryden).[120] 'The most solid observations on human life', he explains, 'express'd with the utmost elegance and brevity, are MORALITY, and not POETRY.'[121] The century had only just ended when the Reverend William Lisle Bowles took the line that *The Rape of the Lock* showed a power of poetic invention which was elsewhere beyond Pope's powers.[122] Disparagement of Pope's poetic powers is evidently regarded not as a novel and exciting discovery of the new century, but as commonplace, and criticism has already begun to seek ways of qualifying the usual judgement. Bowles's judgement was later endorsed by Hazlitt, who wrote that *The Rape of the Lock* is 'the most exquisite specimen of *fillagree* ever invented'.[123] (Hazlitt's 'invented' echoes Bowles's 'invention'.) Meanwhile, among the Romantics themselves, Byron's preference for the moral and didactic poetry of Pope over his contemporaries is notorious. In 1821, Charles Lloyd begins a poem on Pope with a (by now) highly conventional expression of regret at the poet's lack of imagination,[124] but then suddenly decides that he admires his subject deeply, for one simple reason:

> One power has Pope. One, eminently his: –
> And of all powers, the one, with emphasis,

> Which gives th' ephemeral child of Fancy's birth,
> The claim to currency, the stamp of worth,
> This power is *sense!*[125]

With the movement of his mind the 'high' word, 'imagination', is silently replaced by the 'low' word, 'fancy'.

Even Johnson (before delivering a majestically affirmative answer) felt obliged to pose, formally, the question, 'Was Pope a poet?'[126] Long before Matthew Arnold made his famous observation, 'Dryden and Pope are not classics of our poetry, they are classics of our prose',[127] we find Hazlitt writing as if the whole 'prose versus poetry' debate had already begun to be boring: 'The question whether Pope was a poet, has hardly yet been settled and is hardly worth settling; for if he were not a great poet, he must have been a great prose-writer, that is, he was a great writer of some sort.'[128] The idea that Arnold was not answered until our own age is certainly wrong. In the last years of the nineteenth century George Saintsbury wrote, with the air of one tidying up after all the action is over: 'The greater jars of the conflict over the question "Was Pope a poet?" have mostly ceased. Hardly anyone now would dream of denying that he was a poet.'[129]

The nineteenth century in fact produced eulogies of Pope which were quite as intemperate as anything written in the preceding century. When Thackeray lectured on 'Prior, Gay, Swift and Pope' in 1851, he called Pope 'the greatest literary *artist* that England has seen'.[130] Ruskin wildly ranked Pope with Virgil, calling them 'the two most accomplished *Artists*, merely as such, whom I know in literature'.[131] Both Thackeray and Ruskin italicise the word 'artist', presumably in order to isolate an implication of high technical craftsmanship. Ruskin also claimed to perceive in Pope (surely one of the most Frenchified of English poets) 'the true English mind'.[132]

Meanwhile there were always critics who were capable of penetrating the stock antitheses, 'poetic/prosaic', 'imaginative/rational' and the like, and reaching the real complexity and idiosyncrasy of Pope's work. Cowper did not doubt that Pope was a master of verse-music but found something oppressive in that very mastery:

> But he (his musical finesse was such,
> So nice his ear, so delicate his touch)
> Made poetry a mere mechanic art;
> And ev'ry warbler has his tune by heart.[133]

De Quincey noticed that Pope admitted ratiocinative thought to his poetry, but observed that this thought 'proceeded by insulated and discontinued jets'.[134] He further remarked that thought so managed is not a barren, dry affair but is, on the contrary, almost *too* exciting; 'the eye aches', he says; Pope is 'all showers of scintillation and sparkle'.[135] But the old simple opposition of 'poetic' and 'prosaic' is very potent. Charles Lloyd's intelligence was so far dominated by it that he felt that any defence of Pope must dispense with all 'poetic' criteria, so that rhyme and verse-patterning somehow come to be felt as characteristic of the 'wet' opposition, whom he challenges thus:

> How would your matter fare, dismissing rhyme,
> If we should read it destitute of chime?[136]

Yet Pope's poetry 'chimes', if any ever did, and indeed to my ear the effect is commonly not to cloak poverty of thought but to make quite ingenious observations sound more stock than they really are. But the most radical answer to Lloyd is the formalist one, which ascribes a potent efficacy to the very music, as distinct from sense. For this, indeed, we must go to the twentieth century, and to Lytton Strachey, who had his own way of subverting Matthew Arnold: 'Pope's poetic criticism of life', he wrote, 'was, simply and solely the heroic couplet.'[137] The verse speaks itself, and itself is order, which life, alas, is not.

I will not pursue the account farther into the twentieth century, though here, too, the real story is a complex one. James Reeves observes that in our own time Edith Sitwell has admired Pope from an anti-moralist stance and Wilson Knight has admired him from a moralist stance.[138] There seems, indeed, to be general agreement that Arnold was wrong. Even those of us who have our Arnoldian moments, in which it is suddenly blindingly clear that Pope is not a poet as Virgil, Dante, Shakespeare, Milton and Keats are poets, know that he is nevertheless a poet of *some* sort. No other word will do. But we have (I hope) established the somewhat confused general setting for the more specific business of this section, which is the reception and reputation of one poem, the *Essay on Man*.

Pope's essay in philosophical poetry was an immediate success. At first, indeed, it seemed that his position was now more secure than it had ever been when he had satirised individuals. Victims fight back, but highly abstract questions of the intellect, seemingly, might be canvassed in disinterested serenity (see MM, xv–xviii).

Pope's manner of publication, as we have seen, was typically elaborate, with the usual gradual revelation of true authorship (that the poem was really by Pope was not generally known until all four epistles were published together in April 1734, and even then the information was formally withheld from the title-page). The stratagem of anonymity would have allowed Pope to remain obscure if the reception had been harsh. As it was, he had the rare privilege of eavesdropping on a chorus of praise. Johnson suggests that the whole affair was expertly managed by Pope's friends, who went about speaking in awed tones of this new author as a formidable rival whom Pope would do well to respect.[139] Elwin (E & C, II, 275) points to the contrast between Pope's letter of 20 October 1734 to Duncombe and his letter of 15 September of the same year to his more intimate friend Swift. To Duncombe he prates, with a sort of high-minded shrillness, of his hope that the suppression of author-ship would enable him to 'hear truth', adding piously that he is 'more afraid of . . . partial friends than enemies' (*Corr.* III, 438). To Swift he wrote: 'The design of concealing myself was good, and has had its full effect; I was thought a divine, a philosopher and what not? and my doctrine had a sanction I could not have given to it' (*Corr.*, III, 433). Yet in all this 'cant of sensibility' and expert self-advertisement there may have been some real modesty as to his own powers. Pope really was pleased (see *Corr.*, III, 358) that his work was thought to be by such dim figures as Dr Croxall and Dr Secker – real theologians! When he told Duncombe that he was 'diffident enough to distrust my own performance' (*Corr.*, III, 438) this may well have been the truth.

Meanwhile the *Essay* was rapidly gaining readers in other coun-tries. Silhouette translated it into French prose, and Du Resnel produced a far less faithful version in verse. Maynard Mack, follow-ing the findings of Rebecca Price Parkin, observes that within a hundred years or so of its composition the *Essay* was translated into German some twenty-four times, into French sixteen times, into Italian eighteen times, into Polish five times, into Swedish four times, into Latin five times and into Dutch six times. In addition there were various translations into Czech, Danish, Hungarian, Icelandic, Portuguese, Romanian, Russian, Spanish, Turkish and Welsh (MM, xli). Voltaire told correspondent after correspondent that the *Essay* was 'le premier des poèmes didactiques'.[140] The French periodicals fairly buzzed with the name of Pope.[141]

But there was a reaction, and it, too, was swift. It began on the Continent. In June 1736 the *Mémoires de Trévoux*, the Jesuit journal, said that Pope was no theologian. In March and April of the following year, after the publication of Du Resnel's translation, the same journal followed up its first onslaught by publishing two letters, the first attacking the *Essay* in the name of the Faith, the second in the name of morality.[142] Louis Racine, in his poem *La Religion* (1742), accused Pope of Deistical leanings. In response Pope wrote the famous letter in which he affirmed his Roman Catholic orthodoxy, adding (what was true) that Du Resnel's translation had grossly distorted his meaning (*Corr.*, IV, 416). Both Pope's letter and Racine's courteous and apologetic reply were later printed in the *Gray's Inn Journal* for 1756, pages 107–10.

In England a Mr Bridges (forenames unknown) published, in 1738, his *Divine Wisdom and Providence: an Essay Occasion'd by the Essay on Man*. This work, written in verse which everywhere betrays the most abject *stylistic* deference to Pope's authority (for poor Mr Bridges can hardly write a line without echoing the master), discovers gross impiety in Pope's attempt to apply reason to the mysteries of divinity. Even the philosophic criticism, we note, is Popean ('presume not God to scan'). Man, not God's great plan, is the source of evil.[143] As for the suggestion that Heaven sends natural calamities, Bridges simply flinches from the thought, and endeavours to cover the crack in his defence with a poetical conceit:

> O say not this; say Nature Man bemoans,
> Man's is the Guilt, and Nature's are the Groans.[144]

It rapidly becomes clear that philosophy is not Bridges' strongest suit. Heaven's great end is not variety, he explains, but good.[145] That Heaven's prime end should be Heaven's prime good will hardly surprise anyone. Meanwhile the question 'In what does the prime good of creation consist?' is still waiting for an answer. Bridges himself remains almost grotesquely submissive in the face of all problems:

> Be glad to know that GOD is good and wise;
> Tho' these Perfections oft in deep Disguise,
> Are wrapt in their Effects from mortal Eyes.[146]

Indeed, it might be said, certain of God's disguises (as when he plants a cancer) are amazingly convincing.

William Ayre's *Truth* appeared in 1739 and was reissued some four years later expanded by the addition of three further sections, with the title, *Four Ethic Epistles*. Despite the fact that Ayre himself is writing in verse, he professes to feel great indignation that Pope would have Truth 'stoop to *Poetry* and *Wit*'.[147] But in Ayre's poem it has become clear what the main charge against the *Essay* will be: the poem is fatalist and implicitly abolishes morality. Pope's provocative phrase, 'Whatever IS, is RIGHT', begins to receive the strident response it virtually invited:

> If Holiness is Right, why so is Sin.[148]

Ayre becomes mildly hysterical in his counter-assertion that man is free (he uses the same line twice) and almost presents us with a specimen of 'eighteenth century existentialism' when he apostrophises his own species:

> Amazing Being! *made, thyself to make.*
> The very *Source of Power* is lodg'd in Thee.[149]

In the face of such Hermetic ambition, certain of Pope's remarks about human pride might seem highly salutary.

But the principal attack was that launched by the Swiss professor of logic, Jean Paul de Crousaz. Crousaz' critique came in two instalments; the first, based on Silhouette's translation into French prose, was called *Examen de l'essai de M. Pope sur l'homme* (1737) and was translated into English by Elizabeth Carter as *An Examination of Mr. Pope's Essay on Man* (1739); the second was his *Commentaire sur la traduction en vers . . . de l'Essai . . . sur l'Homme* (1738), based on Du Resnel's 'poetic' version. This second work was translated into English, almost certainly by Samuel Johnson, as *A Commentary on Mr. Pope's Principles of Morality, or An Essay on Man* (1742).

Crousaz' objection to Pope is substantially the same as Ayre's. He smells fatalism in the poem, and the extermination of fatalism, it is clear, is Crousaz' main end in life. In the *Examination* the patience of the translator, Elizabeth Carter, seems occasionally to have been strained to breaking-point by Crousaz' obsessive and over-vehement language, for she inserts modest disclaimers in footnotes. Warburton, when he came to write his own great counter-blast to Crousaz, put the matter more frankly: 'Mr. *De Crousaz* . . . is perpetually crying out, *Fate! Fate!* as Men in Distraction call out Fire . . .'[150] Crousaz finds in Pope the Leibnizian system according to which criminals and sinners are necessary to fill out the *plenum* of God's creation (the absence of Cesare Borgia would imply a *defect*, that is, something missing in the divine enterprise of giving existence to the possibles).[151] Against this doctrine Crousaz advanced the old argument from changes in time: are we to suppose that a society in which murder has not yet been thought of is failing to fulfil God's purpose? Crousaz (rather oddly, in view of the staple subject-matter of Greek tragedy) suggests that the ancient Greeks had no conception of parricide and therefore no law to deal with it.[152] Were these, then, failing to perform what God willed?

It will by now be evident that Crousaz, for all his bludgeoning overemphasis and occasional absurdity, is capable of effective criticism. When Pope writes

> See some strange comfort ev'ry state attend
> (II, 271)

Crousaz comments, unanswerably: 'This pretended fact is contrary to Experience.'[153] Like Elwin he can supply picturesque anecdotes from natural history to refute the contention that instinct in animals is infallible (*Essay on Man*, III 94 ff.), for example, the unhappy butterfly who met its end by overeating sugar.[154] He takes Pope's account (at III, 179 ff.) of primitive man learning arts from the animals literally, and doggedly notes that the art of sailing is widely practised while few have ever heard of the little nautilus, which is supposed to have supplied the necessary instructions.[155]

Crousaz is much more powerfully provoked by Pope's account of God as glowing in the stars. Here he scents Spinozism, that is, the identification of God with mere nature. He notices in passing that Pope's language may be construed as meaning that God *causes* these effects, but then at once, without explanation, forgets his reservations and drives furiously on.[156] A little later he reverts to Pope's phrase, 'Glows in the stars, and blossoms in the trees' (I, 272), and writes, 'it should be added too, that he blasphemes in the Prophane, cheats in the Knave, utters Horrors from the Tribunals of the Inquisition, and does Execution upon miserable suspected persons'.[157] Here we see that Crousaz' objection is not only to an implicit Spinozism (though he will repeat this charge in the *Commentary*[158]) but also to Pope's implicit denial of the Fall of Man. For Pope evil must be a temporary illusion; for Crousaz, because the Fall is real, evil should be honestly acknowledged and confessed.

It is therefore not surprising that Crousaz is stung to his most violent language by 'Whatever IS, is RIGHT':

At the Sight of King *Charles* the First's losing his Head on a Scaffold, he ought to have said, THIS IS RIGHT. At the Sight of the Judges who condemn'd him, he must have said too THIS IS RIGHT. On seeing some of those very Judges taken and condemned for having done what was acknowledged to be RIGHT, he must have cried out, DOUBLY RIGHT. When his dear Friend, Lord *Bolingbroke* was disgraced, the System required that he should say THIS IS RIGHT. But Mr. *Pope* himself makes this Prediction:

> When Heroes, Statesmen, Kings in Dust repose
> Whose Sons shall blush their Fathers were their Foes
> Epist. IV, Verse 74

What should they blush at? At that which is right? They could not blush at any Thing else, for

WHATEVER IS, IS RIGHT.[159]

It is the absence of the great biblical narrative which causes all the trouble. 'Has Mr. *Pope* ever read the Scripture?' asks Crousaz in the *Commentary* (apropos of a point present in Du Resnel but missing from the *Essay* – but the question retains a larger relevance).[160] In the *Examination* he had already lodged this fundamental objection: 'The History of the Fall, if the Memory of it had been preserv'd, might have remov'd these Difficulties.'[161] Like Milton (and William Ayre), Crousaz places the blame for evil firmly upon man. But he has his own supplementary explanation (and very curious it is) of natural calamities. These, he suggests, are given to us as a gentle hint of the sort of punishment God might have unleashed upon us had he chosen to deal justly rather than mercifully with our sinful natures.[162] In other words, God having decided not to punish us, relents and punishes us a little after all – just enough, so to speak, to keep us on our toes.

In general Crousaz' later work, the *Commentary,* is less good than the earlier. The *Commentary* is the work which we possess in Johnson's translation, with Johnson's notes. The ascription to Johnson was made by L. F. Powell, the editor of Boswell's *Life of Johnson,* and has since become generally accepted. Here Crousaz spends a great deal of energy on matter never set down by Pope but introduced by his irresponsible 'translator', Du Resnel.[163] Sometimes, indeed, Crousaz seems to confess that 'the Poem of the Abbé Du Resnel',[164] and not Pope's *Essay,* is the object of his criticism (an impression further encouraged by the French title of the work but suppressed in the English title). But in general it remains a fair objection that Crousaz' substitution of Du Resnel's version for Silhouette's leads to the grossest unfairness. Thus he writes, with scorn, 'Mr. *Pope* thought these verses too fine to be left out of his Poem', and it is left to Johnson to comment: 'This Couplet is an Addition by the Translator.'[165]

Crousaz seems to be unequipped mentally for dealing with any sentence in which there is some shadow of irony, or play of metaphor and paradox. Pope's version of Pascal's contradictory man at II, 2–18, completely bewilders him.[166] Pope's scornfully ironic challenge, 'Re-judge his justice, be the GOD of GOD!' (I, 122), simply terrifies him: 'THESE are horrible Expressions,' he exclaims. He is similarly alarmed by Pope's wholly hypothetical picture of a disturbed planetary system at I, 251–2. These lines, he suspects, are written with the express design of frightening readers.[167] But he is uncertainly aware that poetry may be a distinct species of discourse to which his mode of criticism is inapposite. 'But is it not the established Prerogative of Poets to contradict themselves,' he asks himself, and forthwith agrees that the greatest do just that. But it does not and cannot reconcile him to condone nonsense.[168] If Virgil contradicts himself, then so much the worse for him.

The more serious criticisms added by Crousaz in the *Commentary* concern the great Chain of Being, the exaltation of instinct over reason, and Pope's general contempt for Revelation. On the first he has little to say which is really damaging. He observes that we interfere with the nice dependencies of nature when we divert rivers and yet the universe does not fly apart. This is surely to misunderstand what is meant by breaking a link in the chain (a better example would be the complete removal from the order of time and space of some existent). When he goes on to point out that comets swim into the 'Solar Vortex' he is still more unlucky in his example, since comets obey the laws of Newton in an admirably clear fashion.[169] His objection to the exaltation of instinct is merely stock; Crousaz is in general concerned that Pope's metaphysical quietism and general depression of human status will remove the motive of gratitude to God.[170] But on the fact of Pope's neglect of Revelation (one principal index of Deism) he is simply correct.

At this point Warburton, later to be Bishop of Gloucester and already an inveterate controversialist, moved in to defend Pope. The reasons for this sudden allegiance remain obscure. Warburton had earlier shown signs of hostility to Pope and even to the *Essay on Man* (EC, II, 286). At all events, from December 1738, Warburton's letters in defence of Pope began to appear in *The Works of the Learned*. He later published them, with the addition of a sixth letter, as *A Vindication of Mr. Pope's Essay on Man* and then republished them in 1742 with a seventh letter. This final version bears a long title beginning *A Critical and Philosophical Commentary* . . ., but in general the earlier title, *A Vindication*, has stuck, and I shall use that, though my references will be to the text of 1742.

Warburton's *Vindication* is heavy stuff but by no means the incompetent performance it is sometimes described as. He shows some literary acumen when he points out that Pope is the kind of poet who delights in steering between dangerous extremes; thus, the poet is neither Shaftesburian nor Mandevillian, though he is aware of both: 'The *Characteristics* and the *Fable of the Bees*, are two seemingly inconsistent Systems: The Extravagancy of the first is in giving a Scheme of *Virtue without Religion*; and of the latter, in giving a Scheme of *Religion without Virtue*'.[171] Warburton rightly points out that many have believed in a richly interconnected scheme without supposing that this implies fatalism.[172] In reply to Crousaz' loud complaint about 'Whatever IS, is RIGHT', Warburton puts up an answering barrage of sound (and some good sense): '*Whatever is, is right*, is a consequence of his *Principle*, that *partial Evil tends to universal Good*. This shows us the only sense in which the Proposition can be understood, namely that WHATEVER IS, IS RIGHT WITH REGARD TO ITS ULTIMATE TENDENCY'.[173] On the passage beginning 'All are but parts of one stupendous whole' (I, 267 ff.), where Crousaz saw the spectre of Spinoza, Warburton observes that anyone will sound like Spinoza as long as he is describing God's omnipresence in His creation.[174] Pope differs from Spinoza in that in his poem this conception is supplemented by a clear awareness of God's simultaneous transcendence, expressed elsewhere ('The worker from the work distinct was known': III, 229). Warburton is a little embarrassed here by his own scriptural reference (to Acts, XVII, 28); 'For in him we live and move, and have our being' in fact turns Pope's grammar inside out. Pope's language places God in the world, not the world in God. But Warburton sometimes triumphs gloriously over his opponent, as when he grinds under his heel Crousaz' disingenuous claim that Du Resnel's translation was more faithful than Silhouette's.[175] Warburton is scoring points.

Nevertheless, there is something depressing to the spirits in the picture he presents. One sees very clearly how Pope's adventurous treatment of the relation between reason and passion (or instinct) threw his contemporaries into an anxious flurry. Warburton has to choose his quotations with some care in order to crush Pope into an orthodox interpretation.[176] The common form of Warburton's exchanges with Crousaz is as follows: Crousaz finds impiety in Pope in certain places and then, in other places, he finds piety. This, he says, is contradiction. Warburton conversely finds in some places *partial* expressions of theological truth which might imply a heretical or impoverished notion of the Deity, were they not elsewhere *supplemented* by orthodox piety. The later professions do not contradict but, properly understood, *condition* our interpretation of the earlier. The critical difference between the two men is both subtle and important – and curiously difficult to adjudicate. I find it possible myself (by a rather strange private adjustment of the mind) to read the poem in either spirit. It is perhaps not surprising that criticism of the *Essay on Man* has tended ever since to be either Crousazian or Warburtonian.

The eighteenth century itself was innocent of the doctrines of the New Criticism and therefore thought it natural to resolve such questions by examining the author's intentions and manner of composition. If Pope could be shown to have written from a unified, comprehensive awareness of things, Warburton's practice of 'reading-out' extremes by interpreting one passage in the light of another was corroborated. If, on the other hand, Pope's mind could be shown to have operated in a local, piecemeal fashion, then he is the more likely to have inadvertently contradicted himself. Pope's babbling letter of

gratitude to Warburton, written on 11 April 1739, has an important
bearing on this question.

> I think Mr. Crousaz ought never to have another answerer, &
> deserved not so good a one. I can only say you do him too much
> honour and me *too much Right*, so odd as the expression seems, for
> You have made my System as clear as I ought to have done &
> could not. It is indeed the Same System as mine, but illustrated
> with a Ray of your own, as they say our Natural Body is the same
> still, when it is Glorifyed. I am sure I like it better than I did
> before, & so will every man else. I know I meant just what you
> explain, but I did not explain my own meaning so well as you: you
> understand me as well as I do myself, but you express me better
> than I could express myself. (*Corr.*, IV, 171–2)

If one trusts the matter of this letter, Warburton's *Vindication* is
vindicated, by the author's authority. But, if one listens for one
second to the manner (Pope seems to be blinking and rubbing his
eyes), it seems quite clear that much of what Warburton wrote came
as a surprise to Pope.

From the beginning the tension between the *Essay* as a system and
the *Essay* as a miscellany was expressed in terms of the relative
importance of Lucretius (the great didactic poet) and Horace (the
urbane aphorist) as models. Pope himself felt torn. He writes in a
letter (15 September 1734): 'Whether I can proceed in the same
grave march like Lucretius, or must descend to the gayeties of
Horace, I know not' (*Corr.*, III, 433). It is true that Pope here
formally classifies the *Essay* as Lucretian and is probably talking
about the *Moral Essays* when he speaks of Horace. But Bolingbroke's letter to Swift written four or five years before (19 November
1729) says that Pope is as good as any writer and adds: 'I do not
except Horace.'[177] This was written at the time of the conversations
which led to the *Essay*, and it appears that even then Horace was in
Bolingbroke's mind, at least. Jonathan Richardson, who together
with his father regularly visited Pope at Twickenham, said that the
poet never dreamed of the schematic interpretation later applied to
the poem, but actually enjoyed the Horatian irregularity of it all,
jotting down and smoothing off thoughts as they occurred (EC, II,
261). George Sherburn, observing that Pope seems naturally to have
composed in disconnected paragraphs, remarks that it might have

served his reputation better in the long run had he published a string of loosely connected poems. But he grants that Pope, with his ambition to produce a 'System', was not content to do so.[178] Sherburn's sense of the imprudence of such grand 'Systems' is not a purely twentieth-century reaction. Shaftesbury wrote: 'The most ingenious way of becoming foolish is by a system.'[179] Thus, though Pope might have been saved from both the onslaughts of Crousaz and the vindication of Warburton by a fairly simple piece of distributive editing, he chose to present a single didactic poem. Such decisions are part of the public fabric of poetry. We cannot say that the *Essay on Man* is 'really' a collection of fragments disguised as a unity and that Crousaz should therefore have stayed his hand.

The price of Warburton's championship was Pope's friendship with Bolingbroke. For, if Pope (with a little ingenuity) might be cleared of Deism, Bolingbroke certainly could not. It was necessary, therefore, for Warburton to argue that Pope (who invokes Bolingbroke as the presiding genius of the poem), though he understood the deepest mysteries of the faith, had entirely failed to perceive the depravity of Bolingbroke's mind. Pope's own position was indeed unhappy. He was quick to incorporate in his 'Universal Prayer' lines affirming the freedom of the will and to attach the poem as a pendant to the *Essay*. The 'Prayer' is a curiously clinical specimen of Deism (all truly moral, truly rational religions are one) plus free will. It certainly does little to turn Pope into a Christian. In part Pope was a victim of the changing reputation of Deism itself. At first it had seemed to promise the reconciliation of all reasonable Christians in the transcending simplicities of all true religion. Only later was it seen as destructive of Christianity. Pope was very likely to have thought the highly agreeable and civilised talks he had with the noble Lord Bolingbroke a very safe bet; here was reason, civility and a high social gloss; surely all this could only assist his reputation. It is likely that the criticisms of Ayre, Bridges and Crousaz came as a very considerable shock to him. At all events there seems to be a faint note of panic in his gratitude to Warburton. Certainly, some of his earlier professions of admiration for Bolingbroke were now an embarrassment. He could do nothing about the dedication of the *Essay* but he could and did alter his published correspondence. Elwin shows very tellingly (EC, II, 290; VII, 67, n. 1) how Pope changed the text of a letter he wrote to Swift on 14 December 1725, referring to Bolingbroke. In 1741, Pope replaced the words 'he is grown a great Divine' with 'when he writes of anything in this world, he is more than mortal; if ever he trifles it must be when he turns a Divine'.[180] Sherburn in his edition of the *Correspondence* does not notice this change.

Bolingbroke, for his part, was not pleased. 'It cannot be supposed', says Ruffhead in his *Life of Pope* (1769), '. . . that his Lordship took the same delight in seeing his pupil thus reasoned out of his hands.'[181] Ruffhead is a devout disciple of Warburton's, carrying his devotion to the point of eking out his *Life of Pope* with extensive transcriptions from Warburton's *View of Lord Bolingbroke's Philosophy* (1756). The phrase 'reasoned out of his hands' was originally Warburton's.[182] Similarly Ruffhead borrows Warburton's picture of Bolingbroke's system as 'a *pretended* vindication of providence against an imaginary confederacy between *divines* and atheists'.[183] Ruffhead goes on to relate the warm debate which took place between Warburton and Bolingbroke over the moral attributes of God and a subsequent even more acrimonious exchange, in which Bolingbroke attacked Pope, and Warburton defended him.[184] By this time the very 'Memmius' of *An Essay on Man* had taken up his position in the ranks of the enemies.

Ruffhead's narrative of the theft of Pope from under the guns of Bolingbroke may be suspected because of the author's clear partisan interest. Yet Johnson, no uncritical admirer of Warburton, gives a substantially similar account, suggesting that Bolingbroke resented the loss of his manipulable friend but could not say openly why.[185]

Certain of the questions raised by Crousaz and Warburton will always be debated. Warburton was doubtless correct when he claimed that the chain of being was not always linked in people's minds to fatalism, but Crousaz might easily have replied (using one of Warburton's favourite words) that nevertheless the inner *tendency* of the theory is to fatalism. Similarly Warburton's scornful demonstration that Pope was clearly aware of what he called 'partial evil', though it may make Crousaz' jibes look coarsely uncomprehending, cannot eradicate the fact that, by the theology Pope espouses, such partial evils (not merely 'in tendency' but in themselves) are not really evil at all. Moreover (most ironic of all), it may be suggested that here Pope as Crousaz portrays him is more radically pious than the accommodating figure presented by Warburton. We have only to substitute 'Thy will be done' for 'THIS IS RIGHT' in Crousaz' *reductio ad absurdum*, and it all suddenly becomes profoundly traditional.

There will likewise always be arguments about how far one should press the importance of contradictions when they appear in poetry. By and large, Pope's contemporaries, on whichever side they appeared in the debate, considered them important. Pope's frequent use of the *concors discordia* as a local effect is another matter altogether. Such controlled collisions are joyous formal games, built to be resolved; the mind is at first dazzled with a seeming contradiction but then intuits a saving, unifying sense. Mack, seeking to extend the notion of the *concors discordia* beyond its normal, small-scale rhetorical scope, brilliantly observes (MM, xxiv–v) that the cosmology of the poem has a like form: 'All Discord, Harmony, not understood' (I, 291). But none of this, in Pope's eyes or in the eyes of his contemporaries, would license doctrinal contradiction in the poem. Indeed, the major theological discord is no less to be resolved than the minor rhetorical discord, and the agent of resolution is – precisely – doctrine. My own instinct is that our modern impulse to hold back from coarse doctrinal questions may betray a fundamental loss of confidence in didactic literature, as really performing the task it ostensibly sets itself. Were I Pope, watching from a cloud, I should feel more dishonoured by such criticism than by the worst onslaughts of Crousaz. But, indeed, the debate has never ceased. If we consider broad sympathies rather than detailed agreement on all points, Ruffhead is Warburtonian and Johnson is Crousazian. Elwin and Courthope are Crousazian. Maynard Mack is Warburtonian. This book is Crousazian.

Johnson's hostility to the *Essay on Man* is well known. Yet there is a certain tension, a doubleness, in his attitude which shows (if we read attentively) even in the notorious sentence, 'Never were penury of knowledge and vulgarity of sentiment so happily disguised'.[186] The word 'happily' is probably not a further gratuitous insult in the form of ironic praise, but merely sincere. A little later Johnson observes, of the poem's familiar teaching:

It was never till now recommended by such a blaze of embellishment or such sweetness of melody. The vigorous contraction of some thoughts, the luxuriant amplification of others, the incidental illustrations, and sometimes the dignity, sometimes the softness of the verses, enchain philosophy, suspend criticism, and oppress judgement by overpowering pleasure.[187]

But Johnson's philosophy did not long endure its chains. In the very next paragraph he warms once more to his work of demolition.

Certainly Johnson's views shocked Joseph Warton (EC, II, 268 n.), though Warton's own view that the *Essay* was a dry affair enlivened by poetic ornament has much in common with Johnson's.[188] Both perceive a fundamental discontinuity between the intellectual content and the poetic form.

In the first years of the nineteenth century William Lisle Bowles essentially repeated the judgement of Warburton and Ruffhead, finding a happy union of deep thought with appropriate language and imagery.[189] Byron, true to form, claimed to find 'as comfortable metaphysics, and ten times more poetry in the *Essay on Man*, than in *The Excursion*'.[190] This was more than Hazlitt could stomach. Picking on the usual phrase, he observed that Pope proves by the same token that whatever is is wrong.[191] Thus, Hazlitt joins Ayre, Crousaz and the anonymous author of *Sawney and Colley* (1742), who wrote:

> And bravely prove in reason's spite
> That right is wrong, and wrong is right.[192]

De Quincey, who saw Pope not as a classic of prose or an enemy of feeling but, more precisely, as a master of brief verbal spectacle, naturally concluded that the grand systematic enterprise of the *Essay on Man* was the great artistic mistake of Pope's career: 'If the question were asked, What ought to have been the best of Pope's poems? most people would answer, the *Essay on Man*. If the question were asked, What is the worst? all people of judgement would say, the *Essay on Man*.'[193]

The greatest act of critical judgement on Pope carried through in the nineteenth century is that embodied in the edition of Elwin and Courthope. Implacably hostile to Pope, Elwin (for the impetus of the commentary seems to be his) fought his author on every front, personal, philosophical, literary, theological, biographical, with an astonishing weight and ordonnance of intelligent information. The reader is left wondering why, if Elwin despised Pope so much, he was willing to expend so much labour on him. Elwin's want of sympathy with the material is in some ways utterly disabling. There are places where he seems not to know that he is reading poetry at all. Yet at other times the mere energy of his intellectual engagement

leads him to acute literary analysis. For him the *Essay* is never a
picturesque cultural phenomenon. It is a living voice, from which
he, the critic and commentator, dissents.

The twentieth-century answer to Elwin and Courthope, fenced
and guarded with the required depth of scholarship, was provided
by Maynard Mack. The running conflict between Elwin's picture of
the shallow Deist and Mack's picture of Pope as the heir to a rich
Christian tradition permeates this study. Mack is by far the more
accomplished literary critic, yet his edition turns the *Essay* into a
kind of museum. He is highly appreciative of the system of ideas
Pope presents, but the very word 'appreciation' implies a kind of
separateness. Elwin had no leisure for appreciation, for he was a
combatant in the same arena. It is natural that Mack, standing back
from the spectacle, should find an intuitive cultural unity. One suspects that his edition is part of that movement of cultural nostalgia
which swept literary studies in the 1950s, and led to a peculiar kind
of ecumenism, a picture of the-world-we-have-lost as an immense
harmony. Men who while they lived were willing to kill one another
over points of doctrine were seen as profoundly linked by belief in
God and an organic, ordered creation. And perhaps they were. But,
equally, they had their differences. Mack essentially leaves unanswered the question why good Christians like Johnson and Elwin
reacted as strongly as they did against the *Essay*. The problem does
not obtrude because he rarely substitutes for the question, 'Is this
traditional?' the other, coarser question, 'Is this true?' Crousaz, Warburton, Johnson all assumed that this question lay at the heart of any
criticism of didactic poetry. When it is no longer asked something
has died. Perhaps the mere asking of this question indeed 'profoundly linked' them, even while the answers they gave divided
them in opposing camps. The difference between a vivid and a faint
appreciation is a less serious affair.

In general the twentieth century has taken little interest in the
Essay on Man. Yet the questions posed and answered in the poem –
Is God really good? Why, then, did he make a world like this? – are
utterly fundamental for theists, and very large numbers of people
who never enter a church continue to believe in God. It is usual to
speak scornfully of the *Essay* as if it addressed remote, technical
questions which have now been superseded by the advance of civilisation. This position may perhaps be maintained by the atheist. But
any believer is confronted, today, by precisely those questions and,

if they seem remote, that is because he, and not Pope, has his head in the sand. Among modern critics Wilson Knight responded to the *Essay* with real warmth. His view of the poem is like Mack's, but less guarded. Of the poem's doctrine he writes: 'It is not only a poetic philosophy, but the universal philosophy, not so much of poets as of poetry; and is exactly, the philosophy implied by Shakespeare's work.'[194] Elsewhere he exclaims: 'With what imperturbable and untroubled ease, comparable to that of Shakespeare's "cloud-capp'd towers", the couplets roll out their mighty images.' Knight responds with ardour to the vitalist universe which Pope presents. Yet the sentence I quoted is appalling criticism. It badly needs some note of real analysis, of intelligent discrimination. Pope may have things in common with Shakespeare, but criticism is not doing its job if it does not define idiosyncrasy even while it identifies kinship.

This study has attempted to do just that. First, Pope's poem is crammed with philosophical ideas of radical power and importance. It has more of the most strenuous theological thought of the age in it than any other poem of the century. Narrowly literary critics are sometimes dismayed by contradiction and search desperately for a mode of discourse in which such unseemly failures will not obtrude. Philosophers live with, though they do not tolerate, contradiction. The works of Plato are full of contradictions. Dugald Stewart (1753–1828) was a real philosopher and rightly observed that the *Essay on Man* was a remarkable summary of the best that the human mind has been able to excogitate on the moral government of God.[195] Kant, not just a real philosopher, but a great one, notoriously revered Pope and even ranked him higher than Leibniz. In 1755 the Prussian Royal Academy offered a prize for an essay on Pope's 'system'. Kant's notes towards an entry survive and show clearly that his reaction to the poem was profoundly different from that of Crousaz. Where the Swiss logician perceived a latent unity, an underlying fatalism linking Pope and Leibniz, Kant was excited by the difference between Pope and Leibniz. The account of this difference given in Kant's notes is as follows. Leibniz, by means of metaphysical arguments, first established the character of God, for those who were able to understand and willing to applaud. Nothing was then permitted to encroach on this conception. The created world was merely forced into accord with a presumptive harmony. Meanwhile, ordinary people, who wished to trace God in his creation, remained troubled. Pope, conversely, allowed the world to speak with its own voice. Unlike Leibniz, he chose the *a posteriori* road and triumphed. Beginning from the most distressing details of life, he showed how they worked for good. Pope's universe is subject only to the rule of its own 'self-sufficient clockwork' (*allgenugsamen Uhrwesens*) and its perfection is its own, even as it simultaneously displays the goodness of God.[196] Even the love of self is, together with instinct, part of a great natural law of love, transcending individual cases.

Kant's jottings are incomplete (the section ends as if he had been interrupted by the German equivalent of Coleridge's man from Porlock, just when his thought might have been veering sharply). Nevertheless, despite his use of mechanistic language ('clockwork'), he may be said to have seen, far more clearly than the opponents or the friends of Pope, the pre-Romantic streak which runs through the poem. God and his creation may be justified either by metaphysical argument *a priori* or by a quasi-mystical intuition of a blazing, God-filled world. Both of these can be found in Pope's *Essay*. Certain of Pope's attempts to deduce divine benevolence *a posteriori* from the visible character of society are grotesquely inept, and perhaps Kant would have been forced to notice these failures had he pursued his thought. But it appears that he saw in Pope's realignment of Instinct and Reason, Nature and God, an important act of imagination. Kant was not feigning enthusiasm to impress the Academy; his *Allgemeine Naturgeschichte und Theorie des Himmels*, also of 1755, is full of admiring allusions to Pope's *Essay*. Today we may all agree that his comparative placing of Pope and Leibniz is absurd (though it may be that Kant should be left to discuss the question with his peers in the next world – if any can be found). His fundamental intuition that here were certain ideas of radical power remains sane and just.

The *Essay on Man* is a philosophical poem. The philosophy is not systematically consistent but is, rather, an affair of local acuteness (it is, incidentally, frequently impossible to separate 'literary' and 'philosophical' acumen at these moments). It is *the* philosophical poem of the age in that it assembles, in a sort of brilliant disarray, the fractured systems of the age. It tells you more of the thought of the time than any other single literary work. Its virtual exclusion of Revelation and its running tone of urbane compromise and balance (all savage in-fighting of sects transcended by polite reason) stamps it very plainly with the character of a specific period (this is *not* the 'universal philosophy of Shakespeare'). The tense review of the relations between reason and passion, especially, is even more distinctive. Though commentators may still find sources, there is a forward impulse together with a nervous uncertainty in the movement of the poem which suggests that Pope is here thinking for himself. The point may seem a small one, but originality in such matters is rare indeed. The frequency with which I have been forced in this study to use words proper to a later period, such as 'Romanticism', is a mark of Pope's vital power as a thinker and a poet.

I have tried to trace the main lines of the reception of the *Essay*. One work remains which simply refuses to fit into the general picture. *Common Sense a Common Delusion* by 'Almonides, a believing Heathen' appeared in 1751. Some of this writer's objections follow the common track, though he puts them with a rare succinctness, which partly springs from his persona of the artless savage. Commenting on I, 267 ff., 'All are but parts of one stupendous whole', he concludes that God must be 'a prodigious great Animal',[197] and then infers that this animal must share the character of the world: 'In short, if this animal God has any natural Inclinations or Desires at all, he must have all the Inclinations and Appetites of all Souls whatever, because he is the whole, or universal soul.'[198] It follows that we should gratify our desires with all our energy in order to increase the joy of the Big Animal; abstinence might ruin him. In the queer inverted asceticism of this there is a touch of Mandeville (dead, alas, in 1733). The audacious image of the Big Animal recalls Hume's *Dialogues on Natural Religion*.[199] The fluid ironic logic of the persona is Swiftian (*Mr. Collins' Discourse on Freethinking, put into plain English . . . for the Use of the Poor* is a fairly close analogue). Thus, the persona at times permits him to 'kid on the level', and argue that Pope reduces all to mere common sense, a sort of civilised pea-soup. For it is neither common whores nor common gin that is ruining society, 'Almonides' explains, but common sense.[200] Thus, Pope is pilloried, not for intellectual pride and presumption, but for low ambitions. The opening conceit of *An Essay on Man* is turned upon its author. He is found guilty of lack of appetite for God. Much as Blake proved to the followers of Urizen that Jesus Christ broke all ten commandments,[201] so 'Almonides' proves to the followers of Pope that Jesus 'taught nothing but Pride and Ambition; for he commanded his Disciples to seek the Kingdom of Heaven above all things'.[202] Of course it is all a joke, but a serious joke. Perhaps Almonides has laid his finger on the real weakness. Traherne said:

'You must Want like a GOD, that you may be Satisfied like GOD.'[203]
The underlying trouble with Pope and his kind is not rationalism or
futile metaphysics but the fact that they do not want enough.

CHAPTER 4

Coda: The End of Theodicy

(i) RETROSPECT TO VIRGIL

The word 'theodicy' remains in a manner the property of Leibniz, who coined it as the title of a work he published in 1710. But, if we take the term in its general signification, 'vindication of God', it is clear that there were many theodicies before that of Leibniz. The most obvious and the most immediately relevant to Pope's *Essay on Man* is clearly Milton's *Paradise Lost*. But we have seen how Pope set aside the 'Christian story' of Milton and chose another method. It is at this point that it becomes important that we remember Virgil. Virgil lived before Christ but that did not prevent him from writing in the *Georgics* a developed theodicy, a justification of Jupiter. And Pope's rejection of the grand Christian narrative laid him open to the influence of pagan equivalents. We saw how, despite his opting for a philosophical rather than a narrative explanation of evil, Pope was driven back in his third epistle upon a kind of narrative myth, in which the Garden of Eden was secularised as the State of Nature. The modern antecedents of this corruption in Locke and Hobbes we have already noticed. But behind the State of Nature lies the Golden Age of Virgil.

Lovejoy and Boas distinguish two views of the simple life in antiquity: first, 'soft primitivism', which suggests a pastoral existence of leisured ease, the shepherd stretched out in the shade of the beech-tree, playing on his oaten flute; secondly, 'hard primitivism', which conversely suggests that rural existence is hard, and forms the character through labour.[1] Virgil's first major poetic production, the *Eclogues*, was a fairly pure specimen of soft primitivism. But his great didactic poem on practical husbandry, the *Georgics*, introduces the ideal of hard primitivism. By the time we have reached line 46 of the first book the proper mood of the poem has communicated itself. It is the time of spring ploughing.

> Vere novo gelidus canis cum montibus umor
> liquitur et Zephyro putris se glaeba resolvit,
> depresso incipiat iam tum mihi taurus aratro
> ingemere, et sulco attritus splendescere vomer.

[In the new spring, when from the white mountains, the chill mois-
ture melts and the crumbling clods break up under the west wind,
then let my bull begin to groan at the plough, pressed well down,
and let the ploughshare, rubbed by the furrow, glitter.]

(I, 43–6)

Here is a world very different from that of the *Eclogues*, a world in
which the air can be sharp and cold; the groaning of the bull is
answered by the glitter of the iron working in the ground, the darkness of *ingemere* by the brightness of *splendescere*. What has entered
here is energy.

Virgil goes on to explain how the farmer's calendar, the laws and
customs of the earth were laid down at the beginning of time, when
Deucalion (the Greek Noah) saved the human race 'by throwing
stones into an empty world' (I, 62). From these hard stones came
human beings, *durum genus*, 'a hard race' (I, 63). There follows, at
line 121, the crucial passage of theodicy:

> pater ipse colendi
> haud facilem esse viam voluit, primusque per artem
> movit agros, curis acuens mortalia corda,
> nec torpere gravi passus sua regna veterno.
> ante Iovem nulli subigebant arva coloni;
> ne signare quidem aut partiri limite campum
> fas erat: in medium quaerebant, ipsaque tellus
> omnia liberius, nullo poscente, ferebat.
> ille malum virus serpentibus addidit atris,
> praedarique lupos iussit pontumque moveri,
> mellaque decussit foliis, ignemque removit,
> et passim rivis currentia vina repressit,
> ut varias usus meditando extunderet artis
> paulatim et sulcis frumenti quaereret herbam,
> et silicis venis abstrusum excuderet ignem.
> tunc alnos primum fluvii sensere cavatas;
> navita tum stellis numeros et nomina fecit;
> Pleiadas, Hyadas, claramque Lycaonis Arcton;
> tum laqueis captare feras et fallere visco

inventum et magnos canibus circumdare saltus;
atque alius latum funda iam verberat amnem
alta petens, pelagoque alius trahit umida lina;
tum ferri rigor atque argutae lammina serrae
(nam primi cuneis scindebant fissile lignum),
tum variae venere artes. labor omnia vicit
improbus et duris urgens in rebus egestas.

[The Father himself has willed that the farmer's road should not be easy; he first through skill stirred the fields, sharpening men's wits through troubles, not suffering his kingdom to sleep in heavy torpor. Before Jupiter, the land lay subject to no farmer, nor was it lawful even to mark the field or enclose it with boundaries. Men sought what they needed from the common store and the earth herself yielded the more freely what none demanded. It was Jupiter who put in snakes their black venom, who told the wolves to hunt and stirred up the sea; he shook the honey from the leaves, hid the fire, and stopped the wine which had flowed in streams everywhere, so that custom, by taking thought, might gradually hammer out various arts, find out the corn in furrows, and strike out from veins of flint the secret fire. Then first did rivers feel on their backs the hollowed alder tree; then did sailors first number and name the stars, Pleiades, Hyades and Arctos, the shining child of Lycaon. Then men found out how to catch wild beasts in nets, how to deceive with bird-lime and to ring great stretches of woodland with hounds. Now this man lashes the broad stream with a weighted net, searching out the deepest places, while that man trails a wet drag-net. Then came iron's hardness and the blade of the shrill saw (for the first men used to split fissile logs with wedges) and then various arts. Work got the better of all things, obsinate work, and want, which drives when things are hard.]

(I, 121–46)

The passage begins with a firm attribution of all the things which make the farmer's life hard to the will of God, or Jupiter. This dispensation is seen as good for us. We were formed from rocks, and sloth, it is implied, would scarcely have suited our nature. All the fiery energies and ingenuities of man follow from this, in lines that ring with the clash of hammer on anvil and blaze with the sparks of the smithy.

The obverse of this vitality is presented as senile indolence, 'tor-pere . . . gravi veterno' (124). *Veternus*, 'sloth', is etymologically con-nected with *vetus*, 'old'. Thus far, the alignment of values in the passage would seem to be very clear. The childhood of the world would have been, *for human beings*, a perpetual old age, and con-versely the after-time brought youth and vigour in its train.

But none of this will quite do. With half his mind, Virgil rejoices in the hard regimen of Jupiter, but the other half recoils, and rein-vests the primal age with beauty. The deepest pastoral sentiments always lie opposite to hard-primitivist activism. One can trace in pastoral an escalation of radical values, at first political and at last almost mystical. Thus, in Shakespeare's *As You Like It* we move from a condemnation of the hierarchical life of courts to a much more extreme doctrine fenced about with humour and irony but in itself strangely absolute: Jacques weeps for the stricken deer and laments the usurpation by men of the commonwealth of wild crea-tures (II, i, 60–5). In the present Virgilian passage we find pastoral communism ascribed to the First Age (*in medium quaerebant*, l. 127) and, not just the animals as in *As You Like It*, but the earth itself is seen as being harshly subjected by the farmers, who cruelly wrench what before she freely gave. One may even discern an obscure impli-cation of violation in the idea of marking the land with limits. We may remember how in the *Aeneid* the hero, with the truly dreadful confidence of the divinely directed, having arrived in Latium, marked out his new domain without even consulting the Arcadian inhabitants (VII, 157). The Roman gifts of law and government which Aeneas brings seem scarcely to be needed by the native Latins, who, as Latinus explains, are righteous *sponte sua*, spontane-ously, and have no need of sanctions (VII, 203). The idea of spon-taneity is fundamental in pastoral. In these lines it is associated with the world as it was before Jupiter's reformation.

Meanwhile the reforms of Jupiter are not simply bracing. In some ways they come across as positively nasty. He adds black venom to snakes; under the new dispensation man *lashes* (*verberat*) the water and *deceives* (*fallere*) the innocent birds. The references to iron carry a hard-primitivist excitement but by the values of pastoral they are rendered suspect. Iron is unnatural; it is the enemy of green things, the enemy of wood. So here we may discern the beginning of a train of images which is to become especially powerful in the poetry of Andrew Marvell, the scythe which murders the grass in *Upon Apple-*

ton House (394), the iron wedges driven by fate in 'The Definition of Love', the iron gates through which we must drag what pleasures we can seize in life in 'To His Coy Mistress'. Virgil is writing about the loss of Paradise. But he is not content merely to tell the story of the rise of evil. Though his lyric impulse remained firm in its attachment to pastoral values, his piety was of the kind which must justify whatever prevails. So we have here not just a Hesiodic narrative of descent, but a theodicy, and the justification of a fall means the finding of good in evil. This is where hard primitivism can be useful.

Milton justified the ways of God by telling how Adam ate the forbidden fruit. This brought death into the world and all our woe, and yet God permitted it and so it must have been right that it should happen. For Milton the good which justifies the evil is the good of freedom. Adam fell because his generous creator had allowed him an independent will; but, indeed, he demonstrated the reality of his freedom in the most disastrous possible way. Some readers have perceived in the poem a further dimension of justification, this time with more paradoxical consequences. It is not just that evil is justified as a necessary possible consequence of the great gift of freedom, but the idea is planted that, even in the very act of banishing Adam and Eve from Paradise, God was obscurely promoting them to a higher plane. The idea of freedom is still working in the background, but in a different way. Milton avails himself of the ancient doctrine of the *felix culpa*, or 'Happy Fall', whereby Adam, in being expelled from Eden, was really entering an arena of moral testing from which he might make his way to Heaven itself. As Heaven is higher than Eden, the expulsion is at once a challenge and a favour.

This idea is likely to have had a powerful appeal for Milton, because elsewhere his conception of virtue is essentially involved with difficulty and testing. Indeed, one suspects that he would be attracted even to a naturalised version of the *felix culpa*, where the 'promotion' lay not in an accessible heaven, but in the mere fact of being admitted to a world of genuine moral choices. There is a famous passage in *Areopagitica*, which reads:

> I cannot praise a fugitive and cloister'd vertue, unexercis'd & unbreath'd that never sallies out and sees her adversary, but slinks out of the race, where that immortall garland is to be run for, not without dust and heat.[2]

One might infer that in the unbroken contentment of Eden virtue could not exist. There can be no courage where there is no danger, no pity where there is no pain. Heroism and love (to press the point) entered Eden with the Serpent, and man's moral life began with his expulsion into a cold, unsympathising world. That this is no great wrenching of Milton's views can be verified by anyone who turns up the original passage in *Areopagitica*, for there Milton expressly applies these considerations to Adam's coming to know good and evil.

One curious thing about this second-order justification is the hesitation with which scholars commonly put it forward. To be sure, we are now very close to doctrinal contradiction, since the theory implies that what Christian tradition has presented as the greatest disaster ever to affect the human race was really a great boon. Yet this much is clearly implicit in the ancient idea of the Happy Fall. What worries scholars more is the possible presence of the naturalised version, the intuition that, even if Adam and Eve never reach Heaven, their moral existence on earth is already a higher state; their pleasure may be less but their *eudaimonia* is the greater. This seems unacceptable because it smacks of Romantic theory. It is all very well, one senses, to attribute such views to a Shelley or a Blake, but not, surely, to a seventeenth-century Puritan.

Milton lived before the Romantics but he lived after Virgil. The idea tentatively advanced as a faint possibility at the end of *Paradise Lost* is manifest and fully developed in the *Georgics*. Moreover, the idea in Virgil does not turn on the ultimate accessibility of some Platonic Heaven; he simply insists that virtue comes through dust, heat, cold and labour, that is, through testing, so that the Italian farmer, that *durum genus*, is in the deepest sense a happier being than Tityrus, lolling in the shade at the beginning of the *Eclogues*. Adam setting out with Eve into the wide world ('all before them, where to choose': XII, 646) is in one, most important way, happier than he ever was when lying on banks of flowers.

Given this similarity, the differences are highly instructive. In Milton, Satan is the immediate agent of change. In Virgil it is God himself who wills the new order. In radical Christian theology the implication is faced that God (since he is omniscient and omnipotent) must have been willing that the Fall of Man should occur. Once again, it is entailed in the very notion of theodicy, that God's part should not be less than crucial. The remorseless Calvin consistently opposed Melanchthon's moderate doctrine that evil happened with

God's permission and instead affirmed with Zwingli that evil happened by God's will.[3]

But, if the later state is genuinely higher than the earlier, why did not an all-powerful God get on with it straight away? Why, so to speak, waste time with the experiment of Eden (for omniscience need never experiment)?

This, too, it might be said, is covered more adequately by Virgil's scheme than it is by Milton's. For in Virgil's story the first, innocent age was ruled over by a different, older God, Saturn; the replacement of one moral order by another is an effect of the replacement in Heaven of Saturn by Jupiter. Thus, where Christianity blames the Serpent, Virgil boldly tells how Jupiter himself put venom in snakes; that which is only intermittently faced in the Christian tradition as a dark implication is squarely asserted in the Latin poem.

Pope, in the third epistle of *An Essay on Man*, founded his State of Nature on the First Age of Virgil and Ovid. Like Virgil, he is nostalgic for the original state of man and something of the old enchantment of pastoral survives in his account. Like Virgil, again, he acknowledges an obligation to justify the seeming descent from that original happiness, but when it comes to method their paths diverge. Virgil through an immense effort of the ethical imagination discovers a new species of good, in mere obstinate work. In the *Georgics* he gives us pastoral energised, and pastoral energised is no longer pastoral but something else. The values of *stasis* are replaced by the dynamic values of *crisis*. Pope chose instead to show that, although there was a fall (from a Lockean state of nature to something like a Hobbesian one), given time, the system proves to be self-adjusting. God is not a visible agent in Pope's story. The work on the spot is done by Nature, a sort of terrestrial regent who can shrink, when necessary, to a mere hypostatised description of events. But still everything that happens must be at least compatible with a benevolent omnipotence. Self-love, a natural given impulse in human beings, as it becomes more aware of consequences, spontaneously composes a system of public harmony; self-love and social are, given a few millennia, the same. Thus, the final values are even more emphatically those of stasis, not of crisis.

But an ethic of stasis is *inherently* unfitted to account for change and destruction. Pope chose a method of defence which almost obliged him to pretend that nothing had really happened. The bloody centuries which lie between us and the State of Nature are a mere hiccup. Virgil is in a manner freed by the Roman conception of an evolving Pantheon to lament the Golden Age and yet, without inconsistency, to welcome the new and different times. Pope, even when (as in the third epistle) he allows himself to be drawn into an explanatory myth, is prevented by an essentially static Deism from giving much reality to his story.

He was forced into myth, as we saw, by an inescapable intuition of corruption, but the dominant mode of his thinking led him to apply to his narrative of descent what is really just another version of the merely statistical optimism that had already failed him. The ethic of stasis, of achieved harmony, will justify both the State of Nature and the recovered stability, brought about by enlightened self-love, but it will never justify the intervening chaos. But the chaos was what needed justification. Pope may tell us that he has in fact implicitly justified the chaos by showing that it is secretly organised, that its inner workings tend to the re-establishment of peace; but peace was universal in the State of Nature and, conversely, its full recovery seems to be indefinitely postponed.

The comparison with Virgil does little for Pope. It enables us to see, a little more clearly, why the third epistle, for all its brilliance, betrays its own best energies and nullifies itself. Whenever Pope's lyric gift is quickened by the ancient intuition of the First Garden we have all lost, the growing pathos must be expertly muffled with a brisk demonstration that by and large, taking the rough with the smooth, considering things in the long run, everything is really working splendidly. But for the example of Virgil, it would have been easy to think that this progressive anaesthesis of sensibility is inherent in theodicy; Pope, in his doctrine of the passions, had the groundwork of another mode, to which he approaches most nearly in those passages where we diagnosed a rising Romanticism. But the self-adjusting natural system of the third epistle is fundamentally inert; it may account, in a fashion, for the cancellation of change, but not for change itself. The difference between the poet of the first Augustan age and the poet of the second is a difference of moral imagination.

(ii) ARCHBISHOP KING'S *ORIGIN OF EVIL*

Virgil's gods changed with the change of human history. The Christian God, though once historically incarnate, is eternally the same.

The stasis of God determines the stasis of theology; the vindication of such a supreme being can never be a story. We have seen how the presence of obvious horrors could temporarily pitch Pope back into the old myth of decline, but decline itself is inconsistent with unchanging perfection and so proves useless as an explanation. Rather, it becomes a mere summary of the evils to be explained. Thus, Pope's one essay in narrative explanation, the myth of the State of Nature in the third epistle, ended by merely cancelling its own majestic story. It would be easy to blame all this on Pope's smart but superficial intelligence, but it would be wrong to do so.

Milton encountered an identical difficulty in *Paradise Lost*. It is in fact inherent in Christianity itself. Milton was a notably tactless thinker (by design, as readers of the *De Doctrina Christiana* may quickly discover for themselves), and Pope was notably clear. When tactlessness is thus succeeded by clarity, certain embarrassments become inescapable. It has been a fashion among certain twentieth-century Christians to despise the determined optimism of Pope and Archbishop King. Yet, if the supposition of an all-powerful, entirely good God does not entail radical optimism, I do not know what would. Christianity is a profoundly optimistic creed. We tend to think of optimism as self-indulgent but, in strictly intellectual terms, it can be an awkward possession. Leibniz, King, Shaftesbury, Pope faced a central implication of Christianity from which subsequent ages have flinched. Much in the reaction against Pope can be ascribed to style. Pope's 'One truth is clear, "Whatever IS, is RIGHT" ' (I, 294) made the mistake of pretending that everything was easy and obvious. This is not the deliberate intellectual brutalism of Milton but an unintended error of rhetoric. Today the same students who will eagerly 'accept the universe' or thrill to Blake's 'Everything that lives is holy'[4] are instantaneously repelled by Pope's line. Yet Pope's formulation is simply the most radical, the most absolute, the most correct. The others, it might be said, survive because they are prudently involved in a Romantic haze.

Archbisop King's Latin *De Origine Mali* was published in 1702, eight years before the *Théodicée* of Leibniz. The translation by Edmund Law, Bishop of Carlisle, with its richly informative commentary by the translator, appeared in 1731. King often sounds very like Pope. He says of wild or venomous animals: 'Must we reckon them entirely useless because we do not know the use of them? Must we say that every Wheel in the Clock is made for no manner of purpose, which a Rustic understands not the design of?' (1731, p. 133). Readers of Locke will recognise the *topos* of 'the famous clock at Strasbourg'.[5] A page later he is almost epigrammatic: 'If you insist that a Lion might have been made without Teeth or Claws, a Viper without Venom: I grant it, as a knife without an Edge.' In the words of Pope:

> Why has not Man a microscopic eye?
> For this plain reason, Man is not a Fly.
>   (I, 193–4)

Like Pope he places great emphasis on the thesis that the world was not made for man:

> They therefore who urge the unfitness of certain Parts of the Earth for the sustenance of Man, as a Fault or Defect of the Divine Skill in making them, are oblig'd to prove that the Earth was made for the sake of Mankind only, and not of the Universe. (1731, p. 106)

Bishop Law in his notes to the translation similarly strikes the Popean note:

> From the Supposition of a Scale of Beings gradually descending from *Perfection* to *Non-entity*, and compleat in every intermediate Rank and Degree . . . we shall soon perceive the absurdity of such Questions as these, Why was not Man made more perfect? Why are not his Faculties equal to those of Angels? Since this is only asking why he is not placed in a quite different Clan of Beings, when at the same time all other classes are supposed to be already full. (1731, pp. 90–1)

The argument assumes real *ad hominem* force when the opponent of theodicy is made to realise that his own existence must be cancelled if God is to measure up to his expectations. Here the arguments run parallel with Pope's lines beginning 'Presumptuous Man!' at I, 35. King fully perceives the special force of this intuition and, like Pope, breaks the usual, third-person, indicative mode of his writing with a challenging second-person singular: 'Know then that it was necessary that you should either be what you are, or not at all' (1731, p. 25). King, in making this point, is saying two things at once: first, that 'your' place in the system is of this kind and, secondly, by a more radical implication, that 'you' must know that your very identity is involved in imperfection, a perfect version of 'you' would not be 'you' at all but something else, so that if God had confined himself to perfection you would never have existed at all.

This argument, while it may tend to induce a mood of gratitude in place of the former mood of shrill philosophical complaint, leaves unanswered the disinterested question, 'Why did God create anything at all?' As long as God existed alone, infinite goodness and power existed; there was, so to speak, nothing lacking in the universe. Creation is therefore, in a curious manner, as much a subtraction from perfection as an addition to it. For God to *create*, he must make something other than himself; for a thing to be other than God, it must be imperfect (for if it were wholly perfect it would simply be God himself all over again and no creation would have occurred). Thus, to create is to introduce defect where before there was only perfection. King is fairly successful in arguing that evil is implicit in creation, and as long as we assume that creation is nevertheless incontrovertibly good in itself we may be satisfied. But the argument, in blocking one criticism, lays itself open to attack in another place. For the very contention that evil is implicit in creation casts doubt on the normally safe assumption that creation is inherently good. Given the prior perfection of God and the necessary imperfection of creation it is difficult, intellectually, to see why God should have created the world at all. A further, still more disastrous inference might lead one to suppose that, since God did create this world, he cannot, after all, have been good. There is no sign of this thought in King or Pope, but it may be glimpsed in Hume.[6] The prior question, 'Why did God create?', is the question which harassed poor Mr Prendergast in *Decline and Fall*. One wonders whether Waugh realised that it had troubled stronger heads than his. Mr Prendergast is in good company. King is certainly so far convinced that creation entails evil that the final effect of his work is much less bland than that of Pope's *Essay*. It really is, as its title implies, a book about evil. So far from being unaware of the universe Voltaire was to thrust upon the attention of the optimists in *Candide*, King writes with that world, and no other, in mind. At the end of his book he quotes Empedocles: *Neikos oulomenon kai deris haimatoessa*, 'The Pestilential Strife and Bloody Fight' (1731, p. 297). Thus, 'the best of all possible worlds', given the horror implicit in creation, may be re-expressed as 'the least evil of all possible worlds'. King virtually says as much on page 117: ''Tis plain that God did not allow of Natural Evils for the sake of any Good; but chose the least out of several Evils; i.e., would rather have Creatures liable to *Natural Evils*, than no Creatures at all.'

The Greek origins of European theology give us two conceptions of God: first the introverted, self-contemplating perfection of Aristotle's *Metaphysics* and, secondly, the 'unstinting' creator of Plato's *Timaeus* (29E–30A) who can refuse being to no potential existent. The first is hard to reconcile with creation, the second easier. The Aristotelian divine introvert occasionally appears in King's book; for example, on page 53 he refers to God's 'Contemplation and Love of himself', but the manifest fact of creation draws him to the other conception, which implies a set of values more congenial to the Romantics than to the Augustans: 'If therefore the Divine Goodness had deny'd existence to created Beings, on account of the concomitant Evils, he might really have been esteemed Envious, since he had allowed none to exist beside himself' (1731, p. 296). Mere fecundity of life, mere plurality, is itself a gigantic good: 'A Being that has Life is (*caeteris paribus*) preferable to one that has not: God therefore animated that Machine which furnishes out provision for more perfect Animals . . . for by this means he gain'd so much Life to the World' (1731, p. 118). Infinite Goodness still urges the Deity to do the very best. 'This moved him to give *Existence* to Creatures which cannot exist without *Imperfections* and *Inequality*.'

Leibniz, whose *Theodicy* seems not to have been influenced by King's work, despite the austerely deductive tone of his philosophy, was similarly driven to suppose that God delighted in mere fecundity. This view has been powerfully urged and documented by Lovejoy, who comments that, for Leibniz, 'the desirability of a thing's existence bears no relation to its excellence'.[7] It will be noticed that this principle, rigorously applied, means that God should have created all the possible worlds, and not just the best possible. In the *Theodicy* he writes, 'La sagesse doit varier' – 'Wisdom needs variety'.[8] Elsewhere he writes, 'Perfectio . . . est . . . in forma seu varietate. Unde iam consequitur materiam non ubique sibi similem esse, sed per formas reddi dissimilarem, alioqui non tantum obtineretur varietatis quantum posset' – 'Perfection lies in form or variety. From which it now follows that material is not everywhere the same, but is rendered diverse in its forms. Otherwise the greatest possible variety would not be achieved.'[9] Elsewhere again he writes that the actual universe is the collection of the possibles 'qui forment le plus riche composé' – 'which form the richest mixture'.[10] He told Malebranche, 'Dieu fait le plus de choses qu' il peut' – 'God makes the greatest number of things he can' – and goes on to say that God deliberately looks for simple laws so that it will be possible to place the greatest number of things under them; the systematic ordering exists for the sake of the great multitude of existents, not the existents for the system.[11]

Thus far the reasoning of King (and of Leibniz, in so far as we have noticed it) has been severely *a priori*. The object of the exercise has been to reconcile the phenomena with what is known, at a higher level, of the nature of God. The perfection of the Creator is a premiss, not a conclusion of the argument. Only thus can apparent defects be explained as necessary moments in a larger plan, itself good. But King, like Pope, cannot resist the temptation to reason backwards, *a posteriori*, from the given excellence of the world to the goodness of God. This method is more vulnerable than the first. Thus, instead of saying that the Great Scheme, which we cannot comprehend, *must* be good, he points to the system as it is available to us and notes its admirable economy. Just as Pope described in the third epistle (43–68) how man feeds and feeds *on* beasts, so King observes: 'An Ox, for instance, or a Calf, is bred nourished and protected for some time, in order to become fit Food for Man . . .' (1731, p. 118). Leibniz normally avoids this trap, but Lovejoy cites a letter in which he says that in the light of his theory of a *plenum*, or 'filled universe', he would have expected zoophytes (beings midway between plants and animals) and predicts that they will be discovered.[12] This is to invert the normal process of his reasoning, and implicitly to accept the relevance of evidence *a posteriori*. He almost puts his theory in such a way that it could be falsified if no zoophytes were found (he is fortuitously protected by the difficulty of proving a negative empirically – it is impossible in practice to show that there are no zoophytes *anywhere*).

Some scholars are surprised that men like King and even, on occasion, Leibniz should be so foolish as to expose their theories in this fashion, when both are strongly armed with a powerful *a priori* theology, but one has only to make a reasonably sustained effort of imaginative sympathy to see why. If God's nature (including his goodness) is wholly independent of that which is given to our comprehension, it is hard to see how we are in a position to apply any adjectives to him at all. 'Good, but in a logically unique sense' is nonsense. No sense is 'logically unique'. Proper names are logically unique, but they carry not a sense but only a bare reference. Moreover, other human individuals are available to our senses. I suspect that eighteenth-century theologians fell back into *a posteriori* 'demonstrations' in the hope of imparting some ethical colour, some warmth, to an increasingly transparent Deity. But the mixed character of the given universe betrayed them; a God so deduced had the mingled, imperfect character of the world.

Probably Pope read King but did not read Leibniz. Nevertheless, I have glanced in passing at the parallel enterprise of Leibniz in order to suggest that certain strains were becoming evident in fundamental theology. There have probably been many occasions earlier in this book when I have seemed more contemptuous of Pope than I really am. It should now be clear that it is no great disgrace to be defeated by problems which no one has solved.

(iii) JOHNSON'S *RASSELAS*

In three consecutive numbers of *The Literary Magazine* in 1757, two years before the appearance of *Rasselas* in England and *Candide* in France, Johnson published a review of Soame Jenyns's *Free Enquiry into the Nature and Origin of Evil*. Johnson identifies the views of Soame Jenyns with those set forth in the *Essay on Man*:

> He . . . adopts the system of Mr. *Pope* . . . little more than a paraphrase of *Pope*'s epistles . . . He then gives us the system adopted by *Pope* . . . a humble detail of *Pope*'s opinion . . . we are next entertained with *Pope*'s alleviations of those evils which we are doomed to suffer . . . This author and *Pope* perhaps never saw the miseries which they imagine thus easy to be born . . . *Pope*'s doctrine is at last exhibited in a comparison . . . a notion to which *Pope* has given some importance.[13]

Johnson has Pope so firmly in mind that this may be considered as much a review of the *Essay* (considered as a piece of theology) as it is of Jenyns's *Free Enquiry*. The tables are now turned indeed. Pope no longer loses credit by being dismissed as the versifier of Bolingbroke. Instead, he is violently attacked, because *Soame Jenyns* is regarded as a mere prose translator of Pope.

Readers of A. O. Lovejoy in the present century have been taught, with a wealth of illustrative example, that the Great Chain of Being was until comparatively modern times a central element in European thought. It is therefore a little surprising to find Dr Johnson referring to it as if it were recondite exotic belief: 'He . . . gives us the system of subordination, not invented, for it was known I think to the *Arabian* metaphysicians, but adopted by *Pope*.'[14] It is tempting to suppose that Johnson is here intent upon some ponderous but obscure jest, bewildering the enemy with a wholly misplaced air of intelligent inquiry, but it is not probable. It is more likely that Johnson 'blanked out': simply did not notice that this strand in Jenyns reappeared daily in other versions. Johnson, having entered upon his subject in this blundering and myopic manner, forthwith produces a philosophical criticism of fundamental importance. He attacks the notion that just so many beings are needed to 'fill' the universe. His criticism could be described as Zenonian (think of Achilles and the Tortoise).

First, the distance between infinity and the highest created being is infinite, thus always leaving room for more created beings; secondly, he says, a like argument applies to the distance between nothingness and the lowest creature (this might be disputed); thirdly, and most crushingly, he observes that the distance between each level of the Creation can be indefinitely subdivided. What is *conceptually* possible for us is clearly *practically* available to God. Thus, a God wishing to fill his universe to the brim with all possible orders of being would produce not a distinct hierarchy but an infinite sequence, the gradations of which would not be detectable by human intelligence. Indeed, it remains conceivable that in the universe taken as a whole, in space and time, God has done this. But Johnson's argument greatly weakens the old sense that the visible hierarchy of creation – the fact that a cabbage is below a dog, and a stone below a cabbage – represented connected steps in the divine plan, that the gradations we see around us are themselves divinely authorised. The scale of creation now shimmers at the far end of speculative thought, no longer distinctly visible nor even imaginable. It is merely *de fide* and can no longer provide a natural bridge to *a posteriori* demonstrations from 'the admirable economy of nature' and the like.

Johnson's has another fundamental philosophical criticism, which is ethical. Proponents of the great argument with which this book has dealt had always felt themselves secure on one point at least: evil was inherent in creation, since any being other than God was less good than he and therefore, so far, evil. The history of this idea is long and august. Johnson looks at it once and drives his great fist through it: 'There is no evil but must inhere in a conscious being, or be referred to it; that is, evil must be felt before it is evil.' The mouse is weaker than the horse, and is therefore *inferior* in point of strength, but this does not mean that we should say that the mouse is in that respect evil, nor that its weakness is an evil. If its weakness led to its being tormented, we might begin to wish to use the term, but this merely confirms Johnson's point about consciousness. Even if we grant that Adam is less good than God (obviously Johnson would agree to this without hesitation), Adam is not, on that account, *evil*. Evil enters only with consciously deviant choice. The implied effect of Johnson's stubborn resistance is to reinstate the old scheme. Deism had tended to reduce the importance of the Fall of Man by insisting that the corruption of our nature was inherent in our existence as created beings. Johnson conversely suggests what Christians have always been brought up to believe, that there was no evil in Paradise. He thus undoes the work of centuries. From this point on, the Problem of Evil begins to turn into the Problem of Pain.

He then cites a marvellously feeble passage from Soame Jenyns:

Poverty, or the want of riches, is generally compensated by having more hopes and fewer fears, by a greater share of health, and a more exquisite relish of the smallest enjoyments, than those who possess them are usually bless'd with. The want of taste and genius, with all the pleasures that arise from them, are commonly recompensed by a more useful kind of common sense, together with a wonderful delight, as well as success, in the busy pursuits of a scrambling world. The sufferings of the sick are greatly relieved by many trifling gratifications imperceptible to others, and sometimes almost repaid by the inconceivable transports occasioned by the return of health and vigour. Folly cannot be very grievous, because imperceptible; and I doubt not but there is some truth in that rant of a mad poet, that there is a pleasure in being mad, which none but madmen know.[15]

This immediately recalls certain lines from the *Essay on Man*:

> The learn'd is happy nature to explore,
> The fool is happy that he knows no more;
> The rich is happy in the plenty giv'n,
> The poor contents him with the care of Heav'n.
> See the blind beggar dance, the cripple sing,
> The sot a hero, lunatic a king . . .
> Each want of happiness by Hope supply'd,
> And each vacuity of sense by Pride . . .
>
> (II, 263–8, 285–6)

This is the soft, vulnerable underbelly of *a posteriori* theology, and Johnson falls to his easy work of drawing and quartering with gusto. He begins quietly enough: '*Poverty* is very gently paraphrased by *want of riches.*' But then his voice rises in indignation to its full volume:

> The poor indeed are insensible of many little vexations which sometimes imbitter the possessions and pollute the enjoyments of the rich. They are not pained by casual incivility, or mortified by the mutilation of a compliment; but this happiness is like that of a malefactor who ceases to feel the cords that bind him when the pincers are tearing his flesh.[16]

Johnson then considers the doctrine of balance, set forth by Pope in his fourth epistle:

> Some are, and must be, greater than the rest,
> More rich, more wise; but who infers from hence
> That such are happier, shocks all common sense. . .
> . . . Heav'n's just balance equal will appear,
> While those are plac'd in Hope, and these in Fear. . .
>
> (50–3, 69–70)

Johnson comments: 'That hope and fear are inseparably or very frequently connected with poverty, and riches, my surveys of life have not informed me. The milder degrees of poverty are sometimes supported by hope, but the more severe often sink down in motionless despondence.'[17]

He then, a little surprisingly, warms to his author, expressing eager agreement with his utilitarian theory of virtue. He seems to place himself firmly behind Pope's view, as it is presented in lines 1–28 of the fourth epistle. Morality, says Johnson, reduced itself to the fact that 'some actions produce happiness, and others misery: so that all moral good and evil are nothing more than the production of natural'.[18] It would be easy to suppose that Johnson wrote in this way through enthusiastic inattention – that so good a man, had he paused to consider, would have seen at once that lying is wrong even when it produces profound complacency – but Johnson immediately adds: 'This alone it is that makes truth preferable to falsehood.'

Within a few pages it becomes clear that Johnson believed his reductive view of morality cleared a space for the higher operations of religion: 'Morality induces them to embrace virtue from prudential considerations; religion from those of gratitude and obedience. Morality, therefore, being abstracted from religion, can have nothing meritorious in it . . . we can claim no regard for self-preservation.'[19] The severe separation of desert from the field of morality is very strained. Johnson senses that his utilitarian definition has removed all that is most important in moral action and he has attempted to locate the residuum in religion. Yet 'gratitude and obedience' remain troubling. One senses that the reference may be, at bottom, to a simple gratitude for heavenly felicity and obedience through fear of Hell. Two pages later this intuition is confirmed: 'No man can be obliged by nature to prefer ultimately the happiness of others to his own. Therefore, to the instructions of infinite wisdom it was necessary that infinite power should add penal sanctions.'[20] The thought is once more thoroughly utilitarian. We observed earlier, in connection with Pope's fourth epistle, that a theologian like Paley could transform Heaven and Hell into utilitarian machinery (see above, p. 132). Religion, so far from supplying the disinterested factor, is brought within the compass of the felicific calculus. The perennial problem of utilitarian theory is the step from the individual's maximising his happiness to the happiness of the many. The evolution of social sanctions from the self-interest of individuals is a shaky business. God can do these things much more effectively. Thus, 'penal sanctions' in the next world motivate us, here, to consult the happiness of others. What, in such obedience, is other than prudential? What merit can there be in wishing to avoid eternal torment?

Johnson's mind is clouded, one senses, by an excessive anxiety.

The mere thought of human happiness released in him a degree of emotion which he could not easily master.

Nevertheless, by the end of his review Johnson has achieved a notable work of destruction. Yet he remained a Christian, and Christianity *of itself* obliges believers to assume that the universe is the work of an all-good, all-powerful God. Therefore, although Johnson has virtually obliterated any concrete or demonstrable form of theodicy, he remains firmly committed to the (Popean) proposition that, if we could but see the whole, we would confess that it is good. This is the clear implication of his opening observation, that the question treated by Soame Jenyns will always trouble us, as long as '*we see* but *in part*'. So far he will allow his thought to proceed, but no farther. He pays far more heed than Pope ever did to the injunction, 'presume not God to scan' (*Essay on Man*, II, 1). His thought is deeply traditional, and one might therefore have expected that he would revert to the explanatory myth of *Paradise Lost*. But Johnson did no such thing. Instead, he wrote a *myth of non-explanation*. In the first two editions, both of which appeared in 1759, it is entitled *The Prince of Abissinia: a Tale*; today it is known as *The History of Rasselas, Prince of Abissinia*.

The story is an 'oriental tale' about a prince who left his idyllic kingdom and travelled the world. At the same time it is a moral fable, about the futility of hope and imagination. The style is utterly unlike that of Pope: it is, except for a very few passages, unironic and grave. There is something deeply refreshing about a mode of writing which disdains the usual flurry of humorous or evasive rhetorical defences, and simply says what it wishes to say. The opening periodic sentence, contracting at last to the imperative 'attend', is majestic: 'Ye who listen with credulity to the whispers of fancy, and pursue with eagerness the phantoms of hope; who expect that age will perform the promises of youth, and that the deficiencies of the present day will be supplied by the morrow; attend to the history of Rasselas, prince of Abissinia.'

Rasselas lives in a good place, where everything is present to delight the eye and content the soul. Yet he leaves the Happy Valley. Voltaire's Candide likewise left the castle of the Baron of Thundertentrunk, but he did so because the Baron kicked him out. Rasselas's reason conversely is internal and obscure. This difference typifies the contrast between Voltaire's fable and Johnson's. Voltaire sought to show the reality of evil, not, as one might have expected, by dwelling with empirical care on the actual sufferings of mankind but by an uproarious, knockabout sequence of horrors. At its best the stylistic effect is complex and powerful. A species of alienation is achieved whereby the real dreadfulness of the Lisbon earthquake reasserts itself behind the heartless celerity of Voltaire's narrative. To say this is to suggest that the comic mode is there to be defeated. But comedy can be very potent. The mere fact that, in *Candide*, the characters pick themselves up and carry on after each disaster (much as the flattened cat in *Tom and Jerry* bounces back into his former shape) begets a habit of optimism in the reader and also, one suspects, in the author. The old woman whose buttock was cut off by the Turks explains that she thought of suicide but decided against it, because, somehow, she loved life too well.[21]

Meanwhile *Candide* is very different philosophically. It sets up a caricature of Leibniz (an extreme *a posteriori* optimism which says that the world we see is luminously perfect) and then knocks it down, over and over again. The *intellectual* high spirits of Voltaire derive in part from the not wholly admirable fact that he has chosen a very easy course. The absurdity he denounces with such robust alacrity is, even without his efforts, glaring. He shows that war and earthquakes hurt people.

Johnson chose a harder path. He sought to show that even the things which seem best of all – good government, philosophy, the simple shepherd's life, poetry, monastic meditation, imagination – do not really lead to happiness. The third chapter is called 'The wants of him that wants nothing'. The muffled closure of thought here suggested is repeated in the title of the last chapter, 'The conclusion, in which nothing is concluded'. It is important to realise that neither of these headings is a joke, as it would have been in Pope.

The prince, whose every material need is met, is assailed by a hunger of the spirit he cannot explain: 'I have already enjoyed too much; give me something to desire.'[22] His learned tutor Imlac strives to quiet the prince by reconciling his mind to the inescapable imperfection of things, and even anticipates the story which is to follow by narrating (in chapter XII) his own extensive travels. But the prince is resolved to make his *'choice of life'*.[23] The phrase is well chosen, exciting, yet vacuous.

Johnson tells the story of the prince's journey to fabled and exotic places in a crushingly monochrome style. The matter of the narrative is full of potential life, but it is all petrified by the steady march of the sentences. This is no artistic error on Johnson's part. The seeming heights and depths of life are deliberately reduced to an endless plain of futility. Yet even despair, if expressed with sufficient majesty, can begin to give a certain satisfaction to the subject. Johnson was puritan enough to fear the seductive power of even his austere yet monumental prose. In the eighteenth chapter the prince meets a wise and happy man, who teaches him to be a Stoic, explaining how the man who rises above passion is 'no longer the slave of fear, nor the fool of hope; is no more emaciated by envy, inflamed by anger, emasculated by tenderness, or depressed by grief'.[24] Rasselas leaves his teacher and then returns, to find him sitting in a half-darkened room; hearbroken because of the death of his daughter. Rasselas addresses him sententiously:

> 'Sir . . . mortality is an event by which a wise man can never be surprised: we know that death is always near, and it should always therefore be expected.' 'Young man, answered the philosopher, you speak like one that has never felt the pangs of separation.' 'Have you then forgot the precepts, said Rasselas, which you so powerfully enforced? Has wisdom no strength to arm the heart against calamity? Consider, that external things are naturally variable, but truth and reason are always the same.' 'What comfort, said the mourner, can truth and reason afford me? Of what effect are they now, but to tell me, that my daughter will not be restored?'
>
> The Prince, whose humanity would not suffer him to insult misery with reproof, went away convinced of the emptiness of rhetorical sound, and the inefficacy of polished periods and studied sentences.[25]

The last sentence echoes in the mind. For it is itself a polished, studied sentence. The words seem to die on the page.

There are no vivid characters in the marmoreal history of Rasselas, but there is an iron realism, so uncompromising as to be almost embarrassing. The loved servant of Nekayah, sister to the prince, is carried off by Arabs. Imlac, distressed by his inability to learn the whereabouts of the servant, avoids meeting Nekayah. She commands his presence, and says in words which recall Johnson's sad anecdote of Pope and Martha Blount:[26] 'I do not much wonder at your absence; I know the unhappy are never pleasing, and that all naturally avoid the contagion of misery.'[27] She has mistaken the reason for Imlac's elusiveness, but the general proposition, uttered without rancour, has a terrible, bleakly factual force.

In *Rasselas* every form of happiness proves hollow. Even something so simple and disinterested as delight in the beauty of nature is stigmatised as childishness. The servant Pekuah explains how the women imprisoned in the Arab's fortress filled their empty lives: 'Part of their time passed in watching the progress of light bodies that floated on the river, and part in marking the various forms into which clouds broke in the sky.'[28] The language is almost lifeless and yet, so subdued is the general imaginative tone of the work, the images of water and cloud are for a moment like rain in a desert. Johnson is describing aesthetic experience and to do this has had to admit for an instant the beauty of the natural world. He deliberately chooses images of instability in order to convey the idea of weakness, but the very transience of floating leaves and dislimning clouds can also be poignant and engage emotions Johnson might prefer to repress. In Dante's *Purgatorio* the pilgrims were held by the song of Casella, forgetting their journey, content as though nothing else touched their minds, but old Cato broke up their brief rapture and drove them on up the hill (II, 112–23). In Johnson's mind there is both a Casella and a Cato but, while Dante breaks up the enjoyment of immediate beauty with a greater life, Johnson merely mortifies the rising happiness of his account: 'They had seen nothing; for they had lived from early youth in that narrow spot.'[29]

Here Johnson attacks the enjoyment of phenomena considered terminally, that is, as immediate ends. But he is equally ready to attack the appetite for transfinite happiness, the yearning which reaches beyond mere phenomena to a good it cannot grasp. The futile pilgrimage of Rasselas began with an incoherent longing, which was only made the more inescapable by the presence of innumerable immediate satisfactions. C. S. Lewis made 'immortal longings' the foundation of his principal argument for the existence of God; the fact that people experience a desire to which no given object can afford an appropriate satisfaction suggested to him that the appropriate object must exist elsewhere; the existence of ordinary hunger does not mean that the hungry person will be fed, but it does suggest that this is a world in which food exists; transfinite longing does not guarantee a place in Heaven but it does powerfully imply that Heaven exists.[30] Perhaps the longing Lewis has in mind has nothing to do with the longing described by Johnson. Lewis's emotion is something which is inexpressibly sweet, while Johnson's seems in comparison a peevish discontent. Yet, even if the emotion were substantially the same, one would expect a difference of 'colour' to flow from the different construction each author places on it. For Johnson such incoherent desires are merely the last absurdity of human nature. The prince and his companions visit the Great Pyramid. They observe the immensity and the uselessness of the building, and Imlac says: 'It seems to have been erected only in compliance with that hunger of the imagination which preys incessantly upon life.'[31] Where Lewis might have delighted in the impractical character of the building, inferring from it a necessarily religious impulse, Johnson finds only a gigantic idiocy. It must be confessed that he has chosen his example well: not a cathedral but a pyramid, not an upward-surging fantasia of stone, but an immense, suffocating weight.

The History of Rasselas is a work of almost pathological pessimism, but is occasionally irradiated by a sense of comedy subtler than anything in Voltaire. The philosopher who, after a page of wonderfully persuasive vacuousness on the folly of deviating from nature, 'rose up and departed with the air of a man that had co-operated with the present system' is justly famous.[32] In his speech and in his response to the prince's questions, the philosopher (without even venturing outside the received 'wisdom' of the age) simply demolishes himself. Johnson is able to deliver the *coup de grâce* merely by echoing the philosopher's own language. The passage is deliciously funny, but the injunction 'Follow nature' was never the same again. The anonymous author of a burlesque 'Plan of an *English* Dictionary' in the *Gray's Inn Journal* for 1756, after various laboriously facetious definitions (*Modesty*, for example, is 'some Custom among the Ancient *British* Ladies'), defines *Nature* as 'Nothing at all'.[33] Johnson knows when to accelerate for comic effect. The elaborate contrivance of wings which so summarily drops its inventor in the lake, and the almost immediate exhaustion of Imlac and Rasselas when they attempt to dig their way out of the Happy Valley, are both admirable pieces of subdued comedy.[34] But the drive towards despair is almost unrelenting.

The imagination is the great enemy. Chapter XLIV has the title 'the dangerous prevalence of imagination'. 'All power of fancy over reason', says Imlac, 'is a degree of insanity.'[35] In the same chapter Pekuah, the princess and the prince formally and in order repent of their imaginings; that is, each repents of his or her dream. Pekuah's was egoistic, imagining herself queen, regulating ceremonies, building palaces, planting trees on the tops of mountains; the princess had a dream of pastoral life, of freeing the lamb from the thicket and driving the wolf from the flock; the prince's dream (saddest of all) was a dream of good government. Johnson's skill here is almost cruel. He contrives a gradual moral ascent from the servant to the master, and then Imlac lays all level with the one damning word 'folly'.[36]

But, although imagination is doctrinally opposed in *Rasselas* and almost extirpated from the sombre prose in which the story is told, Johnson was an artist and could not quite kill the power of imagination in himself. The very rarity of images, the sense that they are vouchsafed, so to speak, through clenched teeth, makes them trebly powerful when they do occur. Most potent of all are certain images so indefinite that some may dispute the propriety of calling them images at all. I mean images of spatial environment.

The fable begins with the conventional, enclosing world of the Happy Valley, peopled with story-book beasts, all behaving 'in character': 'the subtle monkey frolicking in the trees, the solemn elephant reposing in the shade'.[37] This is the manner perfectly caught by Evelyn Waugh's deranged vicar in *A Handful of Dust*, who regales his shivering bronchitic parishioners with sermons written for a tropical garrison chapel: 'we have for companions the ravening tiger and the exotic camel, the furtive jackal and the ponderous elephant'.[38] But when the prince and his companions at last find a way out of the Valley the writing is very different. At first the prince is delighted with the broad prospect which opens before him when he first looks out. But then, when they leave by moonlight:

> The princess and her maid turned their eyes towards every part, and seeing nothing to bound their prospect, considered themselves as in danger of being lost in a dreary vacuity. 'I am almost afraid, said the princess, to begin a journey of which I cannot perceive an end, and to venture into this immense plain where I may be approached on every side by men whom I never saw.' The prince felt nearly the same emotions, though he thought it more manly to conceal them.[39]

The very shape of the landscape seems to have changed. When the prince first looked out, and saw the River Nile winding below, he looked down into a great depth, but now everything lies level before their eyes, frightening and boundless. As they first venture into the great world, they experience agoraphobia.

From this terror of openness, Johnson gradually conducts us, through a succession of disappointments, to the crowning experience of the pilgrimage, which is, precisely, claustrophobia. As they prepare to enter the Great Pyramid

> the favourite of the princess, looking into the cavity, stepped back and trembled. 'Pekuah, said the princess, of what art thou afraid?' 'Of the narrow entrance, answered the lady, and of the dreadful gloom.'[40]

It is as if the Choice of Life has led them only to this: a dark and narrow entry to empty rooms in an enormous tomb.

But the book ends with neither agoraphobia nor claustrophobia. In the 'conclusion, in which nothing is concluded' when, like addicts, they listlessly revert to dreams of reformation and improvement, the accompanying image is that of a vast tidal river, alternately swollen and ebbing. The chapter begins with the river in flood: 'It was the time of the inundation of the Nile: a few days after their visit to the catacombs, the river began to rise.'[41] The chapter and the book end with the thought of the river subsiding: 'They deliberated a while what was to be done, and resolved, when the inundation should cease, to return to Abissinia.'[42]

The evil of the world is not explained, it is only endured. The great narrative of Milton and the spirited vindication of Pope give place to a fable which does not even end. The Aristotelian requirement that every story should show a change of fortune is bleakly refused by this most classical of authors. The stasis of optimistic theology is replaced by a stasis which is close to despair. But, in its very surrender, Johnson's intellect is manifestly more powerful than Pope's. In writing *Rasselas* he built the tomb of eighteenth-century theodicy.

NOTES

1 THE POET

1 See his *Lives of the English Poets*, ed. G. Birkbeck Hill, Vol. III, pp. 196–8.
2 *The Gentleman's Magazine*, vol. XLV (1775), p. 435.
3 W. K. Wimsatt, *The Portraits of Alexander Pope*.
4 James Prior, *The Life of Edmund Malone . . .*, pp. 428–9.
5 See Wimsatt, *Portraits*, p. xxv.
6 Lady Louisa Stuart, 'Introductory anecdotes', in *The Letters and Works of Lady Mary Wortley Montagu*, Vol. I, p. 92.
7 Henry Fielding, *The Journal of a Voyage to Lisbon*, ed. H. E. Pagliaro, pp. 44–5.
8 Johnson, *Lives*, Vol. III, pp. 189–90.
9 See J. V. Guerinot, *Pamphlet Attacks on Alexander Pope: A Descriptive Bibliography*, pp. 2–4.
10 See Norman Ault, *New Light on Pope*, pp. 302–3.
11 See Guerinot, *Pamphlet Attacks*, pp. 115–16.
12 ibid., p. 226.
13 See John Paul Russo, *Alexander Pope: Tradition and Identity*, p. 56.
14 See Guerinot, *Pamphlet Attacks*, p. xxx.
15 'Verses on the Death of Dr Swift', ll. 47–8, in *The Poetical Works of Jonathan Swift*, ed. Herbert Davis, p. 497.
16 Johnson, *Lives*, Vol. III, p. 188.
17 Earl of Chesterfield, *Characters*, ed. Charles Whibley, p. 21.
18 Wimsatt, *Portraits*, p. xxvi.
19 *An Examination of Certain Abuses, Corruptions and Enormities in the City of Dublin*, written in the year 1732, in *The Prose Works of Jonathan Swift*, ed. Herbert Davis, Vol. XII, pp. 220–1.
20 John Donne, *Biathanatos . . .*, p. 17.
21 John Locke, *Epistola de Tolerantia: A Letter on Toleration*, ed. Raymond Klibansky, trans. J. W. Gough, p. 132.
22 John Locke, *Essays on the Law of Nature*, ed. W. von Leyden, p. 26.
23 See Gough's introduction to *Epistola de Tolerantia*, p. 19.
24 See Leslie Stephen, *History of English Thought in the Eighteenth Century*, Vol. I, pp. 118, 125, 141.
25 See his *The Whig Supremacy, 1714–60*, 2nd edn, revised by C. H. Stuart, p. 68.
26 See David Ogg, *England in the Reign of Charles II*, Vol. I, pp. 368–9.
27 J. L. Miller, *Popery and Politics in England, 1660–88*, p. 66.
28 See Russo, *Alexander Pope*, p. 73.
29 See Owen Ruffhead, *The Life of Alexander Pope, Esq. . . .*, p. 542.
30 John Donne, *The Divine Poems*, ed. Helen Gardner, p. xxvii.
31 See *The Memoirs of the Life of Edward Gibbon*, ed. G. Birkbeck Hill, p. 167, and Gibbon's *History of the Decline and Fall of the Roman Empire*, ed. J. B. Bury, Vol. VII, ch. lxxi, p. 308.
32 Chesterfield, *Characters*, p. 22.
33 Johnson, *Lives*, Vol. III, p. 191.
34 R. H. Griffith, *Alexander Pope: A Bibliography*, Vol. II, p. xlvi.
35 Johnson, *Lives*, Vol. III, p. 15.

2 ORDER AND DISORDER

1 Samuel Johnson, *Lives of the English Poets*, ed. G. Birkbeck Hill, Vol. III, pp. 219, 221, 222.
2 In *The Poems of John Dryden*, ed. James Kinsley, Vol. I, p. 311.
3 ibid., p. 322.
4 ibid., p. 443.
5 See Reuven Tsur, *A Perception-Oriented Theory of Metre*, p. 59.
6 See Milton's note on 'the Verse', prefixed to *Paradise Lost*, in *The Poetical Works of John Milton*, ed. Helen Darbishire, p. 4.
7 *The Poetical Works of John Keats*, ed. H. W. Garrod, p. 65.
8 William Empson, *Seven Types of Ambiguity*, p. 70.
9 *The Works of George Herbert*, ed. F. E. Hutchinson, p. 87.
10 Johnson, *Lives*, Vol. III, p. 188.
11 Edith Sitwell, *Alexander Pope*, p. 215.
12 See also George Sherburn, *The Early Career of Alexander Pope*, p. 249.
13 Johnson, *Lives*, Vol. III, p. 92.
14 Samuel Johnson, *The History of Rasselas, Prince of Abissinia*, ed. Geoffrey Tillotson and Brian Jenkins, p. 28.
15 James Boswell, *Life of Johnson*, ed. R. W. Chapman, corrected by J. D. Fleeman, p. 427.
16 Rashleigh Holt-White, *The Life and Letters of Gilbert White of Selborne*, Vol. II, p. 63.
17 See C. S. Lewis, 'Addison', in *Essays on the Eighteenth Century Presented to David Nichol Smith*, pp. 8–9.
18 Suetonius, *Divus Augustus*, 28, in *The Lives of the Caesars*, ed. and trans. J. C. Rolfe, Vol. I, p. 166.
19 In his *Pope's 'Dunciad': A Study of Its Meaning*.
20 *Memoirs of the Life of Gibbon*, p. 167.
21 In Horace, *Satires, Epistles and Ars Poetica*, ed. and trans. H. Rushton Fairclough, p. 452.
22 In Horace, *Odes and Epodes*, ed. and trans. C. E. Bennett, p. 6.
23 *The Poems of John Dryden*, ed. James Kinsley, Vol. I, p. 266.
24 See Maynard Mack, *The Garden and the City: Retirement and Politics in the Later Poetry of Pope, 1731–43*, p. 258.
25 See Henry Martyn Taylor, 'Sir Isaac Newton', *Encyclopaedia Britannica*, 11th edn, Vol. XIX, pp. 583–92.
26 In his controversy with Newton's 'philosophical lieutenant', Samuel Clarke, 1715–17; see G. W. Leibniz and Samuel Clarke, *The Leibniz–Clarke Correspondence*, ed. H. G. Alexander, pp. xv, 11, 16–17, 28–9, 40, 81–2.
27 Sir Isaac Newton, *Opticks*, ed. I Bernard Cohen and H. D. Roller, p. 402.
28 *Leibniz-Clarke Correspondence*, pp. 11, 17–18.
29 David Hume, *A Treatise of Human Nature*, I.iii.12, ed. L. A. Selby-Bigge, p. 139.
30 Leslie Stephen, *History of English Thought in the Eighteenth Century*, Vol. I, pp. 62–234.
31 ibid., Vol. I, p. 69.

3 AN ESSAY ON MAN

1 Joseph Warton, *An Essay on the Genius and Writings of Pope*, Vol. II, pp. 57–8.
2 See *The Poetical Works of William Wordsworth*, ed. E. de Selincourt and Helen Darbishire, Vol. V, p. 2.

3 *The Correspondence of Jonathan Swift*, ed. Harold Williams, Vol. III, p. 359.

4 John Locke, *An Essay Concerning Human Understanding*, ed. Alexander Campbell Fraser, Vol. I, p. 14.

5 See Miriam Leranbaum's *Alexander Pope's Opus Magnum, 1729–1744*, esp. pp. 6–8.

6 On all these points of connection see ibid., pp. 69, 75, 100, 105.

7 William Warburton, *A View of Lord Bolingbroke's Philosophy*, Letter IV, pp. 326–7.

8 Warton, *Essay*, Vol. II, p. 62.

9 See James Boswell, *Life of Johnson*, ed. R. W. Chapman, corrected by J. D. Fleeman, p. 1032.

10 ibid., p. 1033.

11 *The Works of Mr Abraham Cowley*, p. 78.

12 In *An Essay on Man: Reproductions of the Manuscripts in the Pierpont Morgan Library and the Houghton Library with the Printed Text of the Original Edition*, with an introduction by Maynard Mack, Morgan fo. 2 *recto*, Houghton fo. 1 *recto*.

13 In his edition of *An Essay on Man*, p. 77.

14 Leslie Stephen, *History of English Thought in the Eighteenth Century*, Vol. I, p. 245.

15 Samuel Clarke, *A Discourse Concerning the Being and Attributes of God . . .*, Pt II ('Of natural religion'), pp. 6–8.

16 See *An Answer to Remarks upon An Essay Concerning Human Understanding &c.*, in *The Works of John Locke*, Vol. IV, p. 188.

17 *Analogy*, I, ii, 8, in *The Works of Bishop Butler*, ed. J. H. Bernard, Vol. II, p. 39.

18 *Les Essais de Michel de Montaigne*, Vol. II, p. 257.

19 David Hume, *The Natural History of Religion and Dialogues Concerning Natural Religion*, ed. A. Wayne Colver and John Valdimir Price, pp. 28, 33.

20 Voltaire, *Oeuvres complètes*, ed. Louis Moland, Vol. IX, p. 472.

21 In J.-P. Migne (ed.), *Patrologiae Cursus Completus (Patrologia Latina)*, Vol. XL, p. 27.

22 *The Chief Works of Benedict de Spinoza*, trans, R. H. M. Elwes, p. 55.

23 See *Essais de Montaigne*, Vol. II, p. 264.

24 Voltaire, *Dialogues et anecdotes philosophiques*, ed. Raymond Naves, p. 227.

25 See Henry St John, Lord Bolingbroke, *The Philosophical Works*, ed. David Mallet, Vol. I, p. 18.

26 A. O. Lovejoy, *The Great Chain of Being: A Study of the History of an Idea*, pp. 186–9.

27 William King, *An Essay on the Origin of Evil*, p. 106.

28 Locke, *Essay Concerning Human Understanding*, II, xxiii, 12; in Fraser's edition, Vol. I, p. 403.

29 In *The Poetical Works of Joseph Addison, Gay's Fables and Somerville's Chase*, ed. Charles Cowden Clarke, p. 46.

30 Diogenes Laertius, *Lives of Eminent Philosophers*, ed. and trans. R. D. Hicks, Vol. I, p. 40.

31 Decimus Magnus Ausonius, *Ludus Septem Sapientum*, I, 40, in *Works*, ed. and trans. Hugh G. Evelyn White, Vol. I, p. 320.

32 John Laird, *Philosophical Incursions into English Literature*, p. 43.

33 Marcus Tullius Cicero, *Tusculan Disputations*, I, xxii, 52; ed. and trans. J. E. King, p. 62.

34 Robert Burton, *The Anatomy of Melancholy*, II, iii, 7; in A. R. Shilleto's edition, Vol. II, p. 235.

35 Menander, *The Principal Fragments*, ed. and trans. Francis G. Allinson, p. 360.

36 *The Poems of Sir John Davies*, ed. Robert Krueger, p. 47.
37 ibid., p. 10.
38 René Descartes, *Oeuvres philosophiques*, ed. Ferdinand Alquié, Vol. I, p. 603.
39 Benedict de Spinoza, *Ethics*, II, xxiii, in *Opera Quotquot Reperta Sunt*, ed. J. van Vloten and J. P. N. Land, Vol. I, p. 95.
40 ibid., V, xxiii, Vol. I, p. 261.
41 David Hume, *A Treatise of Human Nature*, ed. L. A. Selby-Bigge, p. 252.
42 Walter Hilton, *The Scale of Perfection*, bk I, ch. 54; in Evelyn Underhill's edition, pp. 129–31.
43 Pico della Mirandola, *De Hominis Dignitate, Heptaplus, De Ente et Uno*, ed. Eugenio Garin, pp. 104–6 (*On the Dignity of Man*, trans. Charles Glenn Wallis, pp. 4–5); Hermes Trismegistus, *Corpus Hermeticum*, ed. A. D. Nock, trans. A.-J. Festugière, Vol. II, pp. 301–2.
44 Blaise Pascal, *Pensées sur la religion et sur quelques autres sujets*, ed. Louis Lafuma, Vol. I, p. 85.
45 *Works of Mr Abraham Cowley*, p. 39 of the Pindarique Odes.
46 Pierre Charron, *De la sagesse*, ed. M. Amaury Duval, Vol. I, p. 2.
47 In 'The study of poetry', in *The Complete Prose Works of Mathew Arnold*, ed. R. H. Super, Vol. IX, p. 181.
48 *The Poems of John Donne*, ed. H. J. C. Grierson, Vol. I, p. 237.
49 See, for example, Hume, *Treatise of Human Nature*, II, iii, 3, pp. 414–15.
50 Laird, *Philosophical Incursions*, p. 43.
51 *Works of Bishop Butler*, Vol. I, p. 5.
52 ibid., Vol. I, p. 57; cf. Vol. I, p. 151, Vol. II, p. 263.
53 Charron, *De la sagesse*, II, iii; in Duval's edition, Vol. II, p. 80. The translation is mine.
54 Bernard Mandeville, *The Fable of the Bees*, ed. F. B. Kaye, Vol. I, p. 56.
55 ibid., Vol. II, p. 178.
56 *Works of Bishop Butler*, Vol. I, pp. 16–20, 138–49.
57 See Anthony Ashley Cooper, Earl of Shaftesbury, *Characteristics of Men, Manners, Opinions, Times*, ed. John M. Robertson, Vol. II, pp. 57–8; *Works of Bishop Butler*, Vol. II, pp. 51–67; see also Stephen, *History of English Thought*, Vol. II, p. 41.
58 Bernard Mandeville, *The Fable of the Bees*, ed. Irwin Primer, p. 16.
59 See J. M. Rist, *Stoic Philosophy*, p. 25.
60 Marcus Tullius Cicero, *De Officiis*, ed. and trans. Walter Miller, I, xx, 67, p. 68.
61 Lucius Annaeus Seneca, *De Constantia Sapientis*, x, 4, in *The Moral Essays*, ed. and trans. John W. Basore, Vol. I, p. 80.
62 Shaftesbury, *Characteristics*, Vol. II, pp. 22–3.
63 *Works of Bishop Butler*, Vol. I, p. 48.
64 Mandeville, *Fable*, ed. Kaye, Vol. I, p. 51.
65 *The Works of Alexander Pope*, ed. W. Elwin and W. J. Courthope, Vol. II, p. 401.
66 Aristotle, *Metaphysics*, 1072b, in *The Works of Aristotle*, ed. W. D. Ross, Vol. VIII (no page numbers).
67 Dante Alighieri, *Paradiso*, canto VI, 11. 11–12, in *The Divine Comedy*, trans. John D. Sinclair, Vol. III, p. 87.
68 Thomas Hobbes, *Leviathan*, IV, 46, in *The English Works of Thomas Hobbes*, ed. Sir William Molesworth, Vol. III, p. 678.
69 David Hume, *Dialogues Concerning Natural Religion*, ed. Norman Kemp Smith, p. 171.
70 Philip Dormer Stanhope, Earl of Chesterfield, *Characters*, ed. Charles Whibley, p. 21.

71 See *The Poems of Jonathan Swift*, ed. Harold Williams, p. 1141.
72 William Paley, *Natural Theology*, ch. III; in Lord Brougham's edition, pp. 17–36.
73 See C. F. A. Pantin, 'Organic design', *Report of the British Association for the Advancement of Science*, Vol. 8 (1951–2), pp. 138–9; and Sir Alister Hardy, *The Living Stream*, pp. 226–7.
74 J. P. de Crousaz, *A Commentary on Mr Pope's Principles of Morality, or Essay on Man*, trans. Samuel Johnson, p. 180.
75 Samuel Daniel, *The Complete Works in Prose and Verse*, ed. A. B. Grosart, Vol. I, pp. 260–1.
76 John Locke, *An Essay Concerning the True, Original Extent and End of Civil Government*, VI, 76, in *Two Treatises of Government*, ed. Peter Laslett, p. 336.
77 ibid., I, 6, p. 289.
78 Hume, *Natural History*, ed. Colver and Price, p. 26.
79 Augustine, *City of God*, XIV, 13; Marcus Dods translation, Vol. II, p. 25
80 See Sigmund Freud, *Totem and Taboo and Other Works*, trans. James Strachey and others, IV, 5, p. 141; and his *Civilisation and Its Discontents*, trans. Joan Rivière, ed. James Strachey, pp. 68–70.
81 King, *Origin of Evil*, p. 146.
82 ibid., p. 222.
83 Johnson, 'Milton', in *Lives of the Poets*, ed. Hill, Vol. I, p. 249.
84 See above, pp. 111–12.
85 Bolingbroke, *Philosophical Works*, Vol. IV, p. 296.
86 Hume, *Dialogues Concerning Natural Religion*, ed. Smith, p. 211.
87 See, for example, Plato, *The Republic*, 354a, in *The Dialogues*, trans. Benjamin Jowett, Vol. III, p. 226.
88 ibid., Vol. IV, p. 61.
89 John Stuart Mill, *Utilitarianism*, ed. Samuel Gorovitz, ch. II, p. 20.
90 *Moral Philosophy*, I, vii, in *The Works of William Paley, DD*, Vol. III, p. 20; cf. *Evidences of Christianity*, II, ii, in ibid., Vol. II, pp. 156 ff.
91 In *The Poems and Fables of John Dryden*, ed. James Kinsley, p. 197.
92 *The Poems and Letters of Andrew Marvell*, ed. H. M. Margoliouth, revised by Pierre Legouis and E. E. Duncan-Jones, Vol. I, p. 51.
93 ibid., Vol. I, p. 51.
94 ibid., Vol. I, p. 51.
95 ibid., Vol. I, pp. 14–15.
96 Oliver Goldsmith, *The Life of Henry St John, Lord Bolingbroke* (1770), in *The Collected Works of Oliver Goldsmith*, ed. Arthur Friedman, Vol. III, p. 439.
97 Jonathan Swift, *An Enquiry into the Behaviour of the Queen's Last Ministry* (1715), in *The Prose Works of Jonathan Swift*, ed. Herbert Davis, Vol. VIII, p. 134.
98 12 December 1749 (Old Style), in *The Letters of Lord Chesterfield*, ed. Bonamy Dobrée Vol. IV, p. 1462.
99 Laird, *Philosophical Incursions*, p. 49.
100 Augustine, *Confessions*, XI, 14; ed. and trans. William Watts, Vol. II, p. 238.
101 *Annual Register*, vol. XIV (1771), p. 253.
102 See Shaftesbury, *Sensus Communis: An Essay on the Freedom of Wit and Humour* (1709), III, 1, in his *Characteristics*, Vol. I, pp. 69–71.
103 John Donne, *The Elegies and the Songs and Sonnets*, ed. Helen Gardner, p. 63.
104 See William McDougall, *An Introduction to Social Psychology*, 30th edn, esp. pp. 73–4, 172–3, 180–96; and Ian Dishart Suttie, *The Origins of Love and Hate*.
105 *Essay on Man: Reproductions of the Manuscripts*, ed. Mack, Morgan fos 21 *verso* and 22 *verso*.
106 Jean de La Bruyère, *De l'homme*, 128, in his *Les Caractères ou les mœurs de ce*

siècle, ed. Robert Garapon. This paragraph was added in the 4th edn. of *Caractères*, 1689.

107 See Alexis de Tocqueville, *L'Ancien Régime*, ed. G. W. Headlam, III, 4, p. 181.

108 Crousaz, *Commentary*, p. 223.

109 Edward Hyde, Earl of Clarendon, *The History of the Rebellion and Civil Wars in England*, ed. W. Dunn Macray, VII, 218, Vol. III, p. 178. For Falkland's weakly and unattractive appearance, see the passage cited in *Selections from 'The History of the Rebellion' and 'The Life by Himself'*, ed. G. Huehns, p. 62.

110 C. S. Lewis, *English Literature in the Sixteenth Century, Excluding Drama*, p. 324.

111 See *Essay on Man: Reproductions of the Manuscripts*, ed. Mack, Morgan fo. 23 *verso*.

112 In George Chapman, *Bussy D'Ambois*, ed. Nicholas Brooke, p. 62.

113 ibid., p. 65.

114 ibid., p. 132.

115 Thomas Babington Macaulay, *Essays*, p. 138.

116 George Crabbe, *The Borough*, bk III, 11. 142–9, in *The Poetical Works of George Crabbe*, ed. A. J. and R. M. Carlyle, p. 118.

117 Letter (in English) to Nicholas Claude Thieriot, 26 October 1726, in *Voltaire's Correspondence*, ed. Theodore Besterman, Letter 294, Vol. II, p. 36.

118 William Ayre, *Memoirs of the Life and Writings of Alexander Pope, Esq.*, Vol. II, p. 389.

119 Dedication to his *Essay on the Genius and Writings of Pope*, Vol. I, p. 10.

120 ibid., Vol. I, p. iv.

121 ibid., Vol. I, p. v.

122 'Memoirs of the life and writings of Pope', prefixed to *The Works of Alexander Pope, Esq.*, ed. William Lisle Bowles, p. xxxiv.

123 *Lectures on English Poets* (1841), in *The Complete Works of William Hazlitt*, ed. P. P. Howe, Vol. V, p. 72.

124 Charles Lloyd, *Poetical Essays on the Character of Pope, as a Poet and Moralist . . .*, p. 1.

125 ibid., p. 3.

126 Johnson, *Lives*, ed. Hill, Vol. III, p. 251.

127 'The study of poetry', in *The Complete Prose Works of Matthew Arnold*, ed. R. H. Super, Vol. IX, p. 181.

128 Hazlitt, *Works*, ed. Howe, Vol. V, p. 6.

129 George Saintsbury, *A Short History of English Literature*, pp. 551–2.

130 W. M. Thackeray, *Henry Esmond, The English Humourists, The Four Georges*, ed. George Saintsbury, p. 594.

131 *Lectures on Art* (1870), in *The Works of John Ruskin*, ed. E. T. Cooke and Alexander Wedderburn, Vol. XX, p. 76.

132 ibid., Vol. XX, p. 77.

133 William Cowper, *Table Talk*, 11. 652–5, in his *Poetical Works*, ed. H. S. Milford, p. 14.

134 'The poetry of Pope', in *The Collected Works of Thomas De Quincey*, ed. David Masson, Vol. XI, p. 62.

135 'Lord Carlisle on Pope', in De Quincey, *Works*, ed. Masson, Vol. XI, p. 119.

136 Lloyd, *Poetical Essays*, Vol. IV, p. 3.

137 Lytton Strachey, 'Pope', in his *Literary Essays*, p. 90.

138 James Reeves, *The Reputation and Writings of Alexander Pope*, pp. 15–16.

139 Johnson, *Lives*, ed. Hill, Vol. III, p. 161.

140 See his letter to Pierre Joseph Thoulier, 26 March 1754, and his letter to Marie de Vichy de Chamrond, 19 May 1754, in *Voltaire's Correspondence*, ed. Besterman, Vol. XXIV, pp. 162 and 260.

141 See E. Audra, *L'Influence française dans l'œuvre de Pope*, p. 91.
142 ibid., p. 92.
143 Bridges, *Divine Wisdom and Providence* . . ., p. 12.
144 ibid., p. 12.
145 ibid., p. 10.
146 ibid., p. 18.
147 William Ayre, *Truth. A Counterpart to Mr Pope's Essay on Man: Epistle the first*, p. 1.
148 ibid., p. 2.
149 ibid., p. 11.
150 William Warburton, *A Critical and Philosophical Commentary on Mr Pope's Essay on Man* . . ., p.148.
151 See J. P. de Crousaz, *An Examination of Mr Pope's Essay on Man*, trans. Elizabeth Carter, p. 303.
152 ibid., p. 26.
153 ibid., p. 132.
154 ibid., p. 149.
155 ibid., p. 153.
156 ibid., pp. 104 ff.
157 ibid., p. 141.
158 J. P. de Crousaz, *A Commentary on Mr Pope's Principles of Morality, or Essay on Man*, p. 74.
159 Crousaz, *Examination*, pp. 30–1.
160 Crousaz, *Commentary*, p. 44.
161 Crousaz, *Examination*, p. 83.
162 ibid., pp. 87–8.
163 See A. T. Hazen, 'Crousaz on Pope', *The Times Literary Supplement*, 2 November 1935, p. 704; and MM, p. xxi.
164 Crousaz, *Commentary*, p. 158.
165 ibid., p. 53.
166 ibid., p. 91.
167 ibid., p. 71.
168 ibid., p. 176.
169 ibid., pp. 70–1.
170 ibid., pp. 167–80.
171 Warburton, *Commentary*, p. 18.
172 ibid., p. 21.
173 ibid., pp. 54–5.
174 ibid., pp. 46–7.
175 ibid., p. 168.
176 ibid., pp. 90–1.
177 See *The Correspondence of Jonathan Swift*, ed. Harold Williams, Vol. IV, p. 359.
178 See his 'Pope at work', in *Essays on the Eighteenth Century Presented to David Nichol Smith*, p. 61.
179 Shaftesbury, *Characteristics*, Vol. I, p. 189.
180 *The Works of Alexander Pope, in Prose*, Vol. II (quarto), p. 43. In this quarto the letter is wrongly dated '10 December'.
181 Owen Ruffhead, *The Life of Alexander Pope, Esq.* . . ., p. 223.
182 See William Warburton, *A View of Lord Bolingbroke's Philosophy*, p. 328.
183 Ruffhead, *Life of Pope*, p. 218; cf. Warburton, *View*, p. 55.
184 Ruffhead, *Life of Pope*, pp. 220 and 522.
185 Johnson, *Lives*, ed. Hill, Vol. III, pp. 168 ff.
186 ibid., Vol. III, p. 243.

187 ibid., Vol. III, p. 244.
188 Warton. *Essay on the Genius and Writings of Pope*, Vol. II, pp. 58–9.
189 *Works of Pope*, ed. Bowles, Vol. III, p. 10.
190 *The Works of Lord Byron: Letters and Journals*, ed. R. E. Prothero, Vol. IV, p. 489.
191 *Lectures on English Poets*, in *Works of Hazlitt*, ed. Howe, Vol. V, p. 76.
192 Cited in W. L. MacDonald, *Pope and His Critics: A Study in Eighteenth Century Personalities*, p. 139.
193 'The poetry of Pope', in *Collected Works of De Quincey*, ed. Masson, Vol. XI, p. 86.
194 G. Wilson Knight, *Laureate of Peace: On the Genius of Alexander Pope*, p. 43.
195 *The Philosophy of the Active and Moral Powers of Man*, III, 1, in *The Collected Works of Dugald Stewart*, ed. Sir William Hamilton, Vol. VII, p. 133.
196 'Uber Optimismus', *Reflexionen zur Metaphysik*, *3703–5*, in *Kants Gesammelte Schriften*, Vol. XVII, pp. 233–4.
197 'Almonides', *Common Sense a Common Delusion*, p. 11.
198 ibid., p. 14.
199 cf. Hume, *Dialogues*, ed. Smith, pt VI, p. 171.
200 'Almonides', *Common Sense*, p. 2.
201 'The Marriage of Heaven and Hell', in *The Poetry and Prose of William Blake*, ed. Geoffrey Keynes, p. 191.
202 'Almonides', *Common Sense*, p. 30.
203 Thomas Traherne, *Poems, Centuries and Three Thanksgivings*, ed. Anne Ridler, I, 44, p. 183.

4 CODA: THE END OF THEODICY

1 A. O. Lovejoy and G. Boas, *Primitivism and Related Ideas in Antiquity*, esp. pp. 9–11.
2 John Milton, *Areopagitica* (1644), p. 12; in the Scolar Press facsimile *Prose Works*, Vol. II.
3 See Adam Mitchell Hunter, *The Teaching of Calvin: A Modern Interpretation*, p. 137.
4 'The Marriage of Heaven and Hell' (etched about 1793), in *The Poetry and Prose of William Blake*, ed. Geoffrey Keynes, p. 193.
5 John Locke, *An Essay Concerning Human Understanding*, II, vi, 9; in Fraser's edn. Vol. II, p. 64.
6 David Hume, *Dialogues Concerning Natural Religion*, ed. Norman Kemp Smith, XI, p. 211.
7 A. O. Lovejoy, *The Great Chain of Being: A Study of the History of an Idea*, p. 222.
8 G. W. Leibniz, *Théodicée*, 124, in *Die Philosophischen Schriften*, ed. C. I. Gerhardt, Vol. VI, p. 179.
9 G. W. Leibniz, *Philosophische Abhandlungen*, VIII, 12–13, in ibid., Vol. VII, p. 290.
10 Letter to Louis Bourguet, December 1714, in ibid., Vol. III, p. 573.
11 22 June 1679, in ibid., Vol. I, p. 331.
12 Lovejoy, *Great Chain of Being*, pp. 144–5.
13 Samuel Johnson, 'Review of *A Free Enquiry*', in *Prose and Poetry*, ed. Mona Wilson, pp. 351, 352, 353, 356, 357, 359, 361.
14 ibid., p. 353.
15 ibid., p. 356.
16 ibid., p. 357.

17 ibid., p. 357.
18 ibid., p. 367.
19 ibid., p. 369.
20 ibid., p. 371.
21 Voltaire, *Candide*, ch. XII, in *Romans et contes*, ed. F. Deloffre and J. van den Heuvel, p. 172.
22 Samuel Johnson, *The History of Rasselas, Prince of Abissinia*, ch. III, ed. Geoffrey Tillotson and Brian Jenkins, p. 8.
23 ibid., ch. XII, p. 37.
24 ibid., ch. XVIII, p. 50.
25 ibid., ch. XVIII, p. 51.
26 See above, pp. 3–4.
27 Johnson, *Rasselas*, ed. Tillotson and Jenkins, ch. XXXV, p. 91.
28 ibid., ch. XXXIX, pp. 103–4.
29 ibid., ch. XXXIX, p. 104.
30 See C. S. Lewis's sermon, 'The weight of glory', in his *They Asked for a Paper*, esp. pp. 199–202.
31 Johnson, *Rasselas*, ed. Tillotson and Jenkins, ch. XXXII, p. 85.
32 ibid., ch. XXII, p. 60.
33 Vol. II, p. 236.
34 Johnson, *Rasselas*, ed. Tillotson and Jenkins, ch. VI, p. 18, and ch. XIII, p. 39.
35 ibid., ch. XLIV, p. 114.
36 ibid., ch. XLIV, pp. 115–17.
37 ibid., ch. I, p. 2.
38 Evelyn Waugh, *A Handful of Dust* (London: Chapman & Hall, 1951), p. 60.
39 Johnson, *Rasselas*, ed. Tillotson and Jenkins, ch. XV, p. 42.
40 ibid., ch. XXXI, pp. 82–3.
41 ibid., ch. XLIX, p. 133.
42 ibid., ch. XLIX, p. 134

BIBLIOGRAPHY

For more complete lists, see R. H. Griffith, *Alexander Pope: A Bibliography*, 2 vols (Austin, Tex.: University of Texas Press, 1922–7; reprinted London: Holland Press, 1962), James Edward Tobin, *Alexander Pope: A List of Critical Studies Published from 1895 to 1944* (New York: Cosmopolitan Science and Art Service, 1945). and Wolfgang Kowalk, *Alexander Pope: An Annotated Bibliography of Twentieth Century Criticism, 1900–1979* (Frankfurt: Peter D. Lang, 1981).

This bibliography is divided into three sections: (i) Works by Pope; (ii) Works Written before 1800; and (iii) Works Written after 1800. I have added occasional explanatory notes, especially to the very early or very recent works. For translations of *An Essay on Man*, see under the name of the translator.

(i) WORKS BY POPE

The Correspondence of Alexander Pope, ed. George Sherburn, 5 vols (Oxford: Clarendon Press, 1956).

An Essay on Man, Being the First Book of Ethic Epistles. To Henry St John, L. Bolingbroke (London: printed by John Wright for Lawton Gilliver, 1734). The first collected edition, containing all four epistles, was advertised in 1734 as being available in large folio, small folio and quarto. All were described as incorporating 'the author's corrections', but in fact only this edition, the quarto, contains the full set of revisions made by Pope in the fourth epistle by this date (he made further changes later). Available in facsimile reproduction by Scolar Press (Menston, 1969); the Scolar facsimile includes as an appendix the 'Index to the ethic epistles', which Pope tried to suppress.

An Essay on Man, ed. Maynard Mack, the Twickenham Edition (London: Methuen, 1950).

An Essay on Man, ed. Mark Pattison (Oxford: Clarendon Press, 1869).

An Essay on Man: Reproductions of the Manuscripts in the Pierpont Morgan Library and the Houghton Library with the Printed Text of the Original Edition, with an introduction by Maynard Mack (Oxford: printed for presentation to the members of the Roxburghe Club, 1962).

The Poems of Alexander Pope, ed. John Butt (London: Methuen, 1968). A one-volume edition of the Twickenham Edition text, with selected annotations; a corrected reprint of the edition of 1963.

The Poems of Alexander Pope, the Twickenham Edition, general editor John Butt, 11 vols in 12 (London: Methuen, 1950–69).

The Works of Mr Alexander Pope, in Prose, Vol. II (London: J. and P. Knapton, C. Bathurst and R. Dodsley, 1741). This volume was published separately in quarto.

The Works of Alexander Pope, Esq., ed. William Lisle Bowles, 10 vols (London: J. Johnson and others, 1806).

The Works of Alexander Pope, ed. W. Elwin and W. J. Courthope, 10 vols (London: John Murray, 1871–89).

The Works of Alexander Pope, Esq. . . . together with the Commentary and Notes of Mr Warburton, 9 vols (London: A. Millar, J. and R. Tonson, H. Lintot and C. Bathurst, 1760). *An Essay on Man* is in Vol. III. This edition contains material not in the earlier Warburton edition of 1752. Elwin and Courthope reprinted Warburton's commentary and notes in their edition. The commentary itself is an abridged and modified version of Warburton's *Critical and Philosophical Commentary* (see under Warburton in section (ii) below).

(ii) WORKS WRITTEN BEFORE 1800

Addison, Joseph, *The Poetical Works of Joseph Addison, Gay's Fables and Somerville's Chase*, ed. Charles Cowden Clarke (London: Cassell, Petter & Galpin, n.d.).

'Almonides' (pseudonym), *Common Sense a Common Delusion, or, The generally received Notions of Natural Causes, Deity, Religion, Virtue, &c. As exhibited in Mr Pope's Essay on Man, proved Ridiculous, Impious etc.* (London: T. Reynolds, 1751).

Annual Register (London: Dodsley, 1758–).

Anonymous, 'Plan of an *English* Dictionary', *Gray's Inn Journal*, Vol. II (1756), pp. 231–6.

Aristotle, *The Works of Aristotle*, trans. under the editorship of W. D. Ross, 12 vols (Oxford: Clarendon Press, 1928–52).

Armstrong, John (pseudonym 'Lionel Temple'), *Sketches or Essays on Various Subjects*, in *Harrison's British Classics*, Vol. VIII (London: Harrison & Co., 1787).

Augustine, *The City of God*, trans. Marcus Dods, 2 vols (Edinburgh: T. and T. Clark, 1872).

Augustine, *Confessions*, with an English translation by William Watts, the Loeb edition, 2 vols (London: Heinemann, 1951).

Augustine, *De Diversis Quaestionibus*, in J.-P. Migne (ed.), *Patrologiae Cursus Completus*, Latin Series (commonly known as *Patrologia Latina*) (Paris, 1844–64), Vol. XL (1845), pp. 11–147.

Ausonius, Decimus Magnus, *Works*, with a translation by Hugh G. Evelyn White, the Loeb edition, 2 vols (London: Heinemann, 1961).

Ayre, William, *Memoirs of the Life and Writings of Alexander Pope, Esq.*, 2 vols (London: printed for the author, 1745).

Ayre, William, *Truth. A Counterpart to Mr Pope's Essay on Man: Epistle the first* (London: R. Minors, 1739). The same work was reprinted with three other epistles in Ayre's *Four Ethic Epistles, opposing some of Mr Pope's Opinions of Man, as Set Forth in His Essay* (London: Samuel Paterson, 1753).

Blake, William, *Poetry and Prose of William Blake*, ed. Geoffrey Keynes (London: Nonesuch Press, 1956).

Bolingbroke, Henry St John, Lord, *The Philosophical Works*, ed. David Mallet, 5 vols (London, 1754).

Boswell, James, *Life of Johnson*, ed. G. Birbeck Hill, revised and enlarged by L. F. Powell, 6 vols (Oxford: Clarendon Press, 1934–64).

Boswell, James, *Life of Johnson*, ed. R. W. Chapman, corrected by J. D. Fleeman (London: Oxford University Press, 1970).

Bridges, ———, *Divine Wisdom and Providence; an Essay Occasioned by the Essay on Man* (London: T. Worral, 1738).

Burton, Robert, *The Anatomy of Melancholy*, ed. A. R. Shilleto, 3 vols (London: Bell, 1903–4).

Butler, Joseph, *The Works of Bishop Butler*, ed. J. H. Bernard, 2 vols (London: Macmillan, 1900).

Chapman, George, *Bussy D'Ambois*, ed. Nicholas Brooke (London: Methuen, 1964).

Charron, Pierre, *De la sagesse*, ed. M. Amaury Duval, 3 vols (Paris: Chassériau, 1820–4).

Chesterfield, Philip Dormer Stanhope, 4th Earl of, *Characters*, ed. Charles Whibley (London: Peter Davies, 1927). The text follows the first edition of *Miscellaneous Works* (1778), supplemented and corrected with reference to Lord Mahon's edition of 1854.

Chesterfield, Philip Dormer Stanhope, 4th Earl of, *The Letters*, ed. Bonamy Dobrée, 6 vols (London: Eyre & Spottiswoode, 1932).

Cicero, Marcus Tullius, *De Officiis*, with an English translation by Walter Miller, the Loeb edition (London: Heinemann, 1913).

Cicero, Marcus Tullius, *Tusculan Disputations*, with an English translation by J. E. King, the Loeb edition (London: Heinemann, 1960).

Clarendon, Edward Hyde, 1st Earl of, *The History of the Rebellion and Civil Wars in England*, ed. W. Dunn Macray, 6 vols (Oxford: Clarendon Press, 1888).

Clarendon, Edward Hyde, 1st Earl of, *Selections from 'The History of the Rebellion' and 'The Life by Himself'*, ed. G. Huehns (Oxford: Oxford University Press, 1978).

Clarke, Samuel, *A Discourse Concerning the Being and Attributes of God, the Obligations of Natural Religion, and the Truth and Certainty of the Christian Revelation* (London: J. Knapton, 1716). The Boyle Lectures for 1704 and 1705.

Collins, Anthony, *A Discourse of Free-Thinking, occasioned by the rise and growth of a sect call'd Free-Thinkers* (London, 1713).

Cowley, Abraham, *The Complete Works in Verse and Prose of Abraham Cowley*, ed. Alexander B. Grosart, 2 vols (New York: AMS Press, 1967).

Cowley, Abraham, *The Works of Mr Abraham Cowley* (London: Henry Herringman, 1680).

Cowper, William, *The Poetical Works of William Cowper*, ed. H. S. Milford, 4th edn (London: Oxford University Press, 1934; revised reprint, 1967).

Crabbe, George, *The Poetical Works of George Crabbe*, ed. A. J. Carlyle and R. M. Carlyle (London: Oxford University Press, 1908).

Crousaz, J. P. de, *Commentaire sur la traduction en vers de M. l'abbé du Resnel, de l'essai de M. Pope sur l'homme* (Geneva: Pellisari, 1738).

Crousaz, J. P. de, *A Commentary on Mr Pope's Principles of Morality, or Essay on Man* (London: E. Cave, 1742). This is the translation by Johnson and contains his notes. Mack says there is a copy of this work in the Yale Library bearing the date 1739 and a Dodd imprint (MM, p. xxi). See also

A. T. Hazen, 'Crousaz on Pope', *The Times Literary Supplement*, 2 November 1935, p. 704.

Crousaz, J. P. de, *Examen de l'essay de Monsieur Pope sur l'homme* (Lausanne/Amsterdam, 1737).

Crousaz, J. P. de, *An Examination of Mr Pope's Essay on Man*, trans. Elizabeth Carter (London: A. Dodd, 1739). This is a translation of his *Examen de l'essay de Monsieur Pope sur l'homme*.

Daniel, Samuel, *The Complete Works in Prose and Verse*, ed. A. B. Grosart, 5 vols (London; privately printed, 1885–96).

Dante Alighieri, *The Divine Comedy*, with translation and comment by John D. Sinclair, 3 vols (London: Bodley Head, 1958).

Davies, Sir John, *The Poems of Sir John Davies*, ed. Robert Krueger (Oxford: Clarendon Press, 1975).

Descartes, René, *Oeuvres philosophiques*, ed. Ferdinand Alquié, 3 vols (Paris: Garnier Frères, 1963–73).

Diogenes Laertius, *Lives of Eminent Philosophers*, with an English translation by R. D. Hicks, the Loeb edition, 2 vols (London: Heinemann, 1959).

Donne, John, *Biathanatos. A declaration of that paradoxe, or thesis, that Self-homicide is not so Naturally Sinne, that it may never be otherwise* (London: H. Moseley 1648). This is a duplicate of the edition of 1644, with a different title-page.

Donne, John, *The Divine Poems*, ed. Helen Gardner, 2nd edn (Oxford: Clarendon Press, 1978).

Donne, John, *The Elegies and the Songs and Sonnets*, ed. Helen Gardner (Oxford: Clarendon Press, 1965).

Donne, John, *The Poems of John Donne*, ed. H. J. C. Grierson, 2 vols (London: Oxford University Press, 1912).

Donne, John, *The Satires, Epigrams and Verse Letters*, ed. W. Milgate (Oxford: Clarendon Press, 1967).

Dryden, John, *The Poems of John Dryden*, ed. James Kinsley, 4 vols (Oxford: Clarendon Press, 1958).

Du Resnel du Bellay, Jean François (trans.), *Les Principes de la morale (ou essai sur l'homme) et du goût (ou essai sur la critique)* (Paris: Chez Briasson, 1737).

Fielding, Henry, *The Journal of a Voyage to Lisbon*, ed. H. E. Pagliaro (New York: Nardon Press, 1963). First published in 1755.

The Gentleman's Magazine (London: various publishers, 1731–1836).

Gibbon, Edward, *The History of the Decline and Fall of the Roman Empire*, ed. J. B. Bury, 7 vols (London: Methuen, 1911–21).

Gibbon, Edward, *The Memoirs of the Life of Edward Gibbon*, ed. G. Birkbeck Hill (London: Methuen, 1900).

Gildon, Charles, *Memoirs of the Life of William Wycherley Esq., with a Character of his Writings* (London: E. Curll, 1718). Gildon wrote the memoir, Lord Lansdowne the 'character'.

Goldsmith, Oliver, *The Collected Works of Oliver Goldsmith*, ed. Arthur Friedman (Oxford: Clarendon Press, 1966).

Gray's Inn Journal (London: various publishers, 1753–4, 1756). Earlier numbers were published in *The Craftsman* (London, 1727–36).

Herbert, George, *The Works of George Herbert*, ed. F. E. Hutchinson (Oxford: Clarendon Press, 1941).

Hermes Trismegistus, *Corpus Hermeticum*, ed. A. D. Nock, trans. A. J. Festugière, 4 vols (Paris: Société d'Edition 'Les Belles Lettres', 1960).

Hesiod, *Theogony*, ed. M. L. West (Oxford: Clarendon Press, 1966).

Hilton, Walter, *The Scale of Perfection*, ed. Evelyn Underhill (London: John M. Watkins, 1923).

Hobbes, Thomas, *The English Works of Thomas Hobbes*, ed. Sir William Molesworth, 11 vols (London: John Bohn, 1839–44).

Horace (Quintus Horatius Flaccus), *Odes and Epodes*, with an English translation by C. E. Bennett, the Loeb edition (London: Heinemann, 1960).

Horace (Quintus Horatius Flaccus), *Satires, Epistles and Ars Poetica*, with an English translation by H. Rushton Fairclough, the Loeb edition (London: Heinemann, 1961).

Hume, David, *Dialogues Concerning Natural Religion*, ed. Norman Kemp Smith (London: Nelson, 1947).

Hume, David, *The Natural History of Religion*, ed. A. Wayne Colver, and *Dialogues Concerning Natural Religion*, ed. John Valdimir Price, in one volume (Oxford: Clarendon Press, 1976).

Hume, David, *A Treatise of Human Nature*, ed. L. A. Selby-Bigge (Oxford: Clarendon Press, 1888). First published 1739–40.

Jenyns, Soame, *A Free Inquiry into the Nature and Origin of Evil*, in *The Works of Soame Jenyns*, Vol. III, with 'short sketches of the History of the Author's family and also of his life' by Charles Nalson Cole, 4 vols (London: T. Cadell, 1790; republished in facsimile, Farnborough: Gregg International, 1969).

Johnson, Samuel, *The History of Rasselas, Prince of Abissinia*, ed. Geoffrey Tillotson and Brian Jenkins (London: Oxford University Press, 1971). The text is that of the British Museum copy of the first edition (1759) collated with that of the second (also 1759). The title, in both editions, is *The Prince of Abissinia: A Tale*.

Johnson, Samuel, *Lives of Dryden and Pope*, ed. Alfred Milnes (Oxford: Clarendon Press, 1915).

Johnson, Samuel, *Lives of the English Poets*, ed. G. Birkbeck Hill, 3 vols (Oxford: Clarendon Press, 1905).

Johnson, Samuel, *The Lives of the most eminent English Poets with Critical Observations on their Works*, 4 vols (London: for C. Bathurst and others, 1783). This was the latest edition in Johnson's lifetime and one in which he made a few corrections of errors which had appeared in the first edition (1781).

Johnson, Samuel, *The Poems*, ed. David Nichol Smith and Edward L. McAdam (Oxford: Clarendon Press, 1974)

Johnson, Samuel, *Prose and Poetry*, selected by Mona Wilson (London: Hart-Davis, 1957). Contains (pp. 351–74) a good text of Johnson's review of Soame Jenyns's *A Free Inquiry into the Nature and Origin of Evil*. The review appeared in the *Literary Magazine* in three consecutive numbers in 1757: no. 13, pp. 171–5; no. 14, pp. 251–3; no. 15, pp. 301–6. Mona

Wilson's text is taken directly from the British Museum copies of the *Literary Magazine*.

Johnson, Samuel, *Works*, general editor A. T. Hazen (New Haven, Conn.: Yale University Press, 1958–). Vols I–X, XIV already published.

Juvenal, Decimus Junius, *The Satires*, ed. John Ferguson (London: Macmillan, 1979).

Kant, Immanuel, *Allgemeine Naturgeschichte und Theorie des Himmels . . .* (1755), in *Kant's Gesammelte Schriften*, herausgegeben von der Preussischen Akademie des Wissenschaften (Berlin: Vols I–VIII, Georg Reimer; Vols IX–XXIII, Walter de Gruyter, 1910–53). Quotes *An Essay on Man* repeatedly, with approval.

Kant, Immanuel, *Reflexionen zur Metaphysik*, 3703–3705, 'über Optimismus', in *Kant's Gesammelte Schriften*, Vol. XVII, pp. 229–39. Sets Pope above previous optimists, including Leibniz.

Keats, John, *The Poetical Works of John Keats*, ed. H. W. Garrod (Oxford: Clarendon Press, 1958).

King, William, *An Essay on the Origin of Evil* (London: W. Thurlbourn, 1731). The translation and notes are by Edmund Law, Bishop of Carlisle. King's original Latin version, *De Origine Mali*, appeared in 1702.

La Bruyère, Jean de, *Les Caractères ou les mœurs de ce siècle*, ed. Robert Garapon (Paris: Garnier Frères, 1962).

Lactantius, Lucius Caelius Firmianus, *A Treatise on the Anger of God*, in *The Works of Lactantius*, trans. William Fletcher, 2 vols (Edinburgh: T. and T. Clark, 1871), Vol. II, pp. 1–48.

Leibniz, G. W., *Die Philosophischen Schriften*, ed. C. I. Gerhardt, 7 vols (Hildesheim: Georg Olms, 1962). A reproduction of the Weidemann edition (Berlin, 1875–90).

Leibniz, G. W., and Clarke, S., *The Leibniz–Clarke Correspondence*, ed. H. G. Alexander (Manchester: Manchester University Press, 1956).

Locke, John, *Epistola de Tolerantia: A Letter on Toleration*, ed. Raymond Klibansky and trans. J. W. Gough (Oxford: Clarendon Press, 1968). The first edition appeared in Gouda in 1689.

Locke, John, *An Essay Concerning Human Understanding*, ed. Alexander Campbell Fraser, 2 vols (London: Oxford University Press, 1894; reprinted New York: Dover, 1959).

Locke, John, *An Essay Concerning Human Understanding*, ed. Peter H. Nidditch (Oxford: Clarendon Press, 1975; corrected reprint, 1979).

Locke, John, *Essays on the Law of Nature*, ed. W. von Leyden (Oxford: Clarendon Press, 1954).

Locke, John, *The Reasonableness of Christianity* with *A Discourse of Miracles* and part of *A Third Letter Concerning Toleration*, ed. and abridged I. T. Ramsey (London: Black, 1958). *The Reasonableness of Christianity* was first published in 1695.

Locke, John, *Two Treatises of Government*, ed. Peter Laslett (Cambridge: Cambridge University Press, 1960).

Locke, John, *The Works of John Locke*, 10 vols (London: T. Tegg, 1823; reprinted Scientia Verlag Aalen, 1963).

Lucretius (Titus Lucretius Carus), *De Rerum Natura Libri Sex*, ed.

with a translation by Cyril Bailey, 3 vols (Oxford: Clarendon Press, 1947).

Mandeville, Bernard, *The Fable of the Bees; or, Private Vices, Publick Benefits*, ed. with a commentary by F. B. Kaye, 2 vols (Oxford: Clarendon Press, 1924).

Mandeville, Bernard, *The Fable of the Bees; or, Private Vices, Publick Benefits*, ed. Irwin Primer (New York: Capricorn, 1962).

Marvell, Andrew, *The Poems and Letters of Andrew Marvell*, ed. H. M. Margoliouth, revised by Pierre Legouis with E. E. Duncan-Jones, 2 vols (Oxford: Clarendon Press, 1971).

Menander, *The Principal Fragments*, with a translation by Francis G. Allinson, the Loeb edition (London: Heinemann, 1921).

Migne, J.-P. (ed.), *Patrologiae Cursus Completus*, Latin Series (commonly known as *Patrologia Latina*) (Paris, 1844–64).

Milton, John, *Areopagitica* (London: 1644). Available in facsimile in John Milton, *Prose Works, 1641–1650*, Vol. II, *The Divorce Tracts, Areopagitica and Of Education* (Menston: The Scolar Press, 1968).

Milton, John, *The Poetical Works*, ed. H. C. Beeching (London: Oxford University Press, 1938).

Milton, John, *The Poetical Works of John Milton*, ed. Helen Darbishire (London: Oxford University Press, 1958).

Montaigne, Michel, seigneur de, *Les Essais de Michel de Montaigne*, 4 vols (Bordeaux: F. Pech, 1906–20).

Newton, Sir Isaac, *Opticks, or a Treatise of the Reflections, Refractions, Inflections and Colours of Light*, with a foreword by Albert Einstein, an introduction by Sir Edmund Whittaker, a preface by I. Bernard Cohen and an analytical table of contents prepared by Duane H. D. Roller (New York: Dover, 1952). Based on the 4th edn (London, 1730).

Paley, William, *Natural Theology, or Evidences of the Existence and Attributes of the Deity, collected from the Appearances of Nature*, 4th edn (London: R. Faulder, 1803).

Paley, William, *Paley's Natural Theology*, with notes and introduction by Henry, Lord Brougham, 4 vols (London: Charles Knight, 1845).

Pascal, Blaise, *Pensées sur la religion et sur quelques autres sujets*, ed. Louis Lafuma, 3 vols (Paris: Editions du Luxembourg, 1952).

Pico della Mirandola, *De Hominis Dignitate, Heptaplus, De Ente et Uno*, ed. Eugenio Garin (Florence: Vallechi Editori, 1942).

Pico della Mirandola, *On the Dignity of Man*, trans, Charles Glenn Wallis, *On Being and the One*, trans. Paul J. W. Miller, *Heptaplus*, trans. Douglas Carmichael (New York: Bobbs-Merrill, 1940).

Plato, *The Dialogues*, trans. Benjamin Jowett, 4 vols (Oxford: Clarendon Press, 1875).

Racine, Louis, *La Religion, poëme* . . . (Paris: J. B. Coignard, 1742).

Ruffhead, Owen, *The Life of Alexander Pope, Esq., compiled from Original Manuscripts, with a Critical Essay on his Writings and Genius* (London: C. Bathurst, 1769; reprinted Hildesheim: Georg Olms, 1968). Pro-Warburton, against Bolingbroke (and Crousaz); borrows heavily from Warburton.

Seneca, Lucius Annaeus, *Moral Essays*, with an English translation by John W. Basore, the Loeb edition, 3 vols (London: Heinemann, 1958).

Shaftesbury, Anthony Ashley Cooper, Earl of, *Characteristics of Men, Manners, Opinions, Times*, ed. John M. Robertson, 2 vols in 1 (New York: Bobbs-Merrill, 1964).

Shakespeare, William, *The Complete Works*, ed. Peter Alexander (London: Collins, 1951).

Silhouette, Etienne de (trans.), *Essai sur l'homme, par M. Pope* (Amsterdam: J. F. Bernard, 1736).

Spence, Joseph, *Observations, Anecdotes, and Characters of Books and Men*, ed. James M. Osborn, 2 vols (Oxford: Clarendon Press, 1966).

Spinoza, Benedict de, *The Chief Works of Benedict de Spinoza*, trans. R. H. M. Elwes (London: Bell, 1891).

Spinoza, Benedict de, *Opera quotquot Reperta sunt*, ed. J. van Vloten and J. P. N. Land, 4 vols in 2 (The Hague: Martin Nijhoff, 1914).

Sterne, Laurence, *The Life and Opinions of Tristram Shandy, gentleman*, ed. J. A. Work (New York: Odyssey, 1940).

Stewart, Dugald, *The Collected Works of Dugald Stewart*, ed. Sir William Hamilton, 10 vols and supplement (Edinburgh: Constable, 1854–8).

Suetonius (Caius Suetonius Tranquillus), *The Lives of the Caesars*, with an English translation by J. C. Rolfe, the Loeb edition, 2 vols (London: Heinemann, 1960).

Swift, Jonathan, *The Complete Poems*, ed. Pat Rogers (Harmondsworth: Penguin, 1983).

Swift, Jonathan, *The Correspondence of Jonathan Swift*, ed. Harold Williams, 5 vols (Oxford: Clarendon Press, 1963–5).

Swift, Jonathan, *The Poems of Jonathan Swift*, ed. Harold Williams, 3 vols (Oxford: Clarendon Press, 1958).

Swift, Jonathan, *The Poetical Works of Jonathan Swift*, ed. Herbert Davis (London: Oxford University Press, 1967).

Swift, Jonathan, *The Prose Works of Jonathan Swift*, ed. Herbert Davis, 14 vols (Oxford: Blackwell, 1939–68).

Tindal, Matthew, *Christianity as Old as the Creation; or, The Gospel A Republication of the Religion of Nature* (London, 1730).

Toland, John, *Christianity not Mysterious; or A Treatise Shewing, that There Is Nothing in the Gospel Contrary to Reason, nor above it: and that No Christian Doctrine Can Be Properly Call'd a Mystery* (London: Sam Buckley, 1696).

Traherne, Thomas, *Poems, Centuries and Three Thanksgivings*, ed. Anne Ridler (London: Oxford University Press, 1966).

Virgil (Publius Vergilius Maro), *Eclogues, Georgics, Aeneid*, with an English translation by H. Rushton Fairclough, the Loeb edition, 2 vols (London: Heinemann, 1926).

Voltaire, François Marie Arouet de, *Dialogues et anecdotes philosophiques*, ed. Raymond Naves (Paris: Garnier Frères, 1955).

Voltaire, François Marie Arouet de, *Oeuvres complètes*, ed. Louis Moland, 52 vols (Paris: Garnier Frères, 1877–85).

Voltaire, François Marie Arouet de, Romans et contes, ed. F. Deloffre and

J. Van den Heuvel (Paris: Gallimard, 1979). This volume contains both *Micromégas* (pp. 19–37) and *Candide* (pp. 145–233).

Voltaire, François Marie Arouet de, *Voltaire's Correspondence*, ed. Theodore Besterman, 107 vols (Geneva: Institut et Musée Volontaire, 1953–65). Excellent indexes.

Warburton, William, *A Critical and Philosophical Commentary on Mr Pope's Essay on Man. In which is contained A Vindication of the said Essay from the Misrepresentations of Mr De Resnel . . . and of Mr De Crousaz* (London: J. and P. Knapton, 1742). This is the work more commonly known as *A Vindication of Mr Pope's Essay on Man* extended by the addition of a seventh letter.

Warburton, William, *A View of Lord Bolingbroke's Philosophy* (London: A. Millar, J. and R. Tonson, S. Draper, 1756).

Warburton, William: for his notes and commentary in his edition of Pope, see section (i) above.

Warton, Joseph, *An Essay on the Genius and Writings of Pope*, 2 vols (London: J. Dodsley, 1782; reprinted New York: Garland, 1970).

Wollaston, William, *The Religion of Nature Delineated*, with an introduction by Stanley Tweyman (Delmar, NY: Scholars' Facsimiles and Reprints, 1974). This is a facsimile of the corrected reprint of 1724. The work first appeared in 1722.

(iii) WORKS WRITTEN AFTER 1800

Aden, John M., *see* Zoellner, Robert M.

Adler, Jacob H., 'Balance in Pope's *Essays*', *English Studies*, vol. 43 (1962), pp. 457–67.

Alderman, William E., 'Pope's *Essay on Man* and Shaftesbury's *The Moralists*', *Publications of the Bibliographical Society of America*, vol. 67 (1973), pp. 131–40.

Alderman, William E., 'Shaftesbury and the doctrine of moral sense in the eighteenth century', *Publications of the Modern Language Association of America*, vol. 46 (1931), pp. 1087–94.

Aldridge, A. O., 'Milton and Pope's conception of God and man', *Bibliotheca Sacra*, vol. 96 (1939), pp. 444–58.

Arnold, Matthew, 'On translating Homer', in *The Complete Prose Works of Mathew Arnold*, ed. R. H. Super, 11 vols (Ann Arbor, Mich.: University of Michigan Press, 1962–77), Vol. I, *On the Classical Tradition*, pp. 97–216. Contrasts Homer's preoccupation with the object with Pope's preoccupation with style.

Arnold, Matthew, 'The study of poetry', first published in 1880 as the general introduction to *The English Poets*, ed. T. H. Ward, in *The Complete Prose Works of Matthew Arnold*, Vol. IX, *English Literature and Irish Politics*, pp. 161–88.

Atkins, G. Douglas, 'Pope and Deism: a new analysis', in *Pope: Recent Essays by Several Hands*, ed. Maynard Mack and James A. Winn (Brighton: Harvester Press, 1980), pp. 392–415. Argues against the 'Deistical' interpretation of *An Essay on Man*.

Auden, W. H., 'A civilised voice', in his *Forewords and Afterwords*, selected by E. Mendelson (London: Faber, 1973), pp. 109–24.

Audra, E. *L'Influence française dans l'œuvre de Pope* (Paris: Librairie Ancienne Honoré Champion, 1931).

Ault, Norman, *New Light on Pope* (London: Methuen, 1949).

Barker, John, *Strange Contraries: Pascal in England during the Age of Reason* (Montreal: McGill-Queens University Press, 1975).

Beales, A. C. F., *Education under Penalty: English Catholic Education from the Reformation to the Fall of James II, 1547–1689* (London: Athlone Press, 1963).

Beaumont, Charles A., 'The rising and falling metaphor in Pope's *Essay on Man*', *Style*, vol. 1 (1967), pp. 121–30.

Bonnard, G. A., 'Note on the English translations of Crousaz' two books on Pope's *Essay on Man*', *Recueil de travaux* (Lausanne: Faculté des Lettres, 1937), pp. 175–84.

Bowles, William Lisle: for his edition of Pope, see section (i) above.

Brett, R. L., 'Pope's *Essay on Man*', in his *Reason and Imagination: A Study of Form and Meaning in Four Poems* (London: Oxford University Press, 1960), pp. 51–77.

Brower, Reuben A., *Alexander Pope: The Poetry of Allusion* (Oxford: Clarendon Press, 1959). Principally concerned with Pope's use of the classics, but includes a critical account of his philosophy.

Bullough, Geoffrey, 'Changing views of the mind in English poetry', *Proceedings of the British Academy*, vol. 41 (1955), pp. 61–83. Discusses Pope's theory of the Ruling Passion.

Byron, George Gordon, Lord, 'Reply to Blackwood's *Edinburgh Magazine*' (1819), printed as appendix IX in *The Works of Lord Byron: Letters and Journals*, ed. R. E. Prothero, 6 vols (London: John Murray, 1902–4), Vol. IV, pp. 474–95.

Campo, Mariano, *La Genesi del Criticismo Kantiano* (Varese: Editrice Magenta, 1953). Gives an account of Kant's early admiration of Pope.

Cruttwell, Patrick, 'Pope and his church', *Hudson Review*, vol. 13 (1960–1), pp. 392–405. On Pope's Roman Catholicism.

Danielson, Dennis Richard, *Milton's Good God: A Study in Literary Theodicy* (Cambridge: Cambridge University Press, 1982).

De Quincey, Thomas, *The Collected Works of Thomas De Quincey*, ed. David Masson, 14 vols (Edinburgh: Black, 1889–90).

Dobrée, Bonamy, 'Books and writers', *The Spectator*, vol. 186 (1951), p. 418.

Dobrée, Bonamy, *English Literature in the Early Eighteenth Century, 1700–1740* (Oxford: Clarendon Press, 1959).

Edwards, Thomas R., Jnr, *This Dark Estate: A Reading of Pope* (Berkeley, Los Angeles, Calif.: University of California Press, 1963). Contains a chapter dealing with the gap between Pope's philosophy and his own experience: Pope was not 'wholly convinced by his own vision of order'.

Edwards, Thomas R., Jnr, 'Visible poetry: Pope and modern criticism', in

Reuben Brower (ed.), *Twentieth Century Literature in Retrospect*, Harvard English Studies, No. 2 (Cambridge, Mass.: Harvard University Press, 1971), pp. 299–321. Pope's changes of direction were not mere philosophical confusion but a visible expression of 'dissatisfaction with what one can say'.

Empson, William, *Seven Types of Ambiguity* (Harmondsworth: Penguin, 1961). First published 1930.

Erskine-Hill, Howard, *The Social Milieu of Alexander Pope* (New Haven, Conn.: Yale University Press, 1979). A good account of Pope's friendships.

Fabian, Bernhard, 'On the literary background of the *Essay on Man*: a note on Pope and Lucretius' (1973), in Maynard Mack and James A. Winn (eds), *Pope: Recent Essays by Several Hands* (Brighton: Harvester Press, 1980), pp. 416–27.

Fabian, Bernhard, 'Pope and Lucretius: observations on *An Essay on Man*', *Modern Language Review*, vol. 74 (1979), pp. 524–37.

Fleischmann, W. B., 'Alexander Pope and Lucretian "anonymity"', *Neophilogus*, vol. 44 (1960), pp. 216–18.

Friedman, Arthur, 'Pope and Deism', in James L. Clifford and Louis A. Landa (eds), *Pope and His Contemporaries: Essays Presented to George Sherburn* (Oxford: Clarendon Press, 1949), pp. 89–95. Treats Pope's attempts to disengage his reputation from the taint of Deism in *The Dunciad*, bk IV, ll. 459–92.

Freud, Sigmund, *Civilisation and Its Discontents*, trans. Joan Rivière and ed. James Strachey (London: Hogarth Press, 1963).

Freud, Sigmund, *Totem and Taboo and Other Works*, trans. James Strachey in collaboration with Anna Freud, assisted by Alix Strachey and Alan Tyson (London: Hogarth Press, 1955).

Goldgar, B. A., 'Pope's theory of the passions: the background of Epistle II of the *Essay on Man*', *Philological Quarterly*, vol. 41 (1962), pp. 730–43.

Griffin, Dustin H., *Alexander Pope: The Poet in the Poems* (Princeton, NJ: Princeton University Press, 1978). Interesting on the element of personal self-expression discernible in *An Essay on Man*.

Griffith, R. H., 'Pope editing Pope', *University of Texas Studies in English*, vol. 24 (1944), pp. 5–108. Lists Pope's revisions to the printed editions of *An Essay on Man*.

Guerinot, J. V., *Pamphlet Attacks on Alexander Pope: A Descriptive Bibliography* (London: Methuen, 1969).

Hammond, Brean, ' "Know then thyself" and John Gay', *Notes and Queries*, vol. 221, NS, vol. 23 (1976), p. 348.

Hardy, Sir Alister, *The Living Stream* (London: Collins, 1965).

Havens, G. R., 'Voltaire's marginal comments on Pope's *Essay on Man*', *Modern Language Notes*, vol. 43 (1928), pp. 429–39.

Hazen, A. T., 'Crousaz on Pope', *The Times Literary Supplement*, 2 November 1935, p. 704.

Hazlitt, William, *The Complete Works of William Hazlitt*, ed. P. P. Howe, 21 vols (London: Dent, 1930–4).

Holt-White, Rashleigh, *The Life and Letters of Gilbert White of Selborne*, 2 vols (London: John Murray, 1901).

Humphreys, A. R., 'Pope, God and man', in Peter Dixon (ed.), *Alexander Pope* (London: Bell, 1972), pp. 66–100. Compares Pope's conception of God with Hooker's.

Hunter, Adam Mitchell, *The Teaching of Calvin: A Modern Interpretation* (Glasgow: Maclehose Jackson, 1920).

Jones, William Powell, 'Newton further demands the Muse', *Studies in English Literature, 1500–1900*, vol. 3 (1963), pp. 287–306. Newton's *Principia* a more important source than *Opticks* for Pope's *Essay on Man*.

Kallich, Martin, 'The conversation and frame of love: images of unity in Pope's *Essay on Man*', *Papers on Language and Literature*, vol. 2 (1966), pp. 21–37. Discusses, in particular, Pope's use of the image of the circle.

Kallich, Martin, *Heaven's First Law: Rhetoric and Order in Pope's Essay on Man* (Dekalb, Ill.: Northern Illinois Press, 1967). Sticks closely to Pope's use of rhetorical patterns.

Kallich, Martin, 'Unity and dialectic: the structural role of antitheses in Pope's *Essay on Man*', *Papers on Language and Literature*, vol. 1 (1965), pp. 109–24.

Keener, Frederick M., *An Essay on Pope* (New York/London: Columbia University Press, 1974). Contains a chapter dealing with elements of rebellion and submission in *An Essay on Man*.

Knapp, R. G., *The Fortunes of Pope's 'Essay on Man' in Eighteenth Century France* (Geneva: Institut et Musée Voltaire, 1971).

Knight, G. Wilson, *Laureate of Peace: On the Genius of Alexander Pope* (London: Routledge & Kegan Paul, 1954).

Laird, John, *Philosophical Incursions into English Literature* (Cambridge: Cambridge University Press, 1946).

Lawlor, Nancy K., 'Pope's *Essay on Man*: oblique light for a false mirror', *Modern Language Quarterly*, vol. 28 (1967), pp. 305–16. Finds Deism in *An Essay on Man*.

Leavis, F. R., *Revaluation: Tradition and Development in English Poetry* (London: Chatto & Windus, 1936). Contains 'Pope' (pp. 68–100) and 'The Augustan tradition' (pp. 101–53).

Leranbaum, Miriam, *Alexander Pope's Opus Magnum, 1729–1744* (Oxford: Clarendon Press, 1977).

Lewis, C. S., 'Addison', in *Essays on the Eighteenth Century Presented to David Nichol Smith* (Oxford: Clarendon Press, 1945), pp. 1–14.

Lewis, C. S., *English Literature in the Sixteenth Century, Excluding Drama* (Oxford: Clarendon Press, 1954).

Lewis, C. S., *They Asked for a Paper* (London: Bles, 1962).

Lloyd, Charles, *Poetical Essays on the Character of Pope, as a Poet and Moralist; and on the Language and Objects Most Fit for Poetry* (London: C. and H. Baldwyn, 1821).

Lovejoy, A. O., *The Great Chain of Being: A Study of the History of an Idea* (New York: Harper, 1960).

Lovejoy, A. O., 'Milton and the paradox of the fortunate Fall', *ELH*, vol. 4

(1937), pp. 161–79; reprinted in *Critical Essays on Milton from ELH* (Baltimore, Md: Johns Hopkins University Press, 1969), pp. 163–81.

Lovejoy, A. O., 'The parallel of Deism and Classicism', *Modern Philology*, vol. 29 (1932), pp. 281–99.

Lovejoy, A. O., and Boas, G., *Primitivism and Related Ideas in Antiquity* (Baltimore, Md: Johns Hopkins University Press, 1935). Presented as the first volume of 'A Documentary History of Primitivism and Related Ideas', but no more volumes appeared.

Lowell, James Russell, 'Pope', in his *My Study Windows* (Boston, Mass.: Houghton Mifflin, 1888), pp. 385–433.

Macaulay, Thomas Babington, *Essays* (London: Routledge, 1887).

MacDonald, W. L., *Pope and His Critics: A Study in Eighteenth Century Personalities* (London: Dent, 1951).

McDougall, William, *An Introduction to Social Psychology*, 30th edn (London: Methuen, 1950). First published 1908.

Mack, Maynard, *Collected in Himself: Essays Critical, Biographical and Bibliographical on Pope and Some of His Contemporaries* (Newark, Del.: University of Delaware Press; London/Toronto: Associated University Presses, 1982).

Mack, Maynard (ed.), *Essential Articles for the Study of Alexander Pope*, revised and enlarged edn (Hamden, Conn.: Archon, 1968).

Mack, Maynard, *The Garden and the City: Retirement and Politics in the Later Poetry of Pope, 1731–43* (London: Oxford University Press, 1969).

Mack, Maynard, 'On reading Pope', *College English*, vol. 22 (1960), pp. 99–107.

Mack, Maynard, and Winn, James A. (eds), *Pope: Recent Essays by Several Hands* (Brighton: Harvester Press, 1980).

Martindale, C. A., 'Sense and sensibility: the child and the man in *The Rape of the Lock*', *Modern Language Review*, vol. 78 (1983), pp. 273–84.

Maslen, K. I. D., 'New editions of Pope's *Essay on Man*, 1745–48', *Publications of the Bibliographical Society of America*, vol. 62 (1968), pp. 177–88.

Maxwell, J. C., 'Pope's *Essay on Man*, IV, 167–70', *Notes and Queries*, vol. 220, NS, vol. 22 (1975), pp. 491–2.

Medford, Floyd, 'The *Essay on Man* and the *Essay on the Origin of Evil*', *Notes and Queries*, vol. 194 (1949), pp. 337–8. Argues that Pope, in composing *An Essay on Man*, could have had access to the English version of King's work.

Mill, John Stuart, *Utilitarianism, with Critical Essays*, ed. Samuel Gorovitz (Indianapolis, Ind.: Bobbs-Merrill, 1971).

Miller, J. L., *Popery and Politics in England 1660–88* (Cambridge: Cambridge University Press, 1973).

Moore, C. A., 'Did Leibniz influence Pope's *Essay*?', *Journal of English and Germanic Philology*, vol. 16 (1917), pp. 84–102. Concludes: 'No one questions some general resemblances to Leibniz; but they afford no ground for concluding that Pope's philosophical ideas "are to be traced" to the *Théodicée* directly or indirectly.'

Moore, C. A., 'Shaftesbury and the ethical poets in England, 1700–1760',

Publications of the Modern Language Association of America, vol. 31 (1916), pp. 264–325.

Nicolson, Marjorie Hope, *Science and Imagination* (Ithaca, NY: Great Seal Books, 1956).

Nicolson, Marjorie Hope, and Rousseau, G. S., *'This Long Disease My Life': Alexander Pope and the Sciences* (Princeton, NJ: Princeton University Press, 1968). An investigation of Pope's medical history, with further reflections on the effects of science on Pope's imagination.

Nuttall, A. D., 'Fishes in the trees', *Essays in Criticism*, vol. 24 (1974), pp. 20–38. On Pope's love of incongruity and its classical antecedents.

Ogg, David, *England in the Reign of Charles II*, 2nd edn, 2 vols (Oxford: Clarendon Press, 1956).

Pantin, C. F. A., 'Organic design', *Report of the British Association for the Advancement of Science*, vol. 8 (1951–2), pp. 138–50.

Parkin, Rebecca Price, *The Poetic Workmanship of Alexander Pope* (New York: Octagon Books, 1966). Interesting on the element of humour in *An Essay on Man*.

Price, Martin, *To the Palace of Wisdom: Studies in Order and Energy from Dryden to Blake* (Garden City, NY: Doubleday, 1964).

Priestley, F. E. L., 'Pope and the Great Chain of Being', in M. MacLure and F. W. Watt (eds) *Essays on English Literature from the Renaissance to the Victorian Age Presented to A. S. P. Woodhouse* (Toronto: University of Toronto Press, 1964), pp. 213–28. Firmly distinguishes Pope's views from those of Leibniz.

Prior, James, *Life of Edmond Malone, Editor of Shakespeare. With Selections from His Manuscript Anecdotes* (London: 1860).

Ransom, Harry, 'Riddle of the world: a note on Pope and Pascal', *Sewanee Review*, vol. 46 (1938), pp. 306–11. For 'rebut' Pope read 'rebus' and made man into a riddle.

Rawson, C. J., *Gulliver and the Gentle Reader: Studies in Swift and Our Time* (London/Boston, Mass.: Routledge & Kegan Paul, 1973). On the varying threats to order in Augustan literature.

Rawson, C. J., 'Nature's Dance of Death. Part I: Urbanity and strain in Fielding, Swift and Pope', *Eighteenth Century Studies*, vol. 3 (1970), pp. 307–38. A revised version of this essay appears as chapter 2 of his *Henry Fielding and the Augustan Ideal under Stress: Nature's Dance of Death and Other Studies* (London: Routledge & Kegan Paul, 1972).

Rawson, C. J., 'Order and misrule: eighteenth century literature in the 1970s', *ELH*, vol. 42 (1975), pp. 471–505.

Rawson, C. J., 'Pope's *Essay on Man*', *Uttar Pradesh Studies in English*, vol. 1 (1980), pp. 1–8.

Rawson, C. J., 'Pope's Waste Land: reflections on mock-heroic', *Essays and Studies* (1982), pp. 45–65.

Reeves, James, *The Reputation and Writings of Alexander Pope* (London: Heinemann, 1976).

Rist, J. M., *Stoic Philosophy* (Cambridge: Cambridge University Press, 1969).

Rogal, Samuel J., 'Checklist of eighteenth century British literature published in eighteenth century America', *Colby Library Quarterly*, vol. 10 (1973), pp. 231–56. Shows that *An Essay on Man* was far more popular than other works by Pope.

Rogers, Pat, *The Augustan Vision* (London: Weidenfeld & Nicolson, 1974).

Rogers, Pat, *An Introduction to Pope* (London: Methuen, 1975). Suggests that Bolingbroke provided 'moral support' (in the modern sense) rather than philosophical.

Rogers, Robert Wentworth, 'Critiques of the *Essay on Man* in France and Germany, 1736–1755', *English Literary History*, vol. 15 (1948), pp. 176–93. Another version of this piece, revised by J. E. Tobin, appeared in *Philological Quarterly*, vol. 28 (1949), pp. 395–9.

Rogers, Robert Wentworth, *The Major Satires of Alexander Pope* (Urbana, Ill.: University of Illinois Press, 1955). Emphasises the degree to which Pope revised his poem in response to criticism. Rogers's conclusions were powerfully opposed by Maynard Mack in his introduction to the Roxburghe Club facsimile of the manuscripts of *An Essay on Man* (see section (i) above).

Rogers, Robert Wentworth, 'Notes on Pope's collaboration with Warburton in preparing a final edition of the *Essay on Man*', *Philological Quarterly*, vol. 26 (1947), pp. 358–66. Assesses the extent to which Warburton pushed Pope towards greater orthodoxy.

Ruskin, John, *Lectures on Art* (delivered at Oxford in 1870), in *The Works of John Ruskin*, ed. E. T. Cooke and Alexander Wedderburn (London: George Allen, 1903–12), vol. XX, pp. 13–179.

Russo, John Paul, *Alexander Pope: Tradition and Identity* (Cambridge, Mass.: Harvard University Press, 1972).

Ryley, Robert M., 'Another defence by Warburton of the *Essay on Man*', *Notes and Queries*, vol. 224, NS, vol. 26 (1979), pp. 24–5.

Saintsbury, George, *A Short History of English Literature* (London: Macmillan, 1903).

Selden, Raman, 'The eighteenth century Horace: Pope and Swift', in his *English Verse Satire, 1590–1765* (London: Allen & Unwin, 1978). Finds plenty of satire even in the ostensibly non-satirical *Essay on Man*.

Shackleton, Robert, 'Pope's *Essay on Man* and the French Enlightenment', in R. F. Brissenden (ed), *Studies in the Eighteenth Century, II: Papers Presented at the Second David Nichol Smith Memorial Seminar, Canberra, 1970* (Canberra: Australian National University Press, 1973).

Sherburn, George, *The Early Career of Alexander Pope* (New York: Russell & Russell, 1963).

Sherburn, George, 'Pope and "the great shew of Nature" ', in R. F. Jones (ed.), *The Seventeenth Century* (Stanford, Calif.: Stanford University Press, 1951), pp. 306–15.

Sherburn, George, 'Pope at work', in *Essays on the Eighteenth Century Presented to David Nichol Smith* (Oxford: Clarendon Press, 1945), pp. 49–64.

Sherburn, George, 'Two notes on the *Essay on Man*', *Philological Quarterly*, vol. 12 (1933), pp. 402–3.

Sherwood, Margaret, *Undercurrents of Influence in English Romantic Poetry*

(Cambridge, Mass.: Harvard University Press, 1934). Stresses the fragmentary character of *An Essay on Man*.

Simon Irène, '*An Essay on Man*, III, 109–46: a footnote', *English Studies*, vol. 50 (1969), pp. 93–8.

Sitter, John E., 'Theodicy at mid-century: Young, Akenside and Hume', *Eighteenth Century Studies*, vol. 12 (1978), pp. 90–106. The difference between Pope on the one hand and Young and Akenside on the other is like the difference between Locke and Hume.

Sitwell, Edith, *Alexander Pope* (Harmondsworth: Penguin, 1948). First published 1930.

Spacks, Patricia M., *An Argument of Images: The Poetry of Alexander Pope* (Cambridge, Mass.: Harvard University Press, 1971). Interesting on Pope's preoccupation with seeing, both literal and metaphorical.

Sparrow, John, *Independent Essays* (London: Faber, 1963). *An Essay on Man* fails both philosophically and poetically.

Stephen, Leslie, *History of English Thought in the Eighteenth Century*, 2 vols (London: Harbinger Books, 1962). First published 1876.

Strachey, Lytton, 'Pope', in his *Literary Essays* (London: Chatto & Windus, 1961), pp. 79–93. The Leslie Stephen Lecture for 1925.

Stuart, Lady Louisa, 'Introductory anecdotes', in *The Letters and Works of Lady Mary Wortley Montagu*, ed. Lord Wharncliffe (London: Henry G. Bohn, 1861). Written 1837.

Sutherland, John, 'Wit, reason, vision and *An Essay on Man*', *Modern Language Quarterly*, vol. 30 (1969), pp. 356–69.

Suttie, Ian Dishart, *The Origins of Love and Hate* (London: Kegan Paul, 1935).

Taylor, Henry Martyn, 'Sir Isaac Newton', in *Encyclopaedia Britannica*, 11th edn (Cambridge: Cambridge University Press, 1910–11), Vol. XIX, pp. 583–92.

Thackeray, William Makepeace, 'Prior, Gay and Pope', the fourth lecture of *The English Humourists of the Eighteenth Century*, first published in 1853, in his *Henry Esmond, The English Humourists, The Four Georges*, ed. G. Saintsbury (London: Oxford University Press, 1908), pp. 579–620.

Tillotson, Geoffrey, *Pope and Human Nature* (Oxford: Clarendon Press, 1958). Applies to Pope a special distinction between 'primary' and 'secondary' nature.

Tillotson, Geoffrey, 'Pope and the Common Reader', *Sewanee Review*, vol. 66 (1958), pp. 44–78. Pays special attention to *An Essay on Man*.

Tocqueville, Alexis de, *L'Ancien Régime*, ed. G. W. Headlam (Oxford: Clarendon Press, 1904).

Troy, Frederick W., 'Pope's images of man', *Massachusetts Review*, vol. 1 (1960), pp. 359–84. Argues that Pope departs fundamentally from Renaissance classicism.

Tsur, Reuven, *A Perception-Oriented Theory of Metre* (Tel Aviv: The Porter Israeli Institute for Poetics and Semiotics, 1977).

Tuveson, Ernest, '*An Essay on Man* and "the way of ideas"', *ELH*, vol. 26 (1959), pp. 368–86. The effects on Pope of the 'Lockean revolution'. Tuveson further defended his view in '*An Essay on Man* and "the way of ideas": some further remarks', *Philological Quarterly*, vol. 40 (1961), pp. 262–9.

Varey, Simon, 'Rhetoric and *An Essay on Man*', in Howard Erskine-Hill and Anne Smith (eds), *The Art of Alexander Pope* (London: Vision Press, 1979), pp. 132–43. Stresses the element of satire in *An Essay on Man*.

White, Douglas Howarth, *Pope and the Context of Controversy: The Manipulation of Ideas in 'An Essay on Man'* (Chicago, Ill.: University of Chicago Press, 1970). Sees Pope as *playing* with ideas.

Whiteley, Paul, '"Enchained philosophy": Pope's *An Essay on Man*', *Critical Quarterly*, vol. 22, no. 4 (1980), pp. 65–74. Suggests that Pope skilfully induces us to accept, without criticism, the major arguments of his poem.

Williams, Aubrey, *Pope's 'Dunciad': A Study of Its Meaning* (London: Methuen, 1955).

Williams, Basil, *The Whig Supremacy, 1714–60*, 2nd edn, revised by C. H. Stuart (Oxford: Clarendon Press, 1962).

Williams, Charles, *Reason and Beauty in the Poetic Mind* (Oxford: Clarendon Press, 1933). Contains a highly original discussion of *An Essay on Man*.

Wimsatt, W. K., *The Portraits of Alexander Pope* (New Haven, Conn./London: Yale University Press, 1965).

Wordsworth, William, *Poetical Works*, ed. E. de Selincourt and H. Darbishire, 5 vols (Oxford: Clarendon Press, 1949).

Yorke, P. C., 'Henry St John, Lord Bolingbroke', in *Encyclopaedia Britannica*, 11th edn (Cambridge: Cambridge University Press, 1910–11), Vol. IV, pp. 161–4.

Zoellner, Robert M., 'Poetic cosmology in Pope's *An Essay on Man*', *College English*, vol. 19 (1958), pp. 157–62. Relates Pope's first Epistle to Newton's concept of a 'special' universe. Zoellner's views are rebutted in the same issue of *College English* by John M. Aden ('Texture and structure in Pope: a dissent'), p. 358.

INDEX